Anna E. R. and Laura Furness

In memory of their grandfather

Alexander Ramsey

# The American Heritage Book of GREAT ADVENTURES OF THE OLD WEST

# The American Heritage Book of

# GREAT ADVENTURES

## OF THE OLD WEST

Compiled by the Editors of AMERICAN HERITAGE

Introduction by Archibald Hanna, Jr.
Curator, Yale Collection of Western Americana

American Heritage Press · New York

# CONTENTS

# INTRODUCTION

From the beginning, the West has symbolized adventure to Americans. At first it was the land beyond the Appalachians, the mountains that set a western limit to colonial settlement. But within thirty years after the Declaration of Independence that barrier had been breached, and Lewis and Clark were returning from the far Pacific shore. Now it was the trans-Mississippi West—an area so vast it seemed centuries would be needed to explore and settle it—that became the theater of mystery and romance. On its stage, men of more than ordinary stature enacted deeds of daring and high adventure to the applause of the whole nation.

So restless were the Americans, so powerful the westward surge, that in less than a century the land was settled and the frontier officially declared closed. Yet even today, when the plains, mountains, and deserts are spanned by modern highways and dotted with equally modern cities, it is impossible to travel across them without feeling at least an echo of the old romance and adventure. The land may be officially settled, but it is still vast and largely open.

The West is still the land of adventure. But too often, both now and in the past, the public has tended to concentrate its attention on the merely sensational and often fictitious western characters and events. This volume, I hope, will at least partially correct the false view of the West that is still too widely held. Here are deeds as desperate and men and women as heroic as ever appeared in the pages of a novel or on the silver screen— but they are real deeds and real people. I commend them to all those who still respond to the tale of a dangerous journey across strange lands or a battle against relentless odds.

ARCHIBALD HANNA, JR.
*Curator, Yale Collection of Western Americana*

*Members of the Mandan tribe—near whom Lewis and Clark spent the winter of 1804—perform a buffalo dance hoping to lure herds closer to their village.*

# "I GAVE HIM BARKS & SALTPETER..."

By PAUL RUSSELL CUTRIGHT

*O*n February 23, 1803, Thomas Jefferson wrote the following letter to Dr. Benjamin Rush, professor of the Institute of Medicine at the University of Pennsylvania and the foremost American physician of his day:

Dear Sir: I wish to mention to you in confidence that I have obtained authority from Congress to undertake the long desired object of exploring the Missouri & whatever river, heading with that, leads into the Western ocean. About 10 chosen woodsmen headed by Capt. Lewis my secretary will set out on it immediately & probably accomplish it in two seasons. . . . It would be very useful to state for him those objects on which it is most desirable he should bring us information. For this purpose I ask the favor of you to prepare some notes of such particulars as may occur in his journey & which you think should draw his attention & enquiry. He will be in Philadelphia about 2 or 3 weeks hence & will wait on you.

As Jefferson stated to Rush, he had just obtained from Congress the necessary authorization to send a party to explore the unknown reaches of the Missouri River and to find a route to the Pacific. To lead this party he had selected Captain Meriwether Lewis—who would, in turn, ask William Clark, the brother of George Rogers Clark, to share the demanding duties of command. Jefferson's letter to Dr. Rush also suggests that the President, who planned each step of the expedition with almost preternatural care, gave no serious thought at any time to engaging the services of a physician, being content to let Lewis and Clark handle whatever ills and miseries might befall the party.

This decision may have been made easier by his familiarity with Lewis' family background. Lewis' mother was a well-known Virginia herb doctor who had her own herb garden, grew and dispensed her own simples, and ministered regularly and faithfully to the sick of Albemarle County. Lewis shared his mother's interest in herbs and herb therapy and had acquired much of her knowledge. Clark also had medical training of sorts. Like Lewis, he carried in his head the usual frontiersman's storehouse of medical information: how to set a broken limb or remove an imbedded bullet, how to cope with croup, dysentery, and a wide range of other ailments. Being often closer to disease and disaster than to doctors, he found it imperative to know such things.

As Jefferson originally planned it, the expedition was too small to include a doctor; but his willingness to entrust medical matters to Lewis and Clark was no doubt also inspired by his own lack of sympathy with the physicians of his day. Living in the era of depleting remedies—purges, vomits, sweats, blisters—and of the bloodletting lancet, which was still by far the most-used medical instrument, Jefferson had good reason to distrust doctors. And yet, he did not hesitate to ask Dr. Rush to advise Lewis on medical matters relating to the expedition. Not long after the President had done so, Rush wrote back to say that he had furnished Lewis with "some inquiries relative to the natural history of the Indians," and "a few short directions for the preservation of his health." The latter present an interesting lesson in personal hygiene as it obtained early in the last century:

When you feel the least indisposition, do not attempt to overcome it by labour or marching. Rest in a horizontal posture. Also fasting and diluting drinks for a day or two will generally prevent an attack of fever. To these preventatives of disease may be added a gentle sweat obtained by warm drinks, or gently opening the bowels by means of one, two, or more of the purging pills.

Unusual costiveness [constipation] is often a sign of approaching disease. When you feel it take one or more of the purging pills. Want of appetite is likewise a sign of approaching indisposition. It should be obviated by the same remedy.

In difficult and laborious enterprises and marches, eating sparingly will enable you to bear them with less fatigue & less danger to your health.

Flannel should be worn constantly next to the skin, especially in wet weather.

The less spirit you use the better. After being *wetted* or *much* fatigued, or *long* exposed to the night air, it should be taken in an *undiluted* state . . .

Molasses or sugar & water with a few drops of the acid of vitriol [sulphuric acid] will make a pleasant & wholsome drink with your meals.

After having had your feet much chilled, it will be useful to wash them with a little spirit.

Washing the feet every morning in *cold* water, will conduce very much to fortify them against the action of cold.

After long marches, or much fatigue from any cause, you will be more refreshed by lying down in a horizontal posture for two hours, than by resting a longer time in any other position of the body.

Rush would have been pained to learn how many of these rules Lewis and Clark totally disregarded. They ignored his injunctions to rest for two whole hours in a horizontal position with each indisposition and to wash their feet in cold water every morning. The idea of fasting to make difficult marches less fatiguing held no appeal for them whatever. Nor do we find in any of the journals mention of that "pleasant & wholsome" drink compounded of sweetened water and sulphuric acid.

Lewis and Clark's original budget was $2,500. Of this total, $90.69 went for medicines. According to one calculation, their purchases included 1,300 doses of physic, 1,100 of emetic, 3,500 of diaphoretic (sweat-inducer), and fifteen pounds of febrifuge (fever-reducer), not to mention sizable amounts of drugs for blistering, salivation, and increased kidney output. Thus equipped with everything from camphor and calomel to tourniquets and clyster syringes, the medical team of Lewis and Clark seemed ready for almost any contingency.

Their historic journey to the Pacific began at the frontier town of St. Charles, Missouri, on May 21, 1804. The expedition, consisting of some forty men, travelled in three vessels, a fifty-five-foot keelboat and two smaller craft called pirogues. Lewis and Clark would not see St. Charles again until September 21, 1806, two years and four months later.

They were a month and a half out of St. Charles before they encountered their first potentially serious medical problem. On

*The nineteenth-century engravings at top and bottom are rather romanticized versions of some of the difficulties encountered by members of Lewis and Clark's expedition. At center, portraits of Meriwether Lewis (left) and William Clark.*

Wednesday, July 4, 1804, Clark wrote: "ussered in the day by a discharge of one shot from our Bow piece . . . passed the Mouth of a Bayeau . . . Came to on the L.S. [larboard side] to refresh our selves & Jos. Fields got bit by a Snake."

This incident occurred north of present-day Atchison, Kansas, near the mouth of a small stream which Lewis and Clark, in honor of the day, called Independence Creek, the name it still bears. The snake that bit Joseph Fields was apparently innocuous. But since the party was now on unfamiliar terrain where snakes might belie their appearance, Lewis took no chances when he treated Fields, and applied a poultice of bark and gunpowder.

The frontiersman of that day employed many remedies for snake bite, their very multiplicity affording the best evidence possible that none was entirely effective. Mark Twain was conversant with one of the most common. Readers of *Huckleberry Finn* will recall how Nigger Jim, after being struck by a rattler, grabbed the whiskey jug and "begun to pour it down." This was one remedy the victims of snake bite found inviting, and great faith was placed in its ability to neutralize snake venom. Doctors as well as laymen regarded it as a sure-fire antidote. This belief was not only false but dangerous: by speeding the flow of blood, alcohol only hastens distribution and absorption of the venom.

The great majority of the remedies employed for snake bite were in the form of poultices. Favorite materials included garlic, onions, radishes, freshly chewed tobacco, and a wide range of other plants. Poultices of bark and gunpowder, such as Lewis applied, also were used. A poultice today is something of an anachronism, like the powder horn and the potbellied stove. As a general rule it consisted of a warm mass of a glutinous or oleaginous material—bread, lard, corn meal, bran, macerated plant material—which, combined with substances of reputed therapeutic value, was spread on a small piece of cloth and applied to the afflicted part. Doctors of the day thought that poultices would not only draw out the poison or other cause of inflammation but also act as a painkiller, antiseptic, and counterirritant. In those days, panaceas were almost as common as infirmities.

Physicians, however, did not regularly use gunpowder as a therapeutic agent. Explorers, Indian fighters, and frontiersmen regarded it more highly, especially for snake bite. They were known on occasion to slash the bite, pour gunpowder on it, and

13

then set fire to the powder. Many of them used gunpowder as a medicine because they had nothing else available. Some wounds thus treated undoubtedly healed, and, using *post hoc* reasoning, the victims unhesitatingly gave credit to the powder instead of to Mother Nature.

The bark employed by Lewis in treating Joseph Fields could have been that of the slippery elm (*Ulmus fulva*), the inner part of which is mucilaginous and was much used in poultices during the last century. But Lewis and Clark had with them fifteen pounds of pulverized Peruvian bark (cinchona), and when anyone used the word "bark" in those days, it almost always meant cinchona.

Cinchona, which contains quinine, was used for a wide assortment of diseases and afflictions, ranging from measles, dysentery, and dropsy to carbuncles and "ill-conditioned ulcers." One-third of Lewis and Clark's medical outlay had gone into pulverized Peruvian bark, an indication of their high regard for it.

The seventh of July, 1804, along that part of the wide Missouri just below the mouth of the Platte must have been a day of pitiless, penetrating heat. Clark wrote: "one man verry sick,

Struck with the Sun, Capt. Lewis bled him & gave Niter which has revived him much."

The niter employed here in treating sunstroke was potassium nitrate, better known as saltpeter. Even today its usefulness as a diuretic and diaphoretic — for increasing urine discharge and inducing sweats — is recognized, though other drugs are more commonly employed for those purposes. Lewis and Clark had two pounds of saltpeter with them and used it in treating a variety of unrelated disorders.

Saltpeter may have been a relatively harmless remedy, but bloodletting was not — in fact, it may well have killed more patients than it cured. For centuries, beginning even before Hippocrates and continuing almost to the present, doctors believed that practically every malady known to man, from pleurisy and scarlatina to bilious fevers and bubonic plague, could be treated effectively by drawing off blood. The practitioners of this sanguinary art included not only the physician but also the apothecary, the bath keeper, even the barber — hence the blood-red stripes on his barber pole. Many used leeches, and were known as leech doctors, while others insisted on the sharp-edged lancet. Some

*Among the herbs carried on the expedition were (left to right) wild ginger, slippery elm, horsemint, and jalap vine, from which a bitter purge was made.*

had a device known as a scarificator, a box-shaped instrument that made several incisions instead of the lancet's one.

Regardless of what instrument he used, the bloodletter meant business. Disease was serious and demanded vigorous action. With a few, the stock apothegm was, "Bleed until syncope," which meant in essence, draw blood until the patient is unconscious. Those who survived did so, of course, in spite of bleeding; today doctors rarely resort to the treatment. It is sometimes indicated in *polycythemia vera,* a rare disease in which the number of red blood cells has increased abnormally, and in certain grave heart and lung disorders where reducing blood volume is beneficial. Too, bleeding occasionally does seem beneficial for sunstroke. According to Dr. William Osler, the famous teacher at Johns Hopkins, "In the cases in which the symptoms are those of intense asphyxia, and in which death may take place in a few minutes, free bleeding should be practiced ..." But whether or not the treatment helped the sunstroke victim of the Lewis and Clark expedition, it is impossible to say.

Soon after, however, tragedy struck for the first and only time during the whole journey to the Pacific and back. On July 31, just above the mouth of the Platte, Sergeant Charles Floyd noted in his journal, "I am verry Sick and Has been for Sometime but have Recovered my helth again." But his recovery was only temporary. Three weeks later, on August 19, Clark wrote: "Serjeant Floyd is taken verry bad all at once with a Biliose Chorlick we attempt to relieve him without success as yet, he gets worst and we are much allarmed at his Situation ..." Nothing, Clark said, would "Stay a moment on his Stomach or bowels."

The next day Sergeant Floyd died, probably of a ruptured, gangrenous appendix. The journals reveal nothing of measures attempted to save his life. The odds are that Lewis both bled Floyd and purged him with laxatives. If he did the latter, it may well have hastened Floyd's death, either by rupturing the appendix or by adding to the inflammatory material already in the peritoneal cavity. In any event, Lewis' efforts were to no avail; probably the best medical talent of that day could not have saved the sergeant, for surgery then was almost entirely limited to the surface of the body. It was not until 1887 that the first appendectomy was performed by Dr. John Morton in Philadelphia.

The Lewis and Clark expedition passed the first winter in a hastily built but sturdy stockade, Fort Mandan, near the mouth of the Knife River, about fifty-five miles above the present Bismarck, North Dakota. Here, for six months, they lived surrounded by some 4,000 aboriginals—Mandans and Minnetarees (Hidatsas). From the very beginning, these Indians exceeded the bounds of what white men considered conventional hospitality. To the explorers they proffered not only corn, beans, and squash but also wives, daughters, and sisters. To them, as to many other Indian tribes, this was no deviation from rectitude; it was an old, established, and entirely respectable custom. However, even for the Indians there were limits to hospitality, and as the long winter wore on, many of the "squars" began to sell their "favors" for a string of beads, a looking glass, or a piece of ribbon.

Though the Indian men had no scruples about farming their wives out for the night, they were properly resentful if their offers were turned down without good reason. However, the evidence seems firm that Lewis and Clark themselves refused all such offers. It is most unlikely that they would have cheapened themselves in the eyes of their men in this manner and thus jeopardized the success of their mission.

Lewis and Clark had little to say in their journals about the sexual relations between soldiers and squaws, or about the sordid sequelae. On January 14, 1805, at Fort Mandan, Clark noted: "Several men with the venereal cought from the Mandan women." And, a few days later: "one man verry bad with the pox [*i.e.* syphilis]." Again, on March 30, as the expedition prepared to resume the ascent of the Missouri: "Generally helthy except Venerial Complaints which is verry Common amongst the natives and the men Catch it from them."

The expedition leaders had anticipated venereal disease. Both men had served previous enlistments in the Army, and they knew something of the appetites and frailties of the average soldier. Thus, they carried ample supplies of mercury ointment, calomel (mercurous chloride), balsam copaiba, and *saccharum saturni* (sugar of lead), and they had armed themselves with four pewter urethral syringes. Lewis and Clark, however, make mention only of mercury in their treatment of venereal disease, which meant either mercury ointment or calomel or both. (Dr. Rush regarded mercury as the "Samson of the Materia Medica" in the treatment of syphilis.)

As is well known, syphilis manifests itself in three stages: a primary one extending from the appearance of the initial sore, a small red papule, or chancre, until the onset of constitutional symptoms; a secondary stage characterized by skin eruptions (the pox); and the tertiary, which shows up much later, often years after the original infection, in the form of general paresis, locomotor ataxia, or other equally grave disorders.

It is highly unlikely that Lewis cured any syphilitic cases using mercury. This drug may have been effective in clearing up evidences of the primary and secondary stages, but hardly the third. But it is obvious from his statements that Lewis believed that he had cured this disease in his men. For instance, on January 27, 1806, while camped at the mouth of the Columbia River, he said, "Goodrich has recovered from the Louis Veneri [*lues venerea*] which he contracted from an amorous contact with a Chinnook damsel. I cured him as I did Gibson last winter by the use of mercury." However, we note that six months later he admitted: "Goodrich and McNeal are both very unwell with the pox which they contracted last winter with the Chinook women."

If venereal disease was a constant nuisance, subzero weather was the expedition's most stubborn enemy during the long winter stay at Fort Mandan. On some nights the cold gripped the land so firmly that the sentinels relieved each other every half hour. Many of the men had to be treated for frostbite. Private Whitehouse, for instance, had his feet so badly frozen while scouring the snow-covered plains for game that he had to have a horse bring him in. Another man returned from a trip upriver with his face frostbitten. Indians reported one day that two of their men had frozen to death on the prairie while hunting buffalo.

Another tragic incident had its beginning late one afternoon when an Indian arrived at the fort and was much distressed not to find his thirteen-year-old son there. That night, one of the coldest of the winter, the temperature dropped to forty below. In the morning, with the boy still missing, the Indians of the lower village turned out en masse to hunt for him. At about ten o'clock the boy limped into the fort and reported that he had spent the night in the snow protected only by a buffalo robe. Luckily he had survived, though his feet were badly frozen. A week later Lewis had to turn surgeon when it became necessary to amputate the toes on one of the boy's feet.

In this operation, if Lewis followed custom, he seared the cut surfaces with a hot iron. This was done to stop hemorrhage rather than to sterilize. With frozen members, however, there was ordinarily a minimum of bleeding if the surgeon cut through the dead tissue immediately beyond the living flesh. Lewis did not sew up the wounds as would be done today. If he had been cutting off a leg above the knee, for example, he might have taken two or three stitches, but not in minor surgery such

*A handsome chief of the hospitable Missouri River Mandans in ceremonial robes*

as the removal of toes. Wounds were never sewed tight then, because they had to be left open to drain and to allow them to heal from inside out. All surgical steps—excision, cauterization, suturing—were taken, of course, without the aid of anaesthesia: back in the "good old days" surgery was a soul-scarring ordeal.

One of the most memorable events of that winter at Fort Mandan was the appearance of Sacagawea, the Bird Woman, whose name has become almost as familiar to present-day Americans as that of Pocahontas. Sister of a Shoshone chief, she was captured in 1800 by a war party of Minnetarees from the Knife

*Fort Clatsop in the early stages of construction; it was completed in a month.*

River. In the attack, which took place at Three Forks, Montana, the Minnetarees killed several of the Shoshones and took Sacagawea and a number of other girls and boys prisoner. Some time later, a French trader, Toussaint Charbonneau, made her his wife. Since Charbonneau could speak the language of the Minnetarees, Lewis and Clark hired him as an interpreter. They also took along Sacagawea, thinking that she might be of value to them once they reached her people.

On February 11, 1805, Sacagawea gave birth to a son. Lewis, whose obstetrical role was a minor one, described the delivery:

It is worthy of remark that this was the first child which this woman had boarn, and as is common in such cases her labour was tedious and the pain violent; Mr. Jessome [René Jessaume, a Frenchman the expedition hired as an interpreter in the Mandan country] informed me that he had frequently administered a small portion of the rattle of the rattlesnake, which he assured me had never failed to produce the desired effect, that of hastening the birth of the child; having the rattle of a snake by me I gave it to him and he administered two rings of it to the woman broken in small pieces with the fingers and added to a small quantity of water. Whether this medicine was truly the cause or not I shall not undertake to determine, but I was informed that she had not taken it more than ten minutes before she brought forth. perhaps this remedy may be worthy of future experiments, but I must confess that I want faith as to its efficacy.

The child was christened Jean-Baptiste, though nicknamed Pomp (short for Pompey). Later Clark called a prominent rock formation on the Yellowstone, Pompey's Pillar. Pomp, with his mother and father, travelled with the party from Fort Mandan to the Pacific and back. He was seriously ill only once, when he was fifteen months old. On May 22, 1806, beside the Clearwater River, as the expedition waited for the melting of the snows in the Bitterroot Mountains, Lewis wrote:

Charbono's Child is very ill this evening; he is cuting teeth, and for several days past has had a violent lax, which having suddonly stoped he was attacked with a high fever and his neck and throat are much swolen this evening. We gave him a doze of creem of tartar and flour of sulpher and applyed a poltice of boiled onions to his neck as warm as he could well bear it.

Most probably Pomp's trouble was tonsillitis complicated by an infected cervical lymph gland. Lewis and Clark brought him around using not only cream of tartar, flowers of sulphur, and onion poultices but also clysters (enemas) and a plaster of basilicon which was, in Clark's words, "a plaster of sarve [salve] made of the rozen of the long leafed pine, Beeswax and Bears oil mixed."

Cream of tartar (potassium bitartrate) is both diuretic and cathartic. It is best known as an ingredient of baking powder. Combining it with flowers of sulphur, an excellent fungicide and insecticide, would not have altered its effect. Lewis and Clark probably would have used plain warm water, or water with soap, in the enemas they gave Pomp.

Two months after the party left Fort Mandan, Sacagawea herself took sick and nearly died. Her illness, which neither Lewis nor Clark could positively diagnose, occurred on that stretch of the Missouri immediately above the mouth of the Marias River, in present-day Montana. Since Lewis had gone ahead to look for the Great Falls of the Missouri, Clark had charge of her case at first. He seems to have had no idea what was wrong with her, but he was attentive and did all he could. On the first day he bled her, and on the next, her condition having failed to improve, he bled her again. The operation, he noted, "appeared to be of great service to her." On the fourth day he gave her "a doste of salts," which seemed to be of no help at all, for the next morning she was "excessively bad" and her case "somewhat dangerous." She complained of abdominal pain and was "low spirited." Clark applied a bark poultice to "her region."

When Lewis rejoined the main party, he found Sacagawea's pulse rapid, irregular, and barely perceptible, and her condition "attended with strong nervous symptoms, that of the twitching of the fingers and leaders of the arm." He immediately took charge. He continued the "cataplasms [poultices] of bark and laudnumn" instituted by Clark and ordered a cask of mineral water brought from a spring on the opposite side of the river. He had great faith in the efficacy of this water, since it was highly impregnated with sulphur and "precisely similar to that of Bowyer's Sulphur Spring in Virginia." He had Sacagawea drink freely of it and by evening was gratified to find her pulse stronger and more regular, her nervous symptoms somewhat abated, and her abdominal pain less severe. He believed that her trouble "originated principally from an obstruction of the mensis [menstrual fluid] in consequence of taking cold."

The next morning Sacagawea was so far improved that she asked for food and ate as heartily as Lewis would permit of "broiled buffaloe well seasoned with pepper and salt and rich soope of the same meat." To the medicine already prescribed, Lewis now added fifteen drops of oil of vitriol, and considered her in "a fair way to recovery." And she no doubt would have been if her husband, who had been given specific orders to watch her, had prevented her from downing a meal of white apples and dried fish, as a result of which her pains and fever returned. After employing army language to tell Charbonneau what he thought of him, Lewis went to work on his patient again, prescribing "broken dozes of diluted nitre [saltpeter] until it produced perspiration and at 10 P.M. 30 drops of laudnumn."

The latter was, of course, a tincture of opium, widely used in those days to deaden pain and induce sleep. Lewis' customary dose of thirty drops, about two cubic centimeters or one-half teaspoon, was not a big one; its effect would probably be similar to that of a quarter-grain injection of morphine.

Although from here on the Indian woman's recovery was rapid and uncomplicated, her case seems to have been a prime example of the patient's recovering in spite of the treatment. Certainly the purging and bleeding could have had no effect upon the cure except to retard it. How much blood Clark withdrew is speculative. Some of the doctors of the day removed only four to eight ounces; others were not satisfied until they had siphoned off from a pint to a quart. Only a few casehardened dissidents were dead set against withdrawing any at all. The removal of a quart is enough to cause grogginess in an individual, and taking any more induces fainting spells. Phlebotomists probably did not often measure the blood accurately; when they had taken what they thought was enough they applied a tight bandage to stop the flow. Very serious infection sometimes set in at such wounds, and it was by no means unheard of to have the patient die as a result.

One harmful effect of excessive bleeding is to reduce the quantity in the blood of calcium, magnesium, and potassium. The muscle twitching reported by Lewis in Sacagawea may very well have been induced by a deficiency of such important minerals. Also, bleeding in conjunction with purging and fever produces dehydration. If the considerable amount of mineral water Lewis had his patient drink benefited her at all, it was because it relieved dehydration and restored vital minerals.

The journals carry many references to dysentery and constipation, "cholick & griping," "lax" and "relax," "heaviness of the stomach"—all debilitating conditions referable to the gastrointestinal tract. Happily for Lewis and Clark, Missouri River water was not then the devil's brew of topsoil, sewage, and industrial waste it is today. They drank it neat for months on end. Only now and then did they suspect that it might be the cause of any of their gastric or intestinal troubles.

For disorders of the digestive tract, Lewis and Clark dispensed pills and doses of salts as they saw fit. On May 4, 1805, above the mouth of the Yellowstone, Lewis wrote, "Joseph Fields was very sick today with the disentary had a high fever I gave him a dose of Glauber salts, which operated very well, in the evening his fever abated and I gave him 30 drops of laudnum." Glauber's salt (from J.R. Glauber, the German chemist who originally prepared it) was sodium sulphate and was, like Epson salts, a well-known physic. Lewis and Clark had six pounds of it, which cost ten cents a pound, and they did not hesitate to use it.

Early in June, 1805, Lewis, with four of his best men, left the mouth of the Marias River and started on foot up the north bank of the Missouri. Clark and the rest of the party followed by boat. Lewis had been "somewhat unwell with the disentary," but he set out nevertheless. As the day advanced, he developed a violent pain in the intestines and a high fever. Since the medical supplies had been left with the main party, Lewis "resolved to try an experiment with some simples," these being the medicinal plants with which any good herb doctor would be familiar. His eyes soon fell on the chokecherry, a small shrub (probably *Prunus virginiana*) that he had encountered frequently along the Missouri. He had his men gather a number of the twigs and, after stripping off the leaves, cut the twigs into pieces about two inches in length. These were then boiled in water "untill a strong black decoction of an astringent bitter tast was produced." At dusk Lewis drank a pint of this, and about an hour later downed another. By ten o'clock he was perspiring gently, his pain had left him, and his fever had abated. That night, all symptoms which had disturbed him having disappeared, he slept soundly. The next morning at sunrise, fit and refreshed, he took another stiff swig of the drink and resumed his march.

In late July the party arrived at Three Forks, that geographically important site in southwestern Montana where the Jefferson, Madison, and Gallatin rivers (as Lewis and Clark named them) unite to form the Missouri. Clark was sick, "with high fever ... & akeing." Upon learning that Clark had not had a bowel movement for several days, Lewis prevailed upon him to bathe his feet and legs in warm water and to take five Rush's pills, which he had "always found sovereign in such cases." The next morning, the medicine having "opperated," Clark felt better.

Rush's pills, a product of the "genius" of Dr. Benjamin Rush, were well-known in those days and referred to, often with some feeling, as Rush's "thunderbolts." Each consisted of ten grains of calomel and fifteen of jalap (a powdered drug prepared from the purgative tuberous root of a Mexican plant of the morning-glory family); they were a powerful physic. Lewis and Clark carried fifty dozen of these pills and, in treating gastrointestinal disturbances, it seems to have been a coin-tossing proposition whether they used the "thunderbolts" or Glauber's salts.

In mid-September, 1805, Lewis and Clark spent ten arduous days crossing the Bitterroot Mountains to the Columbia watershed. They suffered intensely from fatigue, cold, and hunger. There was great rejoicing when they reached the beautiful valley of the Clearwater River and were greeted by the friendly Nez Percé Indians. Food was again plentiful, but quite different from that to which they had long been accustomed. It consisted almost entirely of such Nez Percé staples as dried salmon and the roots of the camass (*Camassia quamash*), a liliaceous plant whose bulb could be eaten raw or in soups or breads. There was nothing to suggest that more trouble was in the offing—not until Clark found himself "verry unwell all the evening from eateing the fish & roots too freely."

During the next few days practically every man in the party, including Lewis, was sick, some violently. Excerpts from the journals reveal a sorry state of affairs:

CLARK—September 23: Capt Lewis & 2 men Verry Sick this evening.

CLARK—September 24: several 8 or 9 men sick . . . Capt. Lewis scercely able to ride on a jentle horse . . . I gave rushes Pills to the Sick this evening.

SGT. GASS—September 24: The men are generally unwell, owing to the change of diet . . . Captain Clarke gave all the sick a dose of Rush's Pills, to see what effect that would have.

SGT. GASS—September 25: The water is soft and warm, and perhaps causes our indisposition more than anything else.

CLARK—September 25: when I arrived at Camp found Capt. Lewis verry Sick, Several men also verry Sick, I gave Some Salts and Tarter *emetic.*

CLARK—September 26: Capt. Lewis Still verry unwell. Several men taken Sick on the way down, I administered *Salts* Pils Galip [jalap] Tarter emetic &c. I feel unwell this evening.

It is quite apparent that the men were in bad shape. With Lewis sick it was incumbent on Clark, himself "unwell," to take charge. He was an uncertain and much puzzled "doctor," but that did not deter him from prescribing Rush's pills "*to see what effect that would have,"* nor, as the cases multiplied, from taking seriously Hippocrates' maxim: "Desperate diseases required desperate remedies."

The cause of the general "lax" among the men is conjectural. The camass roots may have had a purgative effect on one unaccustomed to them, as Lewis and Clark believed. The next spring, as they ascended the Columbia, they tried to avoid eating them. On the other hand, the trouble may have been due simply to a drastic change in diet.

Lewis and Clark could scarcely credit the high incidence of eye troubles among the Indians of the Columbia River basin. Wrote Clark:

The loss of sight I have observed to be more common among all the nations inhabiting this river than among any people I ever observed. they have almost invariably sore eyes at all stages of life. the loss of an eye is very common among them; blindness in persons of middle age is by no means uncommon, and it is almost invariably a comcammitant of old age. I know not to what cause to attribute this prevalent deficientcy of the eye except it be their exposure to the reflection of the sun off the water to which they are constantly exposed in the occupation of fishing.

When the Indians came to Lewis and Clark to have their eyes treated, as they did increasingly in the succeeding months, Lewis had his own special eyewash: "a solution of white vitriol [zinc sulphate] and the sugar of lead [lead acetate] in the proportion of 2 grs. of the former and one of the latter to each ounce of water." Dropped into the eyes, it brought at least temporary relief.

The prevalence of sore eyes among the natives was not caused by anything as innocent as reflection of the sun from water. It was probably due to trachoma or venereal disease. Both appear to have been common in all stages of development among the Columbia Valley Indians, and in all age groups. Trachoma, a highly contagious form of conjunctivitis characterized by granulations of the conjunctival surfaces, may lead to partial or complete blindness. So may gonorrheal conjunctivitis (ophthalmia neonatorum), which babies can inherit from their mothers at birth.

The journals do not mention Private William Bratton as performing any unusual act of bravery, or being party to any of the more breath-taking moments of the expedition except for once being chased for a mile and a half by a grizzly bear. He was a good soldier and a skilled gunsmith; we would know little else about him if he had not become the only member of the party who was seriously ill for an extended period.

As soon as the expedition reached the Pacific, in mid-November, 1805, Bratton was one of five men detailed to evaporate sea water to obtain salt, the supply of that commodity having been exhausted. Some time later, Lewis and Clark received word that Bratton was "verry unwell," and five days later he showed up "much reduced" at Fort Clatsop, their newly constructed winter quarters at the mouth of the Columbia. The next day, February 16, Clark wrote, "Bratten is verry weak and complains of a pain in the lower part of the back when he moves which I suppose proceeds from debility. I gave him barks and saltpeter."

As time went on, however, Bratton's condition became worse. "He complains," wrote Lewis, "of a violent pain in the small of his back and is unable in consequence to set up we gave him one of our flanel shirts, applyed a bandage of flannel to the part and bathed and rubed it well with some vollatile linniment which I prepared with sperits of wine, camphor, castile soap and a little laudinum."

*Medicine chest belonging to the expedition's medical adviser, Dr. Benjamin Rush*

As the time for the return journey drew near, Bratton still remained an invalid. On March 21 Lewis wrote: "Bratton is now so much reduced that I am somewhat uneasy with rispect to his recovery; the pain of which he complains most seems to be seated in the small of his back and remains obstinate. I believe that it is the rheumatism."

Two days later the expedition left Fort Clatsop and began the long journey back home. Bratton, unable to walk, made the trip to Camp Chopunnish on the Clearwater by boat and by horse. When they arrived, two months later, he was still "verry unwell." His cure came suddenly, even dramatically. In Lewis' words:

[Private] John Shields observed that he had seen men in a similar situation restored by violent sweats. Bratton requested that he might be sweated in the manner proposed by Shields to which we consented. Shields sunk a circular hole of 3 feet diamiter and four feet deep in the earth. he kindled a large fire in the hole and heated well, after which the fire was taken out [and] a seat placed in the center of the hole for the patient with a board at bottom for his feet to rest on; some hoops of willow poles were bent in an arch crossing each other over the hole, on these several blankets were thrown forming a secure and thick orning [awning] of about 3 feet high. the patient being striped naked was seated under this orning in the hole and . . . by that means creats as much steam or vapor as he could possibly bear, in this situation he was kept about 20 minutes after which he was taken out and suddonly plunged in cold water twise and was then immediately returned to the sweat hole where he was continued three quarters of an hour longer then taken out covered up in several blankets and suffered to cool gradually. during the time of his being in the sweat hole, he drank copious draughts of a strong tea of horse mint.

This treatment of alternating heat and cold was effective; it is used successfully in similar cases today. The very next day Bratton was walking about, almost entirely free of pain, and within two weeks he had, Lewis wrote, "so far recovered that we cannot well consider him an invalid any longer, he has had a tedious illness which he boar with much fortitude and firmness."

The obscure lumbar ailment which Bratton endured for four long months cannot be definitely diagnosed at this late date. Medical men suggest sciatica or infectious arthritis or an inflamed sacroiliac joint. Bratton's cure was apparently permanent. He fought in the Battle of Tippecanoe and, later, in the War of 1812. In 1819 he married and in time became the father of eight sons and two daughters.

From beginning to end, the members of the expedition suffered from skin infections—boils, tumors, abscesses, and whitlows, these last being inflammations at the ends of the fingers and toes. Such infections could not be avoided. Cuts and skin abrasions which would allow the entrance of germs occurred daily, especially among the boatmen. Theirs was hardly child's play. In places they toiled waist-deep in water for hours on end, scrambling over sharp-edged rocks which cut moccasins to shreds. At one time Lewis wrote: "Many of them have their feet so mangled and bruised with the stones ... that they can scarcely walk or stand; at least it is with great pain that they do either."

Lewis and Clark, of course, knew nothing of the doctrine of sepsis. Pathogens, such as bacteria, protozoa, and viruses, had yet to be recognized for what they are: almost three-quarters of a century would elapse before the world would know of Louis Pasteur and the germ theory of disease. Physicians of this preantiseptic era treated skin infections with poultices and ointments, and Lewis and Clark followed standard practice. For instance, when Private John Potts' cut leg became inflamed and painful, Clark applied first a poultice of the root of the "Cowes" (*Cogswellia cous*), an herb of the Northwest, and later, another of "the pounded root & leaves of wild ginger [*Asarum caudatum*] from which he found great relief." Another time, when an Indian woman showed up with an abscess on the small of her back, Clark opened it and applied basilicon ointment. This was a salve for external application consisting ordinarily of such ingredients as resin, yellow wax, and lard.

Today, it is difficult to evaluate such treatments. If poultices were applied hot, as frequently happened, they may have been of some benefit. Or if they contained a blistering agent, such as Spanish fly (cantharides) or oil of mustard, they would have been effective as counterirritants. It is safe to say that poultices generally did no harm when applied to skin that was still intact.

Just six weeks before the end of the trip, near the mouth of the Little Missouri, Lewis was felled by a bullet which struck him, according to Sergeant John Ordway, "in his back side." As Lewis described it:

... opposite to the birnt hills there happened to be a herd of Elk ... I determined to land and kill some of them accordingly we put too and

I went out with [Private Peter] Cruzatte only. we fired on the Elk. I killed one and he wounded another, we reloaded our guns and took different routs through the thick willows in pursuit of the Elk; I was in the act of firing on the Elk a second time when a ball struck my left thye about an inch below my hip joint, missing the bone it passed through the left thye and cut the thickness of the bullet across the hinder part of the right thye; the stroke was very severe; I instantly supposed that Cruzatte had shot me in mistake for an Elk as I was dressed in brown leather and he cannot see very well; under this impression I called out to him damn you, you have shot me, and looked towards the place from whence the ball had come, seeing nothing I called Cruzatte several times as loud as I could . . .

Receiving no answer, Lewis rushed to the conclusion that he had been shot by Indians. Therefore, though in great pain, he quickly made his way back to the boat, where he ordered the men there to follow him and "give them battle and relieve Cruzatte." But Lewis' wound soon became so painful and his thigh so stiff that he could go no farther. The rest of the party went ahead and about twenty minutes later returned, bringing Cruzatte with them. They had encountered no Indians. Cruzatte was blind in one eye and nearsighted in the other; he had shot Lewis unintentionally and, because of embarrassment, had kept quiet when Lewis called to him.

Sergeant Gass helped Lewis introduce "tents of patent lint into the ball holes" and, later that evening, they applied a poultice of Peruvian bark. It was a nasty wound. When Clark first dressed it, Lewis fainted dead away.

In those days a tent consisted of a roll of lint, or linen, unsterilized of course. It was supposed to expedite drainage and, by keeping the surface of the wound open, to insure the formation of new tissue from the inside out. If a tent was not used, wounds tended to heal at the surface, thus precluding drainage. In similar situations, surgeons today sometimes employ rubber tubes of various kinds, called drains, some of which are open, others filled with gauze.

On August 22, eleven days after Lewis had been shot, Clark reported, "I am happy to have it in my power to Say that my worthy friend Capt. Lewis is recovering fast, he walked a little to day for the first time. I have discontinued the tent in the hole the ball came out." Four days later he removed the tent from the other wound, and by September 9, his worthy friend could "walk and even run nearly as well as ever he could." And just in time. Two weeks later Lewis was in St. Louis enjoying a hero's welcome. For that, a man needed two good legs under him.

Lewis and Clark, though not medically trained, were men of obvious talent and vast common sense in whom the spirit of inquiry ran high. Of the two leaders, Lewis was better educated and more knowledgeable, with the logical and deductive mind of a good scientist. He was a man of many moods and sought solitude rather than companionship. Clark, on the other hand, was genial and gregarious, the friend of prince and pauper alike. It was to him the men turned with their problems. If, subsequently, either of the captains had studied medicine, it is reasonable to believe that he would have distinguished himself. Lewis, from what we know of him, would have come nearer being the astute, discerning diagnostician. Clark, certainly, would have had much the better bedside manner.

The one incontrovertible fact about the medical practice of Lewis and Clark is that in twenty-eight months of travelling some 8,000 miles in a land of thirsty sands, rampaging rivers, and unpredictable savages, they lost only one man, poor Sergeant Floyd, and the best medical men in the country—even, probably, Dr. Rush—could not have saved him. Thomas Jefferson, it would seem, made no mistake in entrusting the health and welfare, as well as the military command, of the party to these two resourceful, clearheaded frontiersmen. In fact, considering the primitive state of medicine in the world at that time, who can conscientiously insist that the expedition would have fared better in the hands of a qualified doctor than in those of Meriwether Lewis and William Clark?

*The majestic Royal Gorge of the Arkansas River*

# HOW LOST WAS ZEBULON PIKE?

By DONALD JACKSON

*I*n the deepening snows of a high mountain valley, about where Salida, Colorado, now stands, a band of sixteen men were gathered on the day before Christmas, 1806. Earlier they had been separated into straggling parties to forage and explore, but now they were united. Earlier they had been wretchedly hungry, but now they had been so fortunate as to kill several buffalo cows. The timely appearance of these animals at a meaningful season must have seemed providential to the young leader of the band, but he was not a man to dwell for long upon such notions in the journal he was keeping.

"We now again found ourselves all assembled together on Christmas Eve," wrote Zebulon Pike, "and appeared generally to be content, although all the refreshment we had to celebrate that day with, was buffalo meat, without salt, or any other thing whatever."

Pike was in a far worse situation than he realized. Although he thought he was on the headwaters of the Red River, he actually was some three hundred miles to the northwest, high up the Arkansas; and before discovering his error he would spend agonizing days along the frozen river bed and in the bottom of an incredible canyon now called the Royal Gorge. His men—

some of whom had cut up their blankets to wrap around their feet — had every reason to believe that they were now to start for the more moderate climes of home. Yet they still were to face an ordeal of hunger and cold in the Wet Mountain Valley that would leave some of them forever maimed. Certainly neither Pike nor his men could have foreseen that they were about to mistake still another river for the Red, and that within a few weeks they all would be prisoners of the Spanish government in Mexico.

Could Pike have known that these misadventures would occur, it is altogether likely that he would have chosen to go on, for he was not easily deterred by disappointment and physical discomfort. But it would have distressed him greatly to know that even at that moment, back in the East, many of his countrymen were questioning the very aim of his expedition. Although Pike was officially performing a notable chore in the national interest, he soon would face the allegation that secretly his mission was a private one, somehow linked with the Aaron Burr conspiracy. Burr had been accused of plotting hostile inroads into the Spanish Southwest, and even of trying to divide the Union by separating the western states and territories. For at least a while, Pike's reputation as an explorer would depend less upon his own skill and courage than upon the turn of events at home.

At the age of twenty-seven, Zebulon Pike was a man to whom reputation meant nearly everything. He believed that he would find it, and glory besides, in the United States Army. He would not duplicate the drab career of his father, Major Zebulon Pike, whose lifetime of military service had left him poor, lame, and occasionally addled. Even young Pike's own early years in the service, spent routinely in the Ohio and Mississippi valleys, had not quelled his zeal. He attacked every assignment with enthusiasm, studied military tactics and taught himself French and Spanish, and kept a ready eye on the promotion lists sent out by the Secretary of War.

But making it alone in those times was very difficult for a young officer of modest background; it required all the help that a man could find, including the favors of influential men in the Army and the government. Pike knew this. "Send me inclosed some letters ... to any friends of Influence you may have," he once wrote his father, "as I have Schemes in view that require every exertion in my power to accomplish."

Such a man is a born protégé, waiting for a patron. Pike was lucky enough to come under the patronage of the one man in the world with whom it seemed that he could prosper most, the commanding general of the United States Army. In 1805, when Pike was still a first lieutenant whose most important previous assignment had been that of regimental paymaster, he was picked by this general for an expedition up the Mississippi that sent his career into a steep ascent. From that day until his death in the War of 1812, Pike's heart, hand, and sword were dedicated to the service of Brigadier General James Wilkinson.

Saying that Wilkinson was profoundly a knave puts the historian in no danger of losing perspective; the General's misdeeds throughout decades spent in public office, ranging from petty chicanery to treason, are now well documented. To some he was a charming gallant, but he impressed others as too cocksure and pompous: Washington Irving felt that had he not become a general he would have made "an admirable trumpeter." He had been made a brigadier general during the Revolution, had engaged in various civilian enterprises in Kentucky, then had returned to military life. Upon the death of General Anthony Wayne in 1796, he found himself the ranking general of the Army. He was to serve in this status until his failure to take Montreal during the War of 1812 cost him his command. Not until years after his death was it proved that he had taken an oath of allegiance to Spain and had received an annual pension from that country during his service at the head of the United States Army.

The sheer magnitude of Wilkinson's shoddy undertakings is one of the marvels of his time; another is the ease with which he duped such men as Thomas Jefferson and repeatedly escaped disclosure and punishment. It would have been impossible, however, for Wilkinson to serve so long as the commanding general of the Army if he had been *completely* a charlatan. He ran the military affairs of his country, including the many problems of a lengthening frontier, not brilliantly but at least not disastrously. He had a keen interest in geography and natural history, and like most other Americans he was eager to know just what the United States had acquired in 1803 in the vast tract of land called the Louisiana Purchase. Lewis and Clark were already in the Northwest, encouraged by Jefferson's intense and highly personal interest in their success, when Wilkinson was appointed as governor of the territory of Louisiana in 1805. Upon reaching his headquarters in St. Louis, Wilkinson began at once to carry out Jefferson's wishes in regard to further exploration.

But was Wilkinson interested in what lay to the west for his country's sake or because he had private schemes to develop? Here was a large part of the General's secret of success: his private designs so often overlapped those of the country that they could be easily concealed and implemented.

Neither Pike's expedition up the Mississippi in 1805–6 nor his second to the West in 1806–7 was specifically authorized by Jefferson. But Wilkinson kept the President and Secretary of War Henry Dearborn fully informed of Pike's progress, and

*Lieutenant Zebulon M. Pike*

both expeditions were later approved.

About the Mississippi River expedition there was no air of mystery and no suspicion of scandal. Pike was sent by Wilkinson to explore the headwaters of the Mississippi, to purchase sites from the Indians for future military posts, and to assert both to Indians and to Canadian traders the authority of the United States over the lands it had recently acquired. He was also to bring some influential chiefs back to St. Louis for talks with Wilkinson. Leaving St. Louis in August in a single keelboat with twenty men, Pike worked his way to the vicinity of Little Falls, Minnesota, by the onset of winter. Here he built a stockade for the protection of his party, then pushed on with a few men—

*Brigadier General James Wilkinson*

travelling on foot and by dog sled to visit various fur-trading establishments. The uppermost point of his journey was Cass Lake
in northern Minnesota.

Pike returned to St. Louis in April. He had not found the ultimate source of the Mississippi but had come within a few miles
of it. In carrying out the rest of his mission he was only moderately successful. The success of the venture, however, must be
judged not on the basis of Wilkinson's extravagant expectations,
but on what might have been expected from a small party with
an inexperienced leader. The trip seasoned Pike and his men for
their more substantial foray into the West, and it produced a
notable map and journal.

Upon his return, Pike found that Wilkinson was already planning to send him on a second expedition. Some Osage prisoners
taken from the Potawatomis, and a few junketing Osage chiefs,
needed to be escorted to their homes in what is now western
Missouri. Also, a party of Kansas Indians had recently come
down and asked for help in making peace with the Pawnees in
the Kansas-Nebraska area. Wilkinson wanted, furthermore, to
establish contact with the Comanches farther to the west, because
their close association with the Spanish made them seem a dangerous threat to the frontier. And, finally, there was the ever-
present need to know what the Spanish themselves were doing
along the poorly defined western border of the Louisiana Purchase.

In 1806 almost every American citizen expected a war with
Spain, which had not reacted happily to France's sale of Louisiana to the United States. The Secretary of War had instructed
Wilkinson to engage in intelligence operations, using army officers disguised as traders if necessary, to find out what Spain was
up to, and to get an idea of the terrain "to the west of Louisiana." The Secretary had even hinted that a military expedition
against Mexico might become necessary. Some of the government's apprehensions about the Spanish had originated with
Wilkinson himself, and even though they were now merely being
fed back to the General, the official concern gave Wilkinson a
freer rein.

It would soon develop that Wilkinson and Aaron Burr had
been planning a coup in the West. Was it a traitorous movement
to separate the western states and territories from the Union, or
merely a plot to conduct filibustering operations against Spanish-

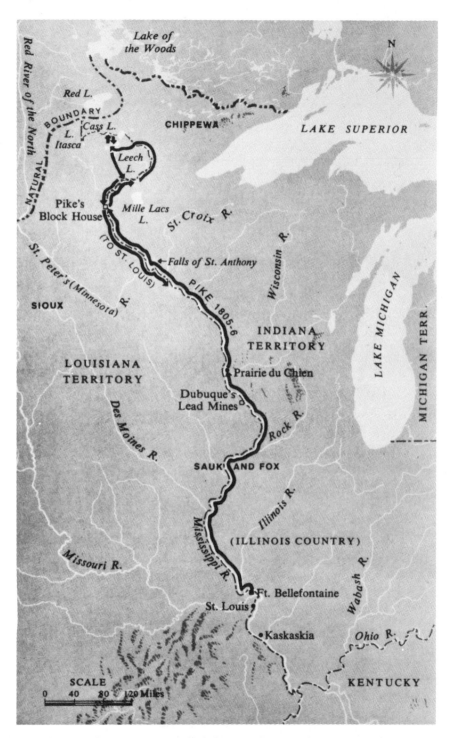

*Pike's first expedition (1805–6) took him north to Leech Lake, which he guessed might be the source of the Mississippi. It was later established that in fact Lake Itasca—just to the west of Pike's route—was the actual source of the river.*

dominated Mexico? The question is still disputed by historians. In either case, the expedition to the Spanish borderlands would serve Wilkinson well. His orders to Pike instructed him to explore the headwaters of the Arkansas and Red rivers, which were presumed to lie just within the western limits of the Louisiana Purchase. When he had completed his reconnaissance he was to descend the Red to Natchitoches. In a separate letter Wilkinson told the young explorer, "you must indeed be extremely guarded with respect to the Spaniards—neither alarm nor offend them unnecessarily."

After some delay because his Osage charges were ill in St. Louis, Pike got his entourage moving on July 15, 1806. The main portion of his command was an assortment of eighteen enlisted men from the First Infantry Regiment, most of whom had been with Pike on his earlier expedition. "A Dam'd set of Rascels," he called them, "but very proper for such expeditions as I am engaged in."

Besides the enlisted soldiers, three other men accompanied Pike. His second in command was Lieutenant James B. Wilkinson, the General's son. The Lieutenant was largely untried, though he had earlier led an unsuccessful Missouri River expedition attempting to reach the mouth of the Platte. His new assignment was to accompany Pike through what is now Missouri and Kansas, as far as the Great Bend of the Arkansas River, then to return down that river and provide the government with a detailed chart and topographic description of the route.

Accompanying the group as interpreter was Baronet Vasquez, usually called Barney by his American friends. He was a young resident of St. Louis, fluent in both French and Spanish, at home among the Indians, and accustomed to living in the wilds. The most mysterious person in the command, a man whose complex motives are still not entirely clear, was Dr. John H. Robinson. He had lately moved west to St. Louis, where he was serving as acting army surgeon, and when he learned of the expedition he is said to have entreated Wilkinson repeatedly for permission to go along as a volunteer.

In the sultriest days of a midwestern summer, the soldiers and Indians moved up the mosquito-ridden Missouri. The supplies and most of the soldiers were in boats, and the Indians kept to the shore—afoot and on horseback. They left the Missouri for the smaller, more tortuous channel of the Osage River—part of

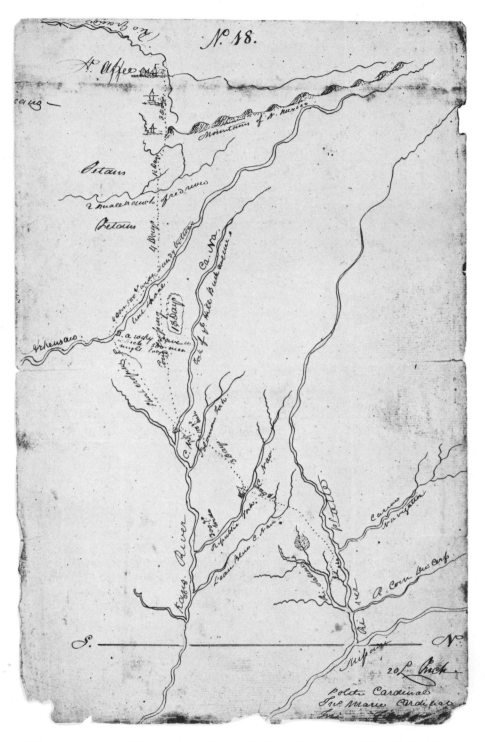

*Pike's own map of his route to Santa Fe from the mouth of the Platte River*

which is now the Lake of the Ozarks — and had reached the two villages of the Osages in western Missouri by August 20. Here the Osage prisoners and chiefs were returned to their people; the party rested, counselled, tried with some success to recruit horses, and then moved on.

Now the expedition veered to the northwest, travelling diagonally across Kansas toward a band of Pawnees then living on the Republican River.* There, in the very center of the Louisiana Purchase, he talked the Pawnee chiefs into hauling down their Spanish flag and running up the Stars and Stripes. His success in persuading them to do so was all the more satisfying to Pike because the village had recently been visited by a contingent of Spanish cavalry. The glitter and dash of the Spanish horsemen, some three hundred of them, no doubt made a strong contrast to Pike's ill-equipped little command. But Pike was a dogged negotiator if not a gifted one, and the King's ensign came down, as least temporarily. The explorer noted in his journal: "I did not wish to embarrass them . . . for fear that the Spaniards might return there in force again, I returned them their flag, but with an injunction that it should never be hoisted again during our stay."

After making a tenuous peace between some Kansas chiefs and the Pawnees, and trying in vain to get some of the Pawnee men to lead him to the Comanches, Pike set out again. He had two chores remaining: he must try to find and proselyte the Comanches, and he must explore the sources of the Arkansas and the Red.

By this time Pike had sent a letter to the General — carried by special messenger — which was to become the theme of every discussion of Pike's motives for years to come. On July 22 he had written:

With respect to the Ietans [Comanches], the Genl. may rest assured I shall use every precaution previous to trusting them — but as to the mode of conduct to be pursued towards the Spaniards I feel more at a loss; as my Instructions lead me into the Country of the Ietans — part of which is no Doubt claimed by Spain — although the Boundary's between Louisi-

* The exact spot has long been disputed by Kansans and Nebraskans, since the river flows close to the border between the two states for several miles and there are remains of Pawnee villages on both sides of the line. Kansans were sufficiently convinced that Pike raised the flag over *their* soil to erect a monument near Republic in 1901. But Pike's tables of course and distance, and his manuscript map of the route, plainly show that he was above the boundary, near Red Cloud, Nebraska.

ania & N. Mexico have never yet been defined—in consequence of which should I rencounter a [Spanish] party . . . in the vicinity of St. Afee [Santa Fe]—I have thought it would be good policy to give them to understand that we were bound to join our Troops near Natchitoches but had been uncertain aboute the Head Waters of the Rivers over which we passed—but that now, if the [Spanish] Commandt. [at Santa Fe] desired it we would pay him a visit of politeness—either by Deputation, or the whole party—but if he refused; signify our intention of pursuing our Direct rout to the posts below—*this if acceded to would gratify our most sanguine expectations*; but if not [would] . . . secure us an unmolested retreat to Natchitoches. But if the Spanish jealousy, and the instigation of traters, should induce them to make us prisoners of War—(in time of peace) I trust to the magnaminity of our Country for our liberation—and a Due reward to their opposers for the Insult, & indignity, offer'd their National Honor.

The phrase italicized here for emphasis was not included in the version of the letter published in the 1810 edition of Pike's journals; it appears only in his retained copy, captured with him and kept by the Spanish. Discovery of this version makes some things quite clear: Pike was eager for firsthand information about the territory around Santa Fe, he had discussed the matter with Wilkinson before his departure, and he would not mind being apprehended by Spanish soldiers in order to gain his objective. Furthermore, this prior understanding—not spelled out in the General's written orders—was a point sufficiently sensitive to call for deletion of the passage before publication.

Actually the letter tells us little about Pike's basic mission that we have not seen elsewhere. Certainly he was collecting information—all he could get by any means—but again the question of motive is crucial. Was he working for Wilkinson, and maybe for Aaron Burr, or did he believe that he was only making an important reconnaissance of a country with which his government might soon be at war?

A more perplexing aspect of the letter is Pike's scheme to explain his presence to the Spanish by claiming to be "uncertain aboute the Head Waters of the Rivers." Within a few months he would be making a claim to Joachín del Real Alencaster, governor of New Mexico, which sounded very much like this. To discover how Pike got into the position of seeming to have predicted his own loss of direction, we must trail him into country more rugged than any he had ever seen.

Beginning October 7, Pike made a trail southward across Kansas. He crossed the Solomon, the Saline, and the Smoky Hill, all typically small prairie rivers lazing through the grasslands, then approached the Arkansas by way of the swampy Cheyenne Bottoms and struck that river at the Great Bend. At this point Lieutenant Wilkinson left the party with a small detachment and began to descend the Arkansas, grumbling as he left that Pike had not given him a fair share of the food, equipment, and ammunition. He was to complete his mission successfully (though three of his five men deserted in the last stages of the descent), and his findings were later incorporated into Pike's published maps and journals.

Pike and the fifteen others started up the Arkansas on October 28, after watching the Lieutenant shove off, and soon found themselves travelling almost due west. Before long they began to scan the horizon for a trace of the Rockies. They were meticulous about following the trail of the Spanish troops who had preceded them, for the chopped-up turf left by the horses' hoofs, and the dozens of cold campfires, offered an excellent guide to—and perhaps through—the mountains. It makes sense that Pike did not try to catch up with the Spanish; he had much work to do before getting involved with them.

By November 11 he was beginning to see that he could not perform his entire mission as quickly as he and General Wilkinson had supposed. But he had survived the previous winter in Minnesota, and this may have encouraged a bold decision: "I determined to spare no pains to accomplish every object even should it oblige me to spend another winter, in the desert." He and his men were wearing cotton uniforms, and they carried no equipment suitable for the snows of the Rockies.

The land was rising now as they entered eastern Colorado. At a point near the junction of the Purgatoire River and the Arkansas, Pike thought he could see mountains on the horizon. He and Dr. Robinson studied the low, blue formation for a while and were sure. "When our small party arrived on the hill," he wrote, "they with one accord gave three *cheers* to the *Mexican mountains*."

A roving band of Pawnees appeared on November 22, about sixty men who had been out hunting for Comanches. They were bent on thievery as they surrounded Pike's men, and it required a good deal of sternness, plus the usual dispensation of presents, to shake them loose and send them on their way.

The expedition reached the site of Pueblo, Colorado, on November 23. Pike had now become fascinated with the great blue peak rising to his right. It was off his course, but he thought he could hike to it in a single day and from its summit make topographic observations of the surrounding area. He was soon to learn that sometimes mountains only *look* close. Early the next day he directed his men in building a small log fortification, and then set out for the mountain with Dr. Robinson and two soldiers.

The four started up Fountain Creek, a branch of the Arkansas that appeared to lead directly to the peak, but they soon abandoned the stream when it seemed to bear too far north (although it would eventually have led them to their goal). They headed northwest across terrain scarred by lightly timbered ridges, but by nightfall were still far from the great mountain that later would bear Pike's name. The next day they reached a formation of lesser peaks that lay between them and the big one. All that day and the next they climbed, and at last reached a high point from which they could see how futile their efforts had been. Still more subsidiary prominences lay between them and the highest mountain. They were in deep snow, in those abominable cotton uniforms, and game was scarce. "The summit of the Grand Peak, which was entirely bare of vegetation and covered with snow," Pike wrote, "now appeared at the distance of 15 or 16 miles from us, and as high again as what we had ascended, and would have taken a whole day's march to have arrived at its base, when I believe no human being could have ascended to its pinacal."

Disappointed, they descended to the prairie and returned to camp. Pike's comments about the difficulty of climbing the mountain can be interpreted in two ways. He may have meant that the peak, which he estimated at more than 18,000 feet (it actually is a little over 14,000), could never be climbed by anyone. Or he may have meant that no one in his situation, cold and hungry and so far from camp, could have made it to the top. Modern tourists who drive to the summit on a good roadway, and who find there a merchant dispensing hamburgers, milk shakes, and souvenirs, usually assume that Pike actually climbed Pikes Peak.

The next significant stop was on the present site of Canon City. Here Pike made one of those crucial decisions that shaped the future of his expedition. He had been following the Arkansas for many days, past several forks, and now he found that it forked again. One branch seemed to reach into the very heart of the mountains, between steep cliffs (the Royal Gorge), and the other veered northward through easier country. This branch, now called Four-Mile Creek, is a sizable affluent of the Arkansas which rises high in the north, at the extremity of the Arkansas River watershed. Pike and Dr. Robinson explored both branches for a short distance. Apparently they did not believe that a main branch could extend very far into the surprising canyon from which the Arkansas actually issues. An added argument for following the north fork was the indication that a party of horsemen had recently ascended it. Whether the horsemen were Spanish troops or a band of Comanches, Pike now wanted to get in touch with them, for he was beginning to feel quite uneasy about his location. In his words, "We determined to pursue them, as . . . the geography of the country, had turned out to be so different from our expectation; we were some what at a loss which course to pursue, unless we attempted to cross the snow cap'd mountains, to the south east of us which was almost impossible."

The expedition followed north along Four-Mile Creek for two days and then chose its western fork. But the branch finally dwindled — and so did the hoof-marked trail they had been tracing. The party then headed straight north. Pike was leading his men toward a high plateau that would later become known as South Park; and there he was surprised to find, on December 12, a river flowing to the east. "Must it not be the head waters of the river Platte?" he wrote in his journal. He was correct; he had found the south fork of the South Platte.

Pike now became convinced that he must head southwest once more and contrive to find the Red River. He had lost the Spanish trail completely and seemed to believe that he had somehow passed above all possible sources of the Arkansas — which actually rises a little farther north, near what later became Leadville. His principal map, and indeed the contemporary map that any sensible explorer would have been delighted to have, was one left in Washington in 1804 by Baron Alexander von Humboldt, the great German naturalist, as one result of a year spent in Mexico. It had been handed down to Pike at the instigation of Wilkinson, and was a remarkable early portrayal of Mexico and the North

American Southwest. But among its many departures from actuality was its handling of the Red River. Humboldt showed this stream rising in the Rocky Mountains, near Santa Fe, when in truth it rises on the plains of northwestern Texas. Pike thought that he could find it by proceeding southwest across the towering ranges.

Abandoning the South Platte, Pike made for a low pass in the mountains, now called Trout Creek Pass and traversed by U.S. Highway 24. His crossing of the pass was not difficult, even in winter — he was still east of the Continental Divide — and when he reached the western foot he made a discovery which sent a shout of joy through the whole command. At a spot just below the present location of Buena Vista, Colorado, they came upon what they assumed was the Red River. It was their highway to home, they thought, for it would lead them to the broad reaches of the Mississippi.

Actually, they were back on the Arkansas, some seventy miles upstream of where they had left it a fortnight earlier. Pike marched northward with two men to probe somewhat deeper into the sources of the river, and sent the rest of his party downstream with urgent instructions to forage for game. The date was December 21; the snow was deep, and the command was short of food, clothing, and ammunition. Pike and his two partners ascended the river to the Twin Lakes region south of Leadville. Here he decided that his "Red River" had nearly played out. Hungry, cold, and separated from his men, he easily convinced himself that he could see the approximate head of the stream where it disappeared into the distant mountains; and, in fact, he was now not far from the source of the Arkansas. He turned back, and on the broadening valley floor where the town of Salida would later appear, beside the carcasses of the buffalo cows which may have saved their lives, he and his men spent Christmas in 1806.

Now they started down the river, seeking a convenient place to await better weather, build boats, and make more side trips before descending to civilization. They worked their way down the valley between towering white peaks, past the present sites of Coaldale, Cotopaxi, and Parkdale. The river was frozen solidly enough to support horses — a fact indicating an extraordinarily low temperature — but Pike had great difficulty moving the animals down the narrow channel among the many rocks impacted in the ice. "Had frequently to cross the river on the ice, horses falling down, we were obliged to pull them over on the ice. . . . We had great difficulty in getting our horses along, some of the poor animals having nearly killed themselves falling on the ice . . . one horse fell down the precipice, and bruised himself so miserably, that I conceived it mercy to cause the poor animal to be shot. Many others were nearly killed with falls received. . . ."

Pike was no literary man. Even with an unusual imagination and a flair for words, both of which qualities he lacked, he could hardly have done justice in his journal to the monstrous cleft in

*The summit of Pikes Peak rises above the small settlement of Colorado City.*

the earth which he and his men were entering as they unknowingly approached, once again, the site of Canon City. He reported that they "encamped at the entrance of the most perpendicular precipices on both sides, through which the river ran and our course lay." So much for the Royal Gorge. Neither Pike nor any of the several parties into which he had divided his men actually descended the whole length of the canyon. Pike travelled about halfway before climbing out.

And now, of course, they had come full circle. Surely in anguish, when he reached the place where the Arkansas left the mountains and recognized it as their old camp, Pike crossed "Red River" off his charts and tables, and penned in the word "Arkansaw."

He had brought his men through a considerable hell, but all was not lost. According to his views of geography, reinforced by Baron von Humboldt's map, he could still find the head of the Red River by working his way through the "white, snow-cap'd Mountains, very high" that lay to the southwest—the Sangre de Cristos. Clearly, it would be a cruel journey.

Because the horses were bruised, exhausted, and sick, Pike now decided to attack the mountains on foot, carrying packs and leaving the horses behind to recuperate. A small stockade was built on the north bank of the Arkansas, within the present limits of Canon City, and Interpreter Vasquez and Private Patrick Smith were detailed to stay with the horses until sent for.

The fourteen-man party left the new stockade on January 14, 1807, and headed up a branch of the Arkansas, now called Grape Creek, which came from the south and offered promise of a route into the mountains. Three days later Pike stood looking across a valley that was to be the scene of his greatest ordeal of cold and hunger, the Wet Mountain Valley. It is a pleasant enough place in fair weather, and today the yellow school buses speed down the middle of it to gather up the ranchers' children; but Pike was entering it with inadequate food and clothing, and he had the bad luck to reach it just before a severe snowstorm.

Where Pike entered the valley there is little vegetation. To find firewood and the shelter of trees, the expedition marched west, to the opposite slope, on January 17. When they camped that night, nine of the men had frozen feet. Two of the victims were Pike's hunters, so designated because of their proficiency in obtaining game, and the party spent a hungry night.

Pike wrote in his journal the next day: "18th January, Sunday. —We started two of the men least injured [to hunt]; the doctor and myself, who fortunately were untouched by the frost, also went out to hunt something to preserve existence, near evening we wounded a buffalo with three balls, but had the mortification to see him run off notwithstanding. We concluded it was useless to go home to add to the general gloom, and went amongst some rocks where we encamped and sat up all night; from the intense cold it was impossible to sleep. Hungry and without cover."

The next day, Pike and Dr. Robinson found and killed a buffalo. They slaughtered it hastily, loaded themselves with meat, and arrived at the camp after midnight. Their men had not eaten for four days.

It now appeared that Privates John Sparks and Thomas Dougherty had been too badly frostbitten to continue. Pike decided to leave them, with some of his supplies, and march on. "I furnished the two poor lads who were to remain with ammunition, made use of every argument in my power to encourage them to have fortitude to resist their fate, and gave them assurance on my sending relief as soon as possible. We parted, but not without tears."

Pike knew that the heights of the Sangre de Cristo range were insurmountable to men so ill-equipped and hungry. He was determined to continue southeast along the base of the range until he encountered a pass. But after marching for a couple of days more, he found his food situation again serious. The snow was waist deep, making hunting almost impossible, and in any case it appeared that the buffalo had quit the valley. He wrote: "I determined to attempt the traverse of the mountain, in which we persevered until the snow became so deep that it was impossible to proceed; when I again turned my face to the plain, and for the first time in the voyage found myself discouraged." Dr. Robinson killed a buffalo the next day, but by this time Private Hugh Menaugh had "froze and gave oute" and had to be left temporarily behind.

A pass now presented itself, and Pike lost no time in entering it. In two days of marching it led him across the Sangre de Cristos and down into the San Luis Valley. At the western foot of the pass he found that unique collection of dunes that has now become the Great Sand Dunes National Monument, and coursing down the middle of the valley was the river then commonly called the Rio del Norte and now named the Rio Grande.

Pike, however, was now lost again. Mistakenly jubilant, he wrote in his tables of course and distance for January 30: "To ye Banks of Red River."

To find logs for a stockade and for building the boats he needed to descend the "Red River," Pike took his men a few miles up a western tributary, the Conejos. Across the stream from a curiously isolated and barren hill, conveniently located for a sentinel's post, they began to construct a small fortification —built of cottonwood logs and surrounded by a moat into which was diverted the water of the Conejos. They were about twelve miles southeast of what today is Alamosa, Colorado. As soon as Pike could get a flag-staff in the ground he unwittingly began to

*A nineteenth-century lithograph showing Santa Fe much as it was in 1807 when Pike arrived — a city of low, cramped adobe huts scattered around a central plaza*

fly the American flag on the soil of His Most Catholic Majesty, the King of Spain.

There is a mistaken belief that Pike would have knowingly trespassed, even if he had actually found the Red River, once he crossed to the far side. But, although the boundary of the Louisiana Purchase was in dispute, the United States laid a firm claim to the Red River and all its waters.

The next episode in the tale belongs to Dr. Robinson. We have seen him thus far as a man with a good shooting eye, but he must have served Pike in other important ways. In a letter to a congressman, Pike later described him as "the right arm of the expedition." The medical ethics of a physician who leaves three men exhausted and freezing in the mountains, while he pushes on with the healthy ones, is open to question; but Dr. Robinson had something on his mind. Armed with a document that gave him authority to collect a debt from an expatriate American near Santa Fe who owed a merchant in Kaskaskia, Illinois, the Doctor set out on foot in the direction of the Spanish settlements. He told Pike that he did not plan to identify himself as a member of the expedition, and that he would return in plenty of time to descend the river when the stragglers had been collected and the boats constructed.

When he reached Santa Fe, Dr. Robinson told Governor Alencaster that he had recently separated from a party of hunters and had come to collect a sum from one Baptiste Lalande. The

Governor immediately reported the incident to his superior, Commandant-General Nemesio Salcedo, in Chihuahua, and he also sent out patrols in the hope of apprehending some of the Doctor's companions. Later, when the Doctor was taken to Chihuahua, he asked General Salcedo for political asylum. He said he wanted to become a Spanish subject and a convert to Catholicism, and that he would repay the Spanish by exploring the lands lying to the north. He asked the General not to betray his wishes to Pike, who had befriended him. Apparently the Spanish officials were suspicious, for he was not allowed to stay.

Pike, meanwhile, sent two relief parties back for the men and horses he had left behind. The detachment dispatched to recover his three crippled soldiers returned with Hugh Menaugh, the only one able to travel. The other two, Sparks and Dougherty, sent Pike bits of their gangrenous toe bones in a kind of macabre supplication not to be abandoned. "Little did they know my heart," wrote Pike, "if they could suspect me of conduct so ungenerous."

Now one of the patrols sent out from Santa Fe found Pike's stockade: on February 26 he was informed by a young Spanish officer that he was encamped on a branch of the Rio Grande. He was surprised, but not ready to argue: "I immediately ordered my flag to be taken down and rolled up, feeling how sensibly I had committed myself, in entering their territory, and was conscious that they must have positive orders to take me in."

After arranging to collect the stragglers, the Spanish patrol escorted Pike's party to Santa Fe. Here his papers were confiscated, and after some questioning he was sent on to Chihuahua. Neither he nor his men were mistreated, but the members of the expedition were now permanently separated. Pike and a few of his men were back in United States territory by June 30, 1807, having been escorted to the border by their captors. Five of the men, for reasons not altogether clear, were detained two years longer, and Sergeant William C. Meek, after killing Private Theodore Miller while drunk, was held for fourteen years.

From here on, the Pike story becomes mainly a wrangle between Spanish and United States officials over the boundary violation, and a long debate in the United States over Pike's intentions. General Salcedo was reprimanded by his government after releasing Pike, for the King and his ministers felt that the exploring party should have been imprisoned until the United

States acknowledged the incursion as a border violation. The officials in Spain somehow never corrected their original, erroneous impression that Pike was apprehended in Texas, near San Antonio, which would have placed him much farther into avowedly Spanish territory.

Pike's return to his country received little notice, for by that time General Wilkinson had charged Aaron Burr with treason and the whole populace was caught up in the electrifying drama. Burr's trial was in progress in Richmond when Pike got back. The Burr story is a complex one, but to consider it in connection

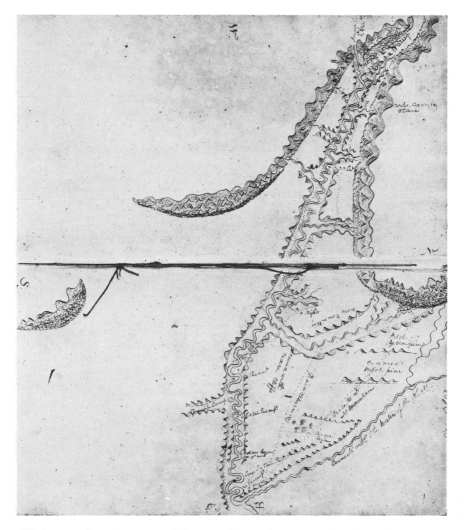

*Pike's own drawing (printed here with North at the right) shows the route he took up the Arkansas River to Pikes Peak (right center) and Royal Gorge, surrounded by mountains (top). At left is a sketch of Pikes Peak and its satellites.*

with Pike we need to distill only two conclusions: first, that Burr's operation seems to have been primarily a planned movement against the Spanish colonies in North America, especially Mexico, and was predicated upon an expected war with Spain; second, that General Wilkinson was surely a co-planner if not an originator of the scheme. The General later found it advisable to extricate himself—in the face of failure—by denouncing Burr.

Almost certainly Pike was not a party to the Aaron Burr movement. His vigorous denials, upon returning from the West, seem to have sprung from a genuine ignorance of the Burr-Wilkinson plan. There is no evidence that he knew of the conspiracy until he read of it in the *Gacetas de Mexico* while in that country.

It is not quite accurate to say that Pike planned to be "captured" by the Spanish. Perhaps it is better to say that he hoped to fall in with a Spanish party and get a chance to visit Santa Fe. Long before he had arrived in the area, word had somehow reached Chihuahua that his expedition was on the way. It is quite possible that Wilkinson himself originated the message. (On the other hand, the Spanish were also quick to learn of the Lewis and Clark expedition and of an abortive American exploration up the Red River, during the same period. Salcedo's orders were to terminate all such expeditions into disputed territory.) It would have been most ingenous of Pike to suppose that Dr. Robinson's visit to Santa Fe would not alert the Spanish garrison there. Yet it does not seem likely that he foresaw his own detention and the loss of his papers.

Besides the lingering suspicion that Pike was in league with Burr and Wilkinson, another charge has lived on—the charge that Pike was never really lost. Historians who build too solidly upon Pike's letter to Wilkinson written in July, 1806 (quoted on page 42), have a difficult task. They must show that Pike—who travelled with defective maps and no true mental image of western geography—conducted an elaborate campaign to convince the Spanish that he was lost. According to this theory, we must believe that Pike knew there was no Red River as far west as the Rockies, despite the information he had from such authorities as Baron von Humboldt; that when he and his men were freezing and starving in the Wet Mountain Valley he was engaging in deliberate subterfuge; and that when he was confronted by a Spanish officer and was told he was encamped on the west side of the Rio Grande, his plea of ignorance was a long-planned lie. Given the faulty knowledge of the West that Pike possessed, the thing is impossible.

Pike published his letter to Wilkinson (with that significant deletion) for all the world to see. To him it was not a damaging letter, for it only projected a plan to *pretend* he was lost if the need should arise. When the time came he actually *was* lost. And, to one who had undergone those awful days along the base of the Sangre de Cristos, the difference was substantial. Apparently Pike thought that the reading public would believe so, too.

Among the papers the Spanish took from Pike was a notebook filled with sketch maps, accompanied by his faithfully made tables of course and distance. These remained in the archives of Mexico for a century before their rediscovery in 1907; later representations by the American government caused them to be transferred to the National Archives in Washington. The documents show the attempt of an earnest and brave but sometimes inept explorer to make a useful record of his travels. When he found that he had mistaken the Arkansas for the Red River, he corrected his maps and tables. Later, when he learned from the Spanish that he was again mistaken, he deleted in one instance the words "Red River" and wrote in "Rio del Nord."

Pike's erratic ramblings, his journal entries, and the evidence revealed by his manuscript maps leave little doubt that he was truly lost — not once, but twice.

When Pike was encamped at the Pawnee village, early in the course of the expedition, word reached him that Meriwether Lewis and William Clark had returned safely from their journey to the Pacific. They had gone up the Missouri, crossed the Rockies, and descended the Columbia. In Pike's correspondence he referred often to Lewis and Clark, sometimes jealously, for he ardently hoped to rank with them as an explorer. His achievement does not quite measure up to theirs, although there is no doubt that he was their equal in courage and endurance. Together, the two undertakings were of vital importance, representing the first extensive probing of the New Louisiana Purchase. Pike's *An Account of Expeditions to the Sources of the Mississippi, and Through the Western Parts of Louisiana,* published in Philadelphia in 1810, was rich in information and became required reading for those whose eyes were turned to the new lands. Along with his "Dam'd set of Rascels," Pike had found a high place among the notable explorers of the American West.

*A trio of travelers passing through the foothills of the towering Canadian Rockies*

# A
# MAN
# TO MATCH THE
# MOUNTAINS

## By ALVIN M. JOSEPHY, JR.

*D*avid Thompson was a short, stocky man with snub nose and hair "cut square" across his forehead in a way that made him resemble John Bunyan. That is all we know about his looks. Until recently, historians knew little about who David Thompson was or what he did, and even today, few people recognize his name. Among those familiar with his exploits, however, he is now deemed one of the most important explorers of the New World, and has been acclaimed as one of the greatest land geographers ever produced by the English-speaking people.

That is high praise, but consider Thompson's achievements. During a twenty-year period, between 1792 and 1812, he crossed and recrossed the unknown wilderness of the northwestern United States and Canada, usually accompanied only by Indians, exploring and mapping the principal features of more than a million and a half square miles of territory, from Hudson Bay to the Pacific Ocean and from the Great Lakes to the Athabaska wasteland of northern Canada. On the maps, when he began his explorations, all that vast region was a blank.

He was the first white man to explore and settle upon the upper Columbia River. He was the first to build white establishments in the present-day states of Montana, Idaho, and Washington. He was the first to make a full survey of the shore line of Lake Superior, and the first to map the relationship between the Missouri River and the principal streams of the central Canadian plains.

In addition, he was the first, and in some cases the only man to gather certain information that is today recognized as indispensable for an accurate history of the early West. He met Blackfeet and other Indians of the plains and Rocky Mountains who told him what it was like when they first got guns, and when they saw their first horse. He heard anecdotes and learned the history of Indian warfare and tribal movements before white men knew of the existence of those tribes. And in the American Northwest, his records have startled historians with references to other white men who were in that remote part of the continent at the same time as Lewis and Clark, including a mysterious second United States exploring expedition about which nothing else has ever been known.

Thompson's discoveries and surveys enriched the world with knowledge of the northwestern part of this continent. But the professional cartographers and engravers who used his information failed to acknowledge him as their source, and the people who in later years followed the routes he pioneered were unaware that he was the author of the maps they used. Similarly, his written records were not published, and no one knew where he had been or what he had done. When he died in 1857—poor, blind, and unknown—he was buried in an unmarked grave in Montreal.

Thompson might have been altogether forgotten had it not been for the curiosity of a Canadian geologist, Dr. Joseph B. Tyrrell, who was working in the West during the 1880's as a member of the Geological Survey of Canada. Tyrrell was struck by the completeness and accuracy of the old government maps he was using, and he became interested in trying to discover their source. His search led to the files of the Crown Lands Department of the Province of Ontario at Toronto, where he uncovered a group of weathered journals and notebooks of David Thompson, as well as a huge manuscript map of the western half of North America between the latitudes of 45 and 60 degrees, which the explorer had made years before. Study of the diaries and notebooks revealed the hitherto unsuspected extent of

Thompson's many journeys as a fur trader and surveyor for the Hudson's Bay and the North West companies, and the map confirmed him as the original source for the government charts of the West that Tyrrell had been using.

In the years that followed, Dr. Tyrrell continued his quest for further information, and eventually learned that while Thompson had been in the service of the fur companies, his maps and reports had been sent by his superiors to Aaron Arrowsmith, the English cartographer, who used them to help prepare his maps of North America. But Arrowsmith never acknowledged Thompson as the source of his information. Dr. Tyrrell also learned that in 1814, while still in the employ of the North West Company, Thompson had completed his own great manuscript map of all the territory he had explored and surveyed. For a while it had hung in the dining hall of the company's post at Fort William, on Lake Superior, where it was seen only by company partners and employees. At the time, the company had no interest in having the map circulated, because its members were then engaged in intense competition with the Hudson's Bay Company, whose traders would have valued the detailed information it contained.

After Thompson retired from the fur trade, he tried on a number of occasions to have his map published, but never succeeded. He settled in eastern Canada with his half-breed wife and their children, and continued as a surveyor. From 1817 to 1827, he was employed by the British Boundary Commission to

Voyageurs *at Fort William, a nineteenth-century trading post on Lake Superior*

survey the international border between Canada and the United States from St. Regis on the St. Lawrence River to the Lake of the Woods, north of Minnesota. Later, he was overcome by a series of misfortunes. Most of his savings disappeared in the unprofitable business ventures of his sons. His eyesight failed. Further difficulties forced him to sell his scientific instruments—and at one time even pawn his coat—in order to eat. When the North West and Hudson's Bay companies merged, a new generation of fur men forgot the name and achievements of David Thompson, the Nor'-Wester.

Thompson's own modest character contributed to his obscurity. Quiet and unobtrusive, he failed to push himself forward or seek recognition. In extreme poverty, on the edge of complete blindness, he managed when more than seventy years old to write a narrative of his explorations, hoping to make a little money from its sale. In some way Washington Irving heard of it and tried to buy it but, according to Thompson's daughter, failed to offer enough money or to satisfy Thompson with regard to acknowledgment of its authorship. There were no other bidders. The narrative, like the great map, remained unpublished, and when Thompson died at eighty-seven, there was sparse evidence for historians to know that he had ever existed.

Thompson was active in the Canadian fur trade during some of its most colorful and exciting days, when agents of the rival trading companies were leapfrogging past each other westward across the unexplored forests and plains of the continent, competing with guns and alcohol for the beaver trade of newly discovered tribes. Thompson was born on April 30, 1770, in Westminster, England, of poor and obscure parents, and after his father's death he received some education at the Grey Coat School, a charitable institution in London. An industrious youth with ability in mathematics and writing, he was bound to the Hudson's Bay Company as a seven-year apprentice, at the age of fourteen. Young Thompson was shipped to the bleak and lonely Churchill Factory post on Hudson Bay, and after a year was sent on foot with two Indian guides to York Factory, 150 miles away. He had a gun, but was given no provisions for the trip, and the difficult journey along the icy, windswept shore of the bay taught the fifteen-year-old boy how to live off the land.

His wilderness education continued at York Factory, where he served as a clerk and hunter; one year later, in 1786, he was sent with an expedition deep into central Canada to establish a new trading post on the south branch of the Saskatchewan River, about as far west as white men had yet penetrated. Though only sixteen, and a quiet, unassuming youth with a devoutly religious turn of mind, he was already considered an unusually capable wilderness man, bold, intelligent, and resourceful, a reliable leader with a sense of responsibility to his companions and a devotion to hard work and duty. The next year he was selected to accompany six men southwestward across the unexplored buffalo plains to find the Blackfeet Indians, teach them to trap beaver, and turn them into providers of furs for the Hudson's Bay Company.

Near present-day Calgary, Alberta, the group found the Blackfeet, and Thompson spent the winter in the lodge of a friendly and aged chief who instructed him in the life and traditions of the Indians inhabiting the country along the eastern side of the Rockies. Much of what Thompson learned that winter, and recorded in his narrative, is the only known account of Indian history in that area before the white man came.

Back on the Saskatchewan River, Thompson became interested in meteorology and surveying, and was instructed by Philip Turnor, the official surveyor of the Hudson's Bay Company. He kept daily records of weather, temperature, and wind, and began to take astronomical readings and learn to solve problems of time, latitude, longitude, and variations of the compass. He acquired a ten-inch brass sextant and, wherever he traveled, made careful observations with compass, watch, and a crude artificial mercury horizon. His thoroughness and skill gradually helped him attain a high degree of precision in his calculations, and Dr. Tyrrell was only the first among many geographers and surveyors who, retracing the ground with modern instruments in later years, were surprised by the accuracy of Thompson's work.

In 1791 his apprenticeship ended, and the following year he became a trader. For a number of years he was assigned to the great watery wilderness west of Hudson Bay. He traveled through thick forests sown with lakes, streams, and mosquito-filled bogs, and across treeless muskeg, stretching in cold and lonely silence toward the Arctic horizon. No white man had been in the country before him, and wherever he went, he surveyed and mapped. He built log huts in the forested areas for the trade of small, isolated groups of Indians, explored canoe routes

61

through muddy, marsh-choked ends of lakes, and charted difficult portages around rushing waterfalls and boulder-strewn
white water.

Usually, his only companions were Indians or half-breeds who
helped him find passages for his canoe and supplied him with
fish and deer and caribou meat. In the face of an unending
procession of hardships and close calls with death, he learned to
live and travel like the natives, moving with speed and exactness
across vast stretches of land, pausing only to seek protection
from gales and blizzards or to gum the leaking seams of his cedar canoe with pine pitch. His sole comforts were the fair-
weather lapping of lake water, the warming flames of evening
fires, and the clean forest smell of pine-needle beds.

Despite his increasing interest in exploring and surveying, the
Hudson's Bay Company wanted him to confine his activities to
trading, and in 1797, when his term with that company ended,
he joined the more aggressive North West Company, whose
partners were more appreciative of his special skills. Unham-
pered by the problems of trade, he set off at once on an unprece-
dented mapping tour for his new employers, traveling south
across the plains to the Mandan Indian villages on the Missouri
River in present-day North Dakota, charting the Red River
country and the wild-rice lake district of northern Minnesota,
coming within a few miles of correctly identifying the source of
the Mississippi River (it was not found until 1832), and going on
to survey for the first time the entire shore line of Lake Superior. During this trip, he met Alexander Mackenzie at Sault Ste.

*Friendly fur trading in Canada, idealized by an eighteenth-century Englishman*

Marie and was told by that great North West Company explorer that he had accomplished more in ten months than the company expected could be done in two years. In those months, which included the worst wintry traveling seasons of the year, Thompson "had covered a total of 4,000 miles of survey."

During the next two years, he mapped Canada's cold and remote Churchill and Athabaska regions, again probing unexplored forests and barrens, knowing the howl of wolves and the nightly call of loons, and charting rapids and gale-whipped lakes across hundreds of miles of bleak, quiet land. In the summer of 1800, he returned to the birch and aspen groves on the eastern slopes of the Rocky Mountains, second in command of a party seeking to cross the mountains and open trade with Indians in the upper basin of the Columbia River, where whites had not yet been. The plan failed when the leader of the expedition came down with an attack of rheumatism, but Thompson reached the high precipices of the Canadian Rockies, west of what is now Banff. There he met some Kutenai Indians from the west side of the mountains, and gathered information about what lay beyond. When the groups parted, Thompson recorded that he sent two of his men, "La Gasse and Le Blanc," to live with the Indians. They were the first two men of white blood from eastern Canada known to have entered the Columbia basin.

For the time being, the North West Company postponed further attempts to expand across the Rockies, and during the following years Thompson continued his exploring and trading activities in the more northerly regions of Lesser Slave Lake, the Peace River, and the "muskrat country" between the Nelson and Churchill rivers.

In 1806, the Canadians were alarmed by the Lewis and Clark expedition, which threatened to flank British traders on the west, and once more the North West Company ordered Thompson to try to cross the Continental Divide.

This time he was successful. Setting out from the Saskatchewan River on May 10, 1807, he led a trade group up the mountains into "stupendous & solitary Wilds covered with eternal Snow, & Mountain connected to Mountain by immense Glaciers, the collection of Ages & on which the Beams of the Sun makes hardly any impression. . . ."

On June 25, they finally topped the pass now called Howse and five days later, after following down the "foaming white"

Blaeberry River, reached the upper Columbia River. Since it flowed north at that point, Thompson did not recognize it as the Columbia. He named it the Kootenai after the Indians of the area, and on it built the "Kootanae House," a crude storage post for his trade goods and furs.*

While there he sought to make contact and open trade with natives farther south. One tribe to whom he sent messengers were the Flatheads of Montana, but on August 13 the messengers returned with the doleful news that the Flatheads had been

*Rival tribes: a Flathead brave with his weapons and a Blackfoot medicine man;*

defeated by a band of Blackfeet and had gone, instead, "to a military Post of the Americans." In explanation, Thompson noted in his journal that the Kutenais "informed me that about 3 weeks ago the Americans to the number of 42 arrived to settle a mili-

* Note the many absurd differences in the modern spelling of this word. Canadian and American officials who were unaware of Thompson's original version, Kootanae, stamped approval on all sorts of later local preferences.

tary Post, at the confluence of the two most southern & considerable Branches of the Columbia & that they were preparing to make a small advance Post lower down on the River. 2 of those who were with Capt. Lewis were also with them of whom the poor Kootanaes related several dreadful stories."

This is a significant addition to history. The only Americans known to be heading for the west at that time, one year after the departure of Lewis and Clark from the Columbia, were a group of fur trappers under a St. Louis trader named Manuel Lisa. But

*a Flathead squaw (with papoose in head flattener) and a Blackfoot sun dancer*

at that moment, Lisa's men were still far east, on the Missouri River in present-day South Dakota. One could assume that the Kutenais might have heard of this party, or had gotten their information mixed up, save for the fact that Thompson's messengers also gave him a letter from the Americans, a copy of which Thompson sent back east across the mountains.

The letter was dated "Fort Lewis, Yellow River, Columbia, July

10, 1807" (when Manuel Lisa and his men were even farther down the Missouri, near the mouth of Nebraska's Platte River) and was signed by "James Roseman, Lieutenant" and "Zachary Perch, Captain & Commanding Officer," and listed American regulations for foreigners who were trading with Indians in territory claimed by the United States. The signers said they were sending Thompson the regulations under "Power delegated to us by General Braithwaite Commander of all the new ceded Territories northward of the Illinois," and added that they had heard about Thompson's trip to trade in the Columbia basin from informants among the Mandans.

U.S. Army records reveal no Lieutenant James Roseman, Captain Zachary Perch, or General Braithwaite, but Thompson's entry takes on even greater drama when it is realized that the position ascribed to "General Braithwaite" was actually held at the time by General James Wilkinson, a master of intrigue and deceit, who was deeply involved in the Aaron Burr conspiracy to establish an empire in the West. Moreover, the regulations given to Thompson closely paralleled advice that had been given by Lieutenant Zebulon Pike to some British traders in northern Minnesota during the winter of 1805–06. Pike had drawn up those regulations in the field, but had given a copy of them to Wilkinson, his commanding officer, when he returned to St. Louis.

On December 24, 1807, Thompson received a second letter from the Americans, who revealed that they were with the Nez Percé Indians of Idaho and had had a fight with the Atsinas, allies of the Blackfeet, and had suffered losses. This letter was signed "Jeremy Pinch Lieut." and, blaming Thompson for arming the Atsinas and causing the Americans their difficulties, threatened him with force if he did not withdraw "with a good grace" from the country. Thompson sent the Americans an answer to this letter, saying that he was "neither authorized nor competent" to discuss the question of who owned the Columbia country, and he forwarded a copy of Pinch's letter to his superiors east of the mountains, adding that "This officer was on a party of Discovery when he wrote the above."

Thompson's journals make no further reference to Jeremy Pinch, who is not listed in army records either, but British archives reveal that Pinch and the mysterious expedition received mention in correspondence in the 1840's during British-American negotiations over Oregon. In addition, later journal entries by Thompson, as will be seen, and also maps made by other Canadian fur men, indicate that some unknown Americans were actually in the country at this time, and had a post near what is now Missoula, Montana.

Pinch, Roseman, and Perch might have been western militia officers, or the pseudonyms of Army Regulars, possibly on a private exploring and trading venture for Wilkinson disguised as an official government mission. A study of General Wilkinson's intrigues in St. Louis shows a number of references to private expeditions he planned to send up the Missouri, as well as correspondence that raises doubt as to whether the United States government was aware of his dispatch of Zebulon Pike's expedition to the southern Rockies in that same year of 1807 until it was well under way. Unlike that of Pike, however, the fate of the Pinch group is not known, but further study of the shadowy and little-known figures revealed by Thompson and other early Canadian traders as having been in the Northwest soon after the time of Lewis and Clark might uncover evidence of a western debacle that has never been recorded.

In the spring of 1808, Thompson started the first of many exploration trips through the Columbia country. Before winter settled in, he sent several of his men under a big, red-bearded clerk named Finan McDonald to establish a trading post on the Kootenai River in Montana. McDonald pitched two skin tepees and built a log storehouse opposite the site of Libby in northwestern Montana. It was the first structure built by whites in the state.

During the next summer, 1809, Thompson also went off to Lake Pend Oreille, where on September 10 he built the Kullyspel House, the first white establishment in Idaho. From this trading post, he explored east and west into mountainous Montana and Washington, making the first white contacts with many Indian tribes.

The winter of 1809–10 found him at still another new post called the Saleesh House, which he built for the Flathead trade on the pine-bordered Clark Fork River near Thompson's Falls in northwestern Montana. In return for beaver furs and provisions of dried meat, he supplied the Flatheads with their first guns; those Indians, long persecuted by the Blackfeet, who already had white men's arms, gave a Blackfeet band the surprise of their lives by opening fire on them with the newly acquired "lightning sticks."

In February, 1810, Thompson referred again to Americans in the area, this time to a mysterious "Mr. Courter," who had apparently had a post near Missoula and was killed by Blackfeet. Thompson rushed to the scene of his death and helped to halt the looting of the dead man's property. Who Courter was, or where he came from, is not known, but he might have been a survivor of the Pinch group, because Thompson's salary payments to the employees of the deceased American indicate that three years' wages were owed to at least one of the men. In addition, another of Courter's companions was a man named Rivet, who had accompanied Lewis and Clark during the first year of their expedition, leaving them in North Dakota.

During the spring, Thompson did some more exploring in northeastern Washington, then took his furs back across the Rockies to a company post in central Canada. This time, when he tried to return to the Columbia, he found his route blocked. The Blackfeet were enraged over the arming of the Flatheads and they were determined to put an end to the white men's trade across the mountains. Their war parties guarded the approaches to the pass Thompson had been using. One of Thompson's colleagues hit on a scheme for putting the Indians to sleep on "high wine," a potent mixture of alcohol and water; though some of the native watchers got "beastly drunk," the plan failed, and Thompson had to look for a new route farther north.

The journey proved to be one of the boldest and most dangerous in Thompson's career, for in the midst of winter it took him through treacherous glacier fields and towering ranges of mountains, across what is now the Jasper National Park in the Canadian Rockies. Aided by Indian and half-breed trappers, he struggled on snowshoes through an unknown country half-hidden by high-altitude clouds and storms. Then, on January 10, 1811, he found the famous Athabaska Pass and eleven days later, worn by the hardships of the trip, he reached the Columbia. He was all for continuing to the coast, but his companions had had enough, and refused to go farther until spring.

It has been suggested by some historians that the detour and delay on the Columbia until the arrival of favorable traveling weather eventually proved costly to British claims to Oregon. The North West Company was aware of the plans of the New

York fur merchant John Jacob Astor to send an American trading expedition to the mouth of the Columbia, and it is possible that Thompson had been directed that year to hasten all the way down the Columbia and build a post on the Pacific Coast before the Americans could get there.

Thompson stated in his journal that he would have liked to head immediately down the Columbia, but his party was too small to risk dangers from the unknown tribes it would meet along the way. First, he said, he would have to return to the Flathead country and enlist additional men from among those he had left at his posts. He made no mention, however, of being under orders to hurry to the coast; his failure to bend every effort to get there, once he did start traveling in the spring, supports a conclusion that can be drawn from a North West Com-

*The Columbia River cuts a trench through the highlands of British Columbia, serving as a natural highway to the Pacific at the Washington-Oregon border.*

pany letter, written that year and recently found, stating that the company would establish a post on the Pacific Coast only if it were supported by the dispatch of a man-of-war and protected against the Americans by the erection of a British government fort.

At any rate, Thompson returned to Montana, where he heard of more Americans in the area—again, none of them known to history—and soon thereafter he finally turned to the formidable business of exploring the lower Columbia. He journeyed to Kettle Falls in northern Washington, built a stout cedar canoe, and on July 3, 1811, he embarked on the downriver voyage.

At the mouth of the Snake River, on the dusty sage-covered plains where Lewis and Clark had reached the Columbia six years earlier, Thompson paused to erect a pole and tie a paper to it, claiming possession of the country for Great Britain and announcing his intention of erecting a North West Company post on the site for trade with the Nez Perces, Walla Wallas, and other Indians in the vicinity. Then he hurried on, sweeping down the Columbia and reaching the coast on July 15. He was too late. Astor's men had arrived at the mouth of the river in March and had already built a fort. The Americans, however, were surprised by Thompson's appearance from the interior, and their chagrin was great to find that the British were already established among the inland Indians.

After collecting the year's furs, Thompson decided to return east by exploring the only part of the Columbia he had not yet seen. From northern Washington, he ascended the river to its big bend, passed many dangerous rapids, and at last reached the camp in which he had rested after his last crossing of the Rockies. Still avoiding the Blackfeet, he went over the Athabaska Pass again and made his way east across Canada to a North West Company post, where he exchanged his furs for more trade goods and supplies. Then, scarcely pausing for rest, he returned across the mountains, descended the Columbia, hastened from Washington to Montana, and finally reached his old Saleesh House among the Flatheads. It had been a whirlwind trip of almost two thousand miles through wild and rugged country of every description, and he had accomplished it in a little more than two months.

Up to now, Thompson and his *engagés* had been the only North West Company men in the Columbia country. Alone, he had explored this vast land, mastered its tangled geography, mapped its routes, opened trade with many Indian tribes, most of whom had never seen a white man before, and prepared the way for traders who would have neither the time nor the ability to start from scratch. A week after his return to the Saleesh House, the first reinforcements of North West traders, clerks, *voyageurs,* and other employees came pouring across the Rockies and down the Columbia, following the charts and directions that Thompson had given them. With their arrival, Thompson's role in the area was finished. He made several more short exploratory tours through Montana, but on April 22, 1812, departed from the region for the last time. He went back up the Columbia and across the Athabaska Pass, and on July 12 reached company headquarters at Fort William, where he was granted permission to return to eastern Canada and work on a map of his explorations. It was the end of his fur-trading days, and his travels.

In the western country that he had left behind him, the newly arrived Nor'Westers followed the routes he had found and filled the posts he had established. Astor's men, coming up from the mouth of the Columbia, met the newcomers, who forced them to withdraw from the country, and the Columbia basin fell firmly into the hands of the North West Company. But that company's existence also was short, and in 1821 a fresh wave of new arrivals took over the region for the Hudson's Bay Company. They knew little, if anything, about Thompson, and the terrain features he had first seen were given the names of Hudson's Bay men. The pass by which he had first found his way to the Columbia became known as the pass of a Johnny-come-lately named Howse, and the region of the icy heights where he had made his heroic crossing of the Athabaska Pass was named for a Hudson's Bay trader called Jasper.

As Thompson's savings and eyesight vanished in the East, obscurity closed around him in the West. When American trappers came back into the Columbia country in the 1830's, all trace of his activities in the interior had vanished. It was known from the records of the Astorians that he had appeared at the mouth of the Columbia in July, 1811. But it was assumed that he had come into the region only once, a late and unimportant arrival. By the time covered-wagon emigrants rolled into Oregon and made that great territory American, David Thompson was a forgotten footnote in the history of the Northwest.

*Hell's Canyon on the Snake River, North America's deepest gorge, cuts deep into two states: the peaks of Idaho are on the right, those of Oregon on the left.*

# ORDEAL IN HELL'S CANYON

By ALVIN M. JOSEPHY, JR.

*O*n October 21, 1810, a large party of fur traders left St. Louis, bound up the Missouri River for the mouth of the Columbia. Before it reached its goal, its members experienced hunger, thirst, and madness, suffering perhaps the most extreme privations and hardships of any westering expedition in American history.

The group, the first to cross the present-day United States after Lewis and Clark, was an overland party of the Pacific Fur Company, which the New York merchant John Jacob Astor had organized to capture the fur trade of the Columbia country. Astor was both visionary and practical, a man quick to perceive an opportunity and quicker to take advantage of it. The reports of Lewis and Clark, confirming the existence of rich beaver streams in the Rockies and the Northwest, had excited him, and more than any other American he possessed the resources and the experience with fur markets to attempt to monopolize the new area before others could overrun it. From years of trading with Canadians, he was familiar with the dynamism and power of the Montreal-based North West Company, and at first he tried to interest that firm, whose fur posts already stretched as far west as the upper part of the Columbia River, in becoming a partner in his plan "to make settlements on the North West Coast of America, [and] to communicate with the inland N W Trade." When the Canadians ultimately turned him down, he went ahead on his own, setting up the Pacific Fur Company and taking into partnership four Americans from the St. Louis area and five experienced Nor'Westers who, for various reasons, had severed connections with the Canadian company.

Astor's plan was to dispatch two expeditions to the mouth of the Columbia, one by ship around Cape Horn, and the other by Lewis and Clark's route up the Missouri River and across the Rocky Mountains.

At the Columbia the two groups would meet and construct a coastal post. The ship would carry on a trade with Indians and with Russian fur posts along the northwest coast, and the land-based personnel would build other trading posts among tribes in promising fur regions found by the overland party in the interior. In time, the ship would take the furs collected in the Northwest to China, dispose of them there, and return to New York or Boston with tea, silk, and other goods for the American market. Other Astor vessels would continue to visit the Columbia River post regularly, bringing supplies and trade goods from the east coast for the Indians and Russians, and taking furs to China.

To strengthen the entire arrangement, Astor planned to build a chain of company forts between the Columbia River and St. Louis so that his men could also move furs and supplies overland across the mountains and along the Missouri River. This high-way, lying wholly within American territory, conformed with the idea of a transcontinental fur route conceived by Thomas Jefferson and supported by Lewis and Clark's report. By using the overland route, especially in conjunction with his ships along the Pacific coast, Astor hoped not only to squeeze the Canadians from the Columbia River basin, but also to bring furs out of the Northwest to the eastern markets faster and cheaper than the Canadians could transport their peltry to Montreal over the difficult wilderness and Great Lakes route across Canada..

Astor's sea party, including four of the five Canadian partners, sailed for the Columbia from New York Harbor on September 6, 1810, in Astor's ship, the *Tonquin*. The following month, the overland group departed from St. Louis, wintered near present-day St. Joseph, Missouri, and started up the Missouri River in earnest in the spring of 1811. Its leader, an unlikely man for

*The* Tonquin *at the entrance to the Columbia River after rounding Cape Horn*

such a demanding assignment, was a youthful merchant of St. Louis, Wilson Price Hunt, who had moved to the Louisiana Territory from Trenton, New Jersey, in 1804. Intelligent, well-educated, and gentlemanly, he had been offered a partnership in the undertaking and the position of agent in charge of the company's operations in the Northwest, as well as leadership of the overland party.

Hunt was brave, persevering, and considerate to his men; he was "a conscientious and upright man—a friend to all, and beloved as well as respected by all," one of them said later. But he was town-bred, more a businessman than an outdoorsman, and he was cautious rather than bold and inspiring. Moreover, he had had no experience with the Indian trade or with wilderness life, and although entrusted with an expedition larger than that of Lewis and Clark, he lacked training, stamina, and ability to lead men. With him were the three other American partners, Ramsay Crooks, Robert McClellan, and Joseph Miller, all veterans of the Missouri River and Illinois fur trade, and the fifth Canadian partner, Donald McKenzie, a tempestuous, strong-willed 300-pounder, the cousin of the great Canadian explorer-trader, Alexander Mackenzie, and the most experienced and able man in the party.

75

Following Astor's instructions, Hunt planned to pursue Lewis and Clark's route up the Missouri. But soon after the party set out, it met John Colter, a Lewis and Clark veteran who had since been a member of trapping expeditions on the upper reaches of the river. Recently returned from the Three Forks region of the Missouri, Colter told Hunt that conditions had changed since Lewis and Clark's day. American trappers had clashed disastrously with Blackfoot Indians, and angry members of the tribe, he said, now made passage of the upper Missouri extremely hazardous. Hunt pondered the warning, but went on. Farther up the Missouri, on May 26, the expedition came on three Kentucky hunters, Edward Robinson, Jacob Reznor, and John Hoback, who had originally gone upriver with a large trapping party under Manuel Lisa of St. Louis in 1807. Robinson, a veteran backwoodsman who had been scalped by Indians in Kentucky and wore a handkerchief on his head to protect the ancient wound, was more than sixty-five years old. With his companions, he had recently lived through nightmarish attacks by Blackfeet and could give Hunt ample confirmation of Colter's warning.

The grizzled trio proposed to Hunt an alternative route to the Columbia. Driven from the Three Forks the year before by the Blackfeet, they and some other Lisa men had made their way south to one of the headwaters of the Snake River, in what is now eastern Idaho, and built a post where they spent the winter in safety. With the coming of spring their group had split up, and Hoback, Reznor, and Robinson, heading for St. Louis, had struck out directly eastward across mountains and plains, staying south of Blackfoot country all the way, and arriving finally at the Missouri River well below the haunts of those Indians. If Hunt would shortly leave the Missouri, they now said, and take the same overland route they had followed, he would reach their old winter quarters on the Snake; then he could travel to the Columbia's mouth by canoe.

Hunt considered the proposal carefully, reluctant to abandon the one cross-country path — Lewis and Clark's — that had been explored and mapped. What the upper stretches of the Snake were like no one yet knew. Still, the Kentuckians' route to the Pacific might be faster and more direct than that of Lewis and Clark, and the Astorians' mission — to locate sites for a chain of interior trading posts among Indians who resided in good beaver country — would not suffer. Hunt finally decided to chance the new route, and, on invitation, the three Kentuckians agreed to guide the party across the country over which they had recently come.

The expedition went on up the Missouri to the mouth of the Grand River in present-day South Dakota, where they purchased horses from the Arikara Indians, and, abandoning the boats, started out across the plains. Altogether, the group now numbered sixty-five people, including the five partners; an Irishman named John Reed who served as clerk; eleven hunters, interpreters, and guides; forty-five French-Canadian *engagés;* and an Indian woman and her two children. She was a stolid and uncomplaining Iowa known as Marie Aioe, the wife of Pierre Dorion, one of the expedition's interpreters.

The travellers crossed South Dakota, guided by Hoback, Reznor, and Robinson, as well as by Edward Rose, a man of dubious character who had also come up the Missouri with Lisa in 1807, and had subsequently lived with the Crow Indians on the plains. The Astorians met a band of Cheyennes, skirted the slopes of the Black Hills, and, entering northeastern Wyoming, travelled across the rough, rolling grassland and the ravines of the Powder River's tributaries toward the Big Horn Mountains. In the foothills of that range a band of Crows joined them, and Hunt was fearful at first that, perhaps assisted by Edward Rose, their former companion, those Indians would pillage the expedition. He and his men maintained their guard; and although Rose gave the others reason to believe he was plotting with the Crows against them, no conflict occurred. The Indians traded amicably, and then helped guide the party to a pass that led across the Big Horns. When the Crows rode away, Hunt offered Rose half a year's wages, three horses, traps, and "some other things" if he would quit the expedition and stay with the Crows. Accepting the offer, Rose hurried after the Indians, and Hunt was glad to be rid of him.

On the west side of the Big Horns, the expedition came on the Bighorn River, and on September 9 turned up the valley of its tributary, the Wind River, down which the three Kentuckians had come earlier in the year. Near present-day Dubois, Wyoming, the men began to suffer from a scarcity of game. Learning from an Indian of a pass that led southwestward across the Wind River Mountains to another river where buffalo were plentiful, Hunt abruptly turned the group in that direction, despite the

*John Jacob Astor, who sought to capture the Northwest fur trade by land and sea*

lateness of the season for mountain travelling and the fact that he was leaving a direct, shorter route to his goal for a longer and more uncertain one. Climbing the Wind River Mountains to present-day Union Pass, the men beheld an inspiring view of the Teton range, still far distant in the west. The Kentuckians told them that those snow-capped peaks overlooked the head of the river on which they had wintered, and the Astorians named them the Pilot Knobs.

Descending the mountains, they arrived at the headwaters of the Green River, which the trappers called the Spanish River because they believed that Spaniards lived along its banks somewhere to the south. The high valley, stirring with herds of buf-

*Wilson Price Hunt, who led Astor's overland party from St. Louis to the Pacific*

falo, was beautiful, carpeted with grass and cut by sparkling streams that tumbled from the mountains. The area was a favorite summer hunting ground and rendezvous area for Shoshonis, and in one of the narrow side canyons the expedition came on a camp of Indians drying buffalo meat for the winter. Some of the natives had had previous contact with parties of Lisa's men, and they were pleased to trade meat and a few beaver skins with the newcomers. Hunt was quick to recognize the area as excellent beaver country. He urged the Shoshonis to continue to hunt beaver, and promised to send a party of his men to live among them and trade for the furs they gathered.

Leaving the Indians on September 24, the expedition moved

79

northwestward over a rugged and difficult divide between the waters of the Green and the Snake and reached a stream which Hoback, one of the Kentuckians, recognized: he had trapped it the previous winter. Following that river, which is still known as the Hoback, the men arrived at the Snake near present-day Jackson, Wyoming, and realized that they would have been there much earlier if they had remained on the Kentuckians' route all the way up the Wind River valley and over the present Togwótee Pass to what is now called Jackson Hole.

The Snake, viewed as a headwater of the Columbia, was greeted with joy. Many of the men, notably Joseph Miller, one of the partners, had had their fill of horseback travel over the rugged, precipitous terrain, and they regarded the rest of the journey as a relatively easy one by water. Hunt spent several days, however, having his men search for trees large enough for the construction of dugout canoes. In the meantime, he sent out four men of the company with orders to stay in the Jackson Hole area and trap its streams. When they had collected a sufficient stock of furs, they were to make their way to the mouth of the Columbia or to any intermediate post that the company might build in the interior.

On October 1, Hunt's men were still trying to find timber suitable for canoes. That day Hunt wrote in his journal, "It rained in the valley and snowed in the mountains." Two days later it rained and sleeted all day. An unexpected crisis arose when an exploratory party under John Reed reported impassable rapids and narrow canyons on the river below them. Despite Miller's objection, Hunt now decided to abandon the plan to take to the river and, instead, to continue by horseback and hurry across the Teton Mountains ahead of him, which he believed were the last on their route. On October 5 the party left the river and, guided by the Kentuckians and two Shoshoni Indians, climbed the mountains and crossed the snow-whitened summit of Teton Pass into present-day Idaho. Three days later, hoping they had seen the last of the menacing snowy heights, the travellers rode through "a beautiful plain" and reached the deserted log huts in which the Kentuckians and their companions, under the leadership of Andrew Henry, had spent the previous winter. Nearby was the north fork of the Snake, known ever since as Henrys Fork, more peaceful and promising than the fork east of the mountains. Timber thick enough for canoes was also available, and Hunt set his men to work constructing craft for the descent of the river. Meanwhile, deciding to use the cabins for a company post, he retained the two Shoshonis to care for the expedition's horses and to watch over the huts until he could send a permanent party back to the area.

Hoback, Reznor, and Robinson, joined by another hunter, now detached themselves from the expedition, planning to trap streams with which they were familiar and to explore new ones. At the same time, Joseph Miller, apparently still smarting from Hunt's failure to take his advice on the eastern side of the Tetons, suddenly announced that he too would remain in this region and try his luck trapping with the Kentuckians. Hunt was crestfallen, but was unable to deter Miller, who was determined to go no farther with him.

The desertion cast a pall over the company, but on October 19 the travellers bade farewell to the five who would stay behind and, leaving the cabins, embarked in fifteen canoes on Henrys Fork, at that point a fast but placid stream. As it turned out, the decision to give up horses and to take to the river was a tragic mistake; but no white man had been on this stretch of the Snake River before, and none of the Astorians could foresee the perils that lay between them and the river's lower section, which they knew that Lewis and Clark had successfully navigated.

At first there was no sign of danger, and Hunt looked forward confidently to a short and swift journey. Then, as the men passed the junction of the two forks of the Snake and the main river broadened, they met rapids and falls that filled their canoes with water, carried off some of their possessions, and forced them to make difficult portages. On October 28, near present-day Burley in southern Idaho, they entered an awesome canyon and shot through a frightening stretch of roaring white water. One of the canoes smashed into a rock, and its French-Canadian steersman was toppled into the water and swept away. The accident brought the expedition to a sober halt. While most of the men waited with the canoes, Hunt and three members of the party climbed laboriously to the top of the basalt cliffs that hemmed the stream and walked thirty-five miles downriver, surveying what lay ahead of them. The river was unlike any they had ever seen or heard about before. It ran fast at the bottom of a deep gash in the level plain, boiling and tossing below barren and precipitous canyon walls that were so high and dangerous that there were only two places where Hunt could climb down to get water to drink. A reconnoitering group that explored along the opposite rim of the canyon came back with a more optimistic report; but four canoes that were portaged six miles down on that side of the river were immediately thereafter swept away with equipment and guns, and the men concluded that further travel by water was impossible.

The expedition was suddenly in a perilous position, without horses, running out of food, and isolated in the vast, unexplored Snake plains, apparently empty of game and as bleak and arid as a desert. In a hurried attempt to solve the problem, Hunt impulsively split up his party and sent out four small groups. One, under Ramsay Crooks, was to walk all the way back to Henry's cabins, which they estimated to be about 340 miles behind them, and return with their horses. Two other groups, under Reed and McClellan, were to continue downriver on foot and search for Indians who could provide them with food. The fourth, under Donald McKenzie, was to strike north across the desolate plain and try to find the Columbia River. The fragmentation of the party seemed the only hope, but it was the start of a breakdown of discipline and morale that would lead eventually to Hunt's loss of control over the men.

Remaining in the canyon with the rest of the party, Hunt buried the company's baggage and equipment in caches and tried unsuccessfully to increase the supply of food by catching fish or beaver. After several days, Crooks's group and two of Reed's men straggled back to camp. The former reported that the travel by land back to Henry's huts had been so slow and disheartening that they had abandoned the attempt. Reed's men were equally discouraging. They had found neither Indians nor food on the route ahead, and had turned back when Reed and the fourth member of their party, arguing that they could be of no help to Hunt, had insisted on pressing ahead.

Hunt and his companions were now alarmed. Winter was approaching rapidly, and none of them knew how far they still had to go, or what mountains and other perils were still ahead of them. But to remain where they were would mean certain starvation. Deciding to follow the direction of McClellan and Reed, the men divided into two bands, to give each one a better chance of survival, and on November 9 started forward on foot along opposite rims of the canyon. Ramsay Crooks, with nineteen men, proceeded down the south side, and Hunt, with twenty-two others, including Marie Dorion and her two children, followed the north rim. The hardy Iowa woman, well advanced in pregnancy, carried a two-year-old on her back and led a four-year-old by the hand, keeping up with the men without a murmur of weariness. The total food supply for all forty-three people, divided between the two groups before they separated, amounted to forty pounds of dried corn, twenty pounds of grease, about five pounds of bouillon tablets, and enough dried meat to allot each person five and a half pounds.

Day after day, the Astorians struggled along through the sagebrush and lava-scarred wastes of the Snake plains, using up their food and suffering from thirst. The river was always below them, but, except on rare occasions, they were unable to make their way down the canyon walls to its banks. The members of Crooks's party were reduced to eating the soles of their moccasins. Hunt's group, lagging behind, finally came on an Indian trail that led them to a miserable straw-hut settlement of impoverished and frightened Shoshonis. The Indians traded them some dried salmon and a dog to eat, and the travellers continued on, passing similar wickiup camps of Shoshonis whose small offerings of food served to keep them alive, but did little to ease their hunger. At length they found Indians with horses and were able to bargain for several animals, on one of which they placed Dorion's wife. Almost due south of present-day Boise, they took the advice of an Indian and, leaving the Snake River, turned north, plodding across a seemingly endless desert and almost dying of thirst. Some of the Canadians in anguish had begun to drink their urine before the party finally reached the banks of the Boise River, near the site of Idaho's future capital city.

Following the Boise to its mouth, they arrived back on the Snake River and moved along it again as it flowed north through barren hills toward a formidable range of mountains capped with snow. At the entrance to a narrow passage where the river began to force its way through steep and rugged basalt cliffs, they paused among another band of Shoshonis, learning from them that white men, travelling on both sides of the river, had preceded them into the canyon. Hunt was cheered to know that Crooks and probably McClellan and Reed were safely ahead of him, and his spirits were roused further when Indians told him that after three sleeps in the mountains, he would meet another

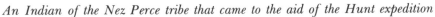

*An Indian of the Nez Perce tribe that came to the aid of the Hunt expedition*

nation of people whom they called the Sciatogas, and that from the homes of those people it was only six more sleeps to the falls of the Columbia River.

The Sciatogas were Cayuses and Nez Perces who often raided the Shoshonis from the north, and the wild and dark defile into which Hunt's people hopefully plunged on November 29 was the forbidding Grand Canyon of the Snake River, the deepest gorge on the North American continent (7,900 feet deep at its maximum)—and to this day one of the least accessible in the United States. No white man had yet been through this awesome mountain trench, which now forms part of the border between Oregon and Idaho, and no one who had known its extent of more than 100 miles would have tried forcing it in winter. But Hunt was unaware of its dangers, and he was in difficulty almost at once. The narrow benchland along the water, hemmed by walls that rose thousands of feet above him, became rocky and impassable, and Hunt tried to climb the cliff. The steep route was dizzying, and the travellers, already weak from hunger, moved along perilous ledges and basalt rimrock, edging close to the cliffsides to keep from falling. On the heights, "so high," wrote Hunt, "that I would never have believed our horses could have got over them," they ran into a snowstorm that "fell so densely on the mountains where we had to go that we could see nothing a half-mile ahead."

At an earlier season they might have gotten through the canyon. But winter had struck, and they were now to pay dearly for their previous delays and false hopes. One whole day they were unable to move in the storm, and remained encamped, eating one of the horses they had traded from the Shoshonis and shivering in the bitter cold. When the weather cleared, they had a dismaying view of the country ahead of them—range upon range of mountains, all covered with snow and extending as far as they could see. They made only a few miles a day, returning occasionally to the river, but climbing again when the dark canyon walls rose close to the water and barred their progress. On December 4, they floundered in snow that came above their knees. The cold dulled their minds and made them sleepy, and on one occasion, Hunt noted, they escaped what seemed a sure death only by coming on a clump of pines that gave them the makings of a roaring fire. The next day the snowfall cut visibility to three hundred yards, and they returned again to the river, slipping and sliding down a rocky slope through a fog that obscured the bottom of the canyon. On December 6, when the fog cleared, they were startled to see a party of men coming through the gorge toward them, but on the opposite side of the river. It was Crooks's group, so wasted from hunger that Hunt scarcely recognized any of them. They stood on the rocks, calling hoarsely across the stream for food, and Hunt had a boat hastily made from the skin of a horse that they had butchered the night before, and sent some meat across to them.

The boat returned with Crooks and one of his men, a Canadian named François LeClerc, who, weak-voiced and scarcely able to stand up unassisted, told Hunt that they had struggled

85

three days farther down the river. There, near the most awe-some part of the chasm, the narrowest and most rugged section, since that time given the name Hell's Canyon, the rock walls had been so close together and the river so wild and frightening that they had climbed with difficulty to the mountain top, where the view of the snow-covered wilderness, still extending as far as they could see, had appalled them. Realizing that they could never get through alive, they had turned back in the hope of finding help before starvation overtook them.

They also had news of the other groups. Several days before their worst trials had begun, they had sighted the parties of Reed and Donald McKenzie trudging downriver along the opposite shore. The burly McKenzie had called across to them that Mc-Clellan's men were also heading north, following a route farther east, which they thought would lead them to the land of the Flat-head Indians.

Hunt had persevered bravely, but the end seemed to have been reached. Discouraged by Crooks's report, he determined to turn the whole party around and get out of the terrifying moun-tains before they all died. During the night, the skin boat was swept away by the current, and the next day an attempt to ferry Crooks and LeClerc back across the stream with some meat for their men failed when a hastily constructed raft proved unman-ageable in the torrent. There was no time to build another craft. Now that the men knew they were going back, out of the canyon, they were impatient to start moving, and Hunt finally ordered the two parties to travel abreast of each other on opposite sides of the river. At first the enfeebled Crooks and LeClerc managed to keep up, but their strength soon gave out, and they began to hold up Hunt's group. As the pace slowed, some of the men be-came panicky and urged Hunt to abandon Crooks. Hunt refused to do so, but could not prevent his party from breaking up as some men, alone or in small groups, slipped away from him. Desperate to save themselves before it was too late, they hurried southward along the rushing river and over the ledges on the canyon walls.

For a while, Hunt and several of his men continued to assist Crooks and LeClerc. But, finally, it was evident that everyone would perish unless Hunt hurried on and found an Indian vil-lage where he could secure food to send back to the starving men. He pushed ahead and, after existing for two days on a solitary beaver skin, came suddenly on a band of Shoshonis who had descended from the mountains to camp along the river. He had meanwhile overtaken the rest of his men; and the sight of so many strangers appearing unexpectedly from the direction of the homeland of their Nez Perce enemies terrified the Shoshonis, who fled in fright, leaving some of their horses behind them. The weakened men managed to catch five of the animals and, after making a meal of one of them, sent a mounted messenger back to Crooks and LeClerc with a supply of meat. The food arrived in time, and shortly afterward they appeared at Hunt's camp.

An attempt was now made to feed the starving men of Crooks's original band, who had arrived on the opposite shore of the river. Another crude boat was made from the skin of a horse, and the food was ferried over to them. On a second trip across the turbulent water, one of Crooks's men, crazed by his suffering, jumped into the craft and, clapping his hands and leaping about in delirium, upset the skin boat. While the others watched in horror, he was swept away by the current and drowned.

When the men's hunger was appeased, the disheartened parties set off again, continuing their doleful retreat from the mountains. Crooks was still too weak to travel; and a Canadian, Jean Baptiste Dubreuil, and a tall, forty-year-old Virginia frontiersman named John Day, who were also too emaciated and feeble to keep up with the rest, stayed behind with him, hoping to regain their strength and eventually catch up with the expedition. The rest of Hunt's men hastened south and on December 16, after three weeks in the canyon, emerged from the mountains and camped near the lodges of a band of Shoshonis on Idaho's Weiser River.

The Shoshonis were surprised to see them and told them that they could never have gotten all the way through the canyon. The information made Hunt worry about the fate of Donald McKenzie and the other men whom Crooks had sighted along the river. The Shoshonis also revealed that there was another, more westerly route to the country of the Sciatogas and the Columbia River; but since it too crossed mountains, it would be unwise to take it at this time of the year. Hunt was impatient to be off, however, and after many pleas and threats, he secured three Indians as guides and ferried his men across the Snake

River in a boat made of two skins. Three French Canadians decided to remain among the Shoshonis, where there was at least some food and the possibility of trapping, but they promised to try to find Crooks and his two companions and eventually make their way with them to the Columbia River. On December 24, Hunt and his men again struck off overland, following an Indian route that led northwest from the country of the Shoshonis to the Grande Ronde Valley of northeastern Oregon. That part of the journey was to be of considerable significance, for it amounted to the discovery by white men of a feasible, short-cut route between the Snake River country of southern Idaho and the Columbia River.

In Hunt's wake, trappers, traders, and other travellers came to use the route regularly, and in time it became an important leg of the famous Oregon Trail.

The Astorians' hardships, however, were not ended. For several days they travelled through rain and snow, crossing cold, blustery plains and high hills; and another Canadian, Michel Carriere, gave up and had to be left behind. On December 30, near the Grande Ronde Valley, Marie Dorion, still plodding along with the others, paused to give birth to her baby. The Do-

*The party Astor sent by the sea route arrived in Oregon in the spring of 1811,*

rion family waited with her, while the rest of the party pushed ahead. The next day, the doughty woman and her family caught up, and Hunt wrote in his journal that the Indian mother "was on horseback with her newborn infant in her arms; another, aged two years, wrapped in a blanket, was slung at her side. One would have said, from her air, that nothing had happened to her."

In the Grande Ronde, a great oval valley of rich grass and marshland, the party came on a small camp of Shoshonis. They lingered with them only briefly, and on January 2, 1812, began to climb the forested Blue Mountains that hemmed the valley on the north and west. After five days of renewed struggle across wooded heights and through snow that was often waist-deep, they reached the northern rim of the cold wilderness and gazed down with cheer and relief on the plains of the Umatilla Valley near present-day Pendleton, Oregon. Before the party could descend from the mountains, the Dorion baby died, and the Astorians paused to bury it. Then they trooped down the hills and arrived at a sprawling village of mat-covered lodges belonging to a band of Cayuses and Nez Perces.

These Indians were bold and picturesque, said Hunt, and pos-

*built Fort Astoria (above) on the Columbia River, and awaited Hunt's arrival.*

sessed huge horse herds and abundant food supplies. The Astorians rested among them for a week, buying horses from them
and rebuilding their strength on a diet of roots and deer meat.
When the travellers pushed off again, Hunt, considering the
Cayuses and Nez Perces likely fur suppliers, promised to send
men back to them to trade for beaver skins.

The worst of the journey was now over. Moving down the
Umatilla Valley, the party finally reached the Columbia on January 21, 1812. It was, wrote Hunt, "for so long the goal of our
desires. We had traveled 1,751 miles, we had endured all the
hardships imaginable. With difficulty I expressed our joy at sight
of this river." The group crossed the Columbia to follow a trail
along the northern shore, and near the present-day city of The
Dalles took to canoes. On February 12, 1812, without further
mishap, Hunt's men reached the Columbia's mouth to find that
the members of the sea group had arrived in March, 1811, and
had built a post which they had named Fort Astor, or Astoria.

In a happy climax to his arrival, Hunt also found eleven of his
own men at the fort. They were the members of the parties of
McKenzie, McClellan, and Reed, who had preceded Crooks and
himself into the great canyon of the Snake. Exhausted and in
rags, they had reached the mouth of the Columbia on January
18, almost a month ahead of Hunt, and they, too, had a story of
hardship to relate. After leaving Hunt on the Snake plains,
where the combined group had abandoned its canoes, their
three parties had searched separately for Indians and food. Failing to find assistance, they had eventually encountered each
other and, rather than return and encumber Hunt, had decided
to hasten forward and try to reach the mouth of the Columbia,
where they had hoped to find the sea party and send back help.

Led by the bold and herculean McKenzie, they had trudged
across the plains that bordered the northern edge of the Snake,
suffering painfully from hunger and thirst. At some point, possibly just below the confluence of the Snake and Weiser rivers in
southwestern Idaho, the men had apparently decided that they
would have a better chance of survival if they again split into
smaller groups and took different routes. Seeking the Flatheads,
who, according to the Lewis and Clark report, lived somewhere
north of where they then were, McClellan and several men
had left the Snake and had climbed northeastward over the
mountains.

Two groups under McKenzie and Reed had continued into the great canyon, but after a while they too had climbed the mountains and had run again into McClellan's party along the divide between the Snake and the Weiser. Together once more, they had traversed rugged country for twenty-one days, urged on by McKenzie's aggressive determination, and living solely on five beavers and two mountain goats that they had shot. During the last five days of their struggle through the high wilderness, they had existed entirely on the skins of the beavers. Finally, they had descended to the Little Salmon River, where they had come on some wild horses, a few of which they had managed to kill for food. Shortly afterward, they had reached the main Salmon River and settlements of friendly Nez Perce Indians, who had given them camas roots and other food and had guided them to the Clearwater River. From there, they had continued by canoe down the Clearwater and Snake to the Columbia and, at last, safely to Astoria. Their success in coming through the dangerous wilderness had been due to the determination and experience of the band's three capable leaders, as well as to their head start, which had permitted them to get across some of the high country just ahead of the deep snows that had worn out and defeated the parties behind them.

The second crossing of the continent through what is now the United States had come to an end. In the months that followed, additional stragglers from Hunt's party reached Astoria, and others were rescued by groups sent into the interior to search for them. Some were found sick, starving, or deranged. Others were robbed and killed by Indians before they reached the fort, or were never found.

The expedition had been a tragedy, but it had not been without its achievements. Although Hunt, the youthful businessman, had been unfit for its leadership, his bravery and persistence in forcing his way through to the Pacific had added greatly to men's knowledge of the geography and terrain of the Northwest. His ordeals on the Snake River would show future travellers where not to venture, but his route as a whole did turn out to be shorter, faster, and easier than that of Lewis and Clark; almost all portions of the trail he blazed were used thereafter by western pioneers.

As for the full Astorian venture, it fell a victim to the War of 1812 and was eventually abandoned. But it lasted long enough to help establish the claim of the United States to the lower Columbia River and the Oregon country. Back in St. Louis, where he became the operator of a large farm, postmaster of the city,

*Fort Astoria, at the mouth of the Columbia River, in 1813, a year after the Hunt*

and a successful dealer in furs until his death in 1842, Hunt had the satisfaction of knowing that his trials on the Snake had provided a major basis for the American claim.

*expedition straggled in on foot and two years after the arrival of the* Tonquin

*Comanche Indians close in for the attack on a tight circle of emigrants' wagons.*

# THE
# BALLAD
# OF
# CYNTHIA ANN

## By DONALD CULROSS PEATTIE

*T*his is an old tale, and not a pretty one; it is a true tale, a real "Western," although it wouldn't go on TV. It sounds to me like a ballad—the ballad of Cynthia Ann.

But Cynthia Ann, fleeing us all on the thunder of Comanche hoofs, is no part of a sentimental ditty. By all accounts, she was a very pretty little girl. One of about eighteen children at Parker's Fort on the Navasota River, she was the kind men pick out for a tweak of the curls or a joking word—even those grim pioneers whose eyes saw less of the beauty around them than visions of the day when the Lord would drive their enemies out of the land. The women, trying to describe her afterwards, said she had blue eyes and light hair—flax-flower eyes, I fancy, wheat-straw hair that curled, as a child's will in hot weather, softly at the temples where the veins show blue in the porcelain flesh. The women would remember that flesh with burning pity. Cynthia Ann was in her ninth year on the last day of Fort Parker, which was May 19, 1836.

The day dawned warm, then turned to a regular east-Texas hot spring morning. For a while the women in Parker's Fort could hear their men's voices out in the fields in the shimmering heat waves. Then the voices drifted away down the long furrows. The women sought cool footing (shoes were for Sunday) as they went about their tasks. Rachel Plummer moved languidly, eight months gone with child. Old Granny Parker (eighty-odd) drove the flies from the parchment of her face.

The people in Parker's Fort numbered only 35 souls. Patriarch of them all was Elder John Parker, who had led his people—the Parkers, the Plummers, the Nixons and other neighbors from back east—across the Red River into the Canaan of Texas soil. And he was a God-fearing, "Two-seed" Baptist, and his son the Reverend James Parker walked in the ways of the Lord also, and so did his brothers Isaac and Silas and Benjamin. And they took unto themselves wives, all except young Benjamin, and begat children. And the names of their children were Rachel and Sara and James and John and the like—all Bible names. All except Cynthia Ann, daughter of Silas, the son of Elder John. Her name, whether her mother knew it or not, was Greek. For "Cynthia" is one of the titles of Artemis, goddess of the moon and protectress of maidens.

But to protect her now there wasn't a soldier left in the fort. The Republic of Texas had pulled them all out some weeks ago, now that the Indian frontier had retreated a hundred miles to the west. Nobody that morning was thinking of Indians; why should they?

Then, suddenly, out of the prairie heat waves—they were there: Comanches and Kiowas, some afoot, some sitting ponies. The braves weren't yelling or brandishing their shields of buffalo hide. They were just staring in silence—a long, deadly stillness. Even the buffalo horns and the eagle plumes of their head-dresses hardly stirred. Their fourteen-foot lances were motionless as a grove of dead saplings, only the feathers near the tips trembling a little in the south wind.

Benjamin Parker, Cynthia Ann's youngest uncle, went out to meet them and play for time—enough for Mrs. Sara Nixon, Cynthia's cousin, to run for the fields with the alarm. Ben talked as long as he could, then came into the fort to say the Indians showed by sign they wanted beef. There was none, so he went back to temporize. He was the first to die. They clubbed, speared, and scalped him.

Now the yells broke. The mounted Indians dashed their ponies in a noose around the fort. They swept up young Mrs. Elizabeth Kellogg; Rachel Plummer, a child in her arms and another inside her, was dragged away by her hair along the ground. The folding gate of wooden slabs yielded to the blows of the hostiles. As it burst in, one scream tore the throats of the ten women, the fifteen children. With them were only four men—old Elder John, and Silas (Cynthia's father), and Robert Frost and his son Samuel. They had time for a single burst of firing, a single yell of triumph from Silas as a few Indians fell. Then all the men were overpowered, killed, stripped, and scalped.

Cynthia Ann heard her mother's voice urging her on, but she couldn't outrun those long coppery legs. A copper hand was in her hair; a hard arm scooped her up by her waist. Her own mother was forced to set her on a pony's back behind a mounted brave, and stand staring after her as she was borne away.

For now from the fields came the rest of the men, crouching as they ran. They were armed, though short of bullets and powder, which were mostly in the fort. Their line of fire was a ragged popping; these were farmers who never before had shot anything more dangerous than a snake or hawk. But they turned back the Comanche charge, and then another, and gained time for the children and women to scatter like quail in the brush down by the Navasota's banks.

The Indians didn't charge again. They were dealing with the milch cows now, filling them full of arrows as so many pin cushions. The farmers could hear the beasts bellowing. Soon they saw the red and yellow flames war-dancing in the standing crops.

Deep in the woods the men began hunting for their families, children for their parents. These refugees were many starving days from safety. The shoeless had to walk all the way on bleeding feet. Yet they all made it back to the eastern settlements. The wounded made it, a woman with child made it. Old Granny Parker, speared and left for dead, played possum till darkness— she made it too. Three nursing mothers somehow brought their babes alive through the flight; Nature wrung the milk out of their gaunt flesh to nourish the frail hopes they carried.

Wouldn't you think they'd had enough of Fort Parker? Then you don't know your own American ancestors. For practically all of these people returned to the fort in a short time. They buried the bones, picked clean by wolves and vultures, of their dead. They planted another crop that year. They begot and bore and raised more children. They brought more Bibles with them, and read aloud together the covenant of Jehovah with those who keep His commandments.

And now the heathen wilderness began to give up some of those ravished away. Elizabeth Kellogg was the first to return. Unbroken in spirit, she had given such a thrashing to a squaw who was beating her that the Ketchaw Indians admiringly named her "Brave Woman." They sold her for $150 in trading goods to some Delawares (always allies of the whites) who brought her home. Rachel Plummer, that same autumn, was purchased by Santa Fe traders and brought back to her husband. Of her son Pratt, taken from her early in captivity, she never lived to hear news. Yet seven years later he was turned over by friendly Indians to the soldiers at Fort Gibson.

*Two years before Comanches attacked Parker's Fort and abducted Cynthia Ann,*

But the Indians had taken Cynthia Ann to a place that no honest white man ever saw—and lived. It is the center of the whirlwind, the ancient and most secret hide-out of the Comanches. It is the lost and inaccessible valley where a stream comes down, between war-paint canyon walls, from the high Llano Estacado through the break of the cap rock. That stream was called the Rio de las Lenguas—"the river of tongues"—for the many tongues that were spoken here: Kiowa, Comanche, Wichita, Jicarilla, Mescallero, a cawing Babel like ravens and geese and whooping cranes all calling together. The Comancheros, white renegades who rode out from New Mexico to trade here for stolen cattle and horses, with a cruel poetry named this spot— where women were sold among the tribes, where children were

*George Catlin painted this canvas of domestic life at a Comanche camp in Texas.*

reft from the clutch of their mothers, and girls knew brutal hands—the Valle de las Lágrimas.

Into that blackness vanished Cynthia Ann.

Years had passed, and Colonel Len Williams, with his fellow trader, Stoat, and the Delaware guide, Jack Harry, were parleying with Pahuaka's band of Comanches down by the bank of the Canadian River. Heat and excitement fevered the Colonel's impatience. Best let the more stoic Stoat negotiate. For the Colonel himself hadn't a doubt of the identity of that blond girl of thirteen among the Comanches. Promptly he had offered to buy her freedom; proudly Pahuaka replied that members of his tribe were not for sale. The Colonel then asked to speak with the girl, and received the startling answer that the chief would have to get the permission of her mother and father.

Now the girl, in Indian dress, walked slowly out of the group and toward him, her eyes on the ground. At the Colonel's feet she sat down, as a modest Comanche girl does before a man, tucked her legs under her skirt, and folded her hands in her lap —the incarnation of obedient attention.

The Colonel spoke, coolly, kindly. Her family had been hunting for her for years. Her playmates remembered her. Her place waited for her, and a warm welcome. And he promised to raise any sum for her ransom that the Indians might ask.

She raised her eyes. And what he saw was nothing he had ever seen before in the gaze of any woman, least of all in the look of a young white girl. In that long glance he saw the Llano—the endless level of the high-lifted short-grass plain, where there is nothing from dawn to sunset to give back an echo. Even the blue of those eyes was like the Llano sky, that arches over the buffalo grass and the curlew lakes, and is unchanging, beyond recollection or fear or pity.

He dropped his own startled gaze. It's no use, he knew. There's nothing we can do with this. Let us go.

Yes, they went, and they let her go back—back to the blanket. For there is no fugitive so difficult to pursue as the freed will of a woman—unless it is a Comanche.

The tribe was, in those days, the whirlwind itself, possessed of the greatest horsemen in history. Greater, said old cavalry officers, than Arabs or Bedouins or Cossacks. It was they, perhaps, who were first of the red men to master horses—beasts descended from strayed or stolen mounts of the Spaniards. From

*The Comanche technique of riding past an enemy while letting fly an arrow*

the moment that the Comanche leaped to the back of that mustang, he changed from the clumsiest Indian afoot into the "red knight of the plains."

With horses, the Comanches' striking power was fluid as the Llano wind. The West Point style of cavalry charge was useless against a foe who could hang by his heels while galloping, and shoot arrows under the horse's neck so fast that he could keep eight of them in the air all the time. The Texas Ranger could get in at most three shots—one from a rifle and one each from a brace of pistols—before he had to reload. In those sixty seconds, a Comanche horseman could close in for the kill.

It was in horses that a Comanche counted his wealth; racing he thought the one sport worthy of a man. Squaws, too, rode like wild spirits of the air; they too could hang by their heels, vault up again to the saddle, or spring from one galloping steed to another. The horse lifted the Comanche woman from a beast of burden to a mate, mounted and proud and free, whose bride-price had been paid by her suitor in those very animals that made of him a red half-god, a centaur out of myth. . . . That was how Peta Nakona, young chief of the Kwahadi band of Comanches, obtained Cynthia Ann from her red foster parents when she would have been about fifteen years old.

In 1851, some Texan travelers fell in with the Kwahadi band along the upper Canadian River. They stared long at the hair of the young chief's wife; it was straight as an Indian's, smelling of the lodge fires, but yellow, yellow. Her skin was tanned to leathery brown; in her eyes, when they questioned her, there was no gleam of recognition. Not even at the name of Cynthia Ann Parker. She was Preloch now (say the *ch* hard, as in the Scottish *loch*). No, she answered in Comanche, she had no desire to return to her white relatives, to leave her two swarthy little sons, and her good husband.

I know, I know. It doesn't fit at all with the ten-gallon legend. It's right in the script that any white woman would spurn the embrace of a no-account, red-handed, scalp-lifting Indian varmint. And the fair-haired girl is always rescued by the Lone Ranger.

All right. I'll play you the banjo tune for a minute — and I'll be telling the truth. That's just what happened.

The Kwahadi band — so went the Texan tune — had to be punished. They'd been raiding; the frontier was aflame. So, in December of 1860, 47 Rangers, under the command of Captain Sul Ross, took the field in vengeance. Joining them was a handful of settlers and cowboys, and 23 dragoons, fight-loving Irishmen. In all, they made a motley force of some eighty, in every kind of uniform or duds, on every sort of mount.

United in their enmity, these outfits had their own ways of fighting; when it came to a scalp-lifting, you couldn't always tell a Texas settler from a Comanche; the dragoons shot squaws as soon as bucks. (Harsh truth drowns out the banjo.) And the Rangers had at last got Colt six-shooters. They were the first to use the Colt on the Comanches, and with it they turned the whole tide of Indian warfare. Now it was they, not the red centaurs, who charged, and their in-fighting was so close they powder-burned the coppery skins.

Thus, on the morning of December 19, the end was clear in the beginning, when the whites surprised the Kwahadi camp on the desolate banks of the Pease. It was the same end, of course, as that which had come to Fort Parker. The Comanches fled, as the Baptists had fled, larruping their wild-eyed ponies, toppling, under the leaden hail, sideways or backwards with a last crazy salute of upflung hands. Only one figure, crouched low on an iron-gray mount, was pacing the wind. She outraced the Rangers, all but outran the bullets, until at their whine around her ears she reined, plunging, and lifted high above her head a swaddled babe, hostage to surrender, pledge of her womanhood.

So they took her. Took her first to Camp Cooper, where the officers' wives were kindly pitying, and cooed over Tautaijah, the tiny red baby. They improved the Indian syllables into Topsannah, and declared it meant "Prairie Flower." (You know how we make up the Indian's poetry for him, to fit our Longfellow notions.) To poor Cynthia Ann Parker they showed every Christian charity—and met the glare of Preloch, a caged female whose mate and cubs were still out in the wild. Twice she stole a horse and with her babe in her arms streaked as only a Comanche could for the open. But the cavalry did its job; she was always brought back. Everybody concerned was glad when Senator (and Colonel) Isaac Parker came and took his niece and her child away.

He brought her home, to the piny eastern part of Texas, to her younger brother Dan Parker's house in Athens.

The state legislature was so good as to vote a pension to Cynthia Ann. But it bought nothing that Preloch wanted in this world. Nor could money save Topsannah when she sickened. For as soon as she was weaned and began taking white man's food, she wasted, and presently was laid beneath a stone.

Her mother did not long survive her. Some say she died of sorrow, some that she starved herself to death. By 1864 she was buried in the old Fosterville cemetery. No doubt they put a cedar by her head, to point the way to heaven. No doubt they planted periwinkle; they usually do, on a woman's grave, down south. Its kitten-eyed blue flowers bring to mind the little girl who vanished a quarter-century before, by the salt river of tongues, in the war-paint valley of tears.

So ends the ballad, my ballad of Cynthia Ann. So, you might think, ends the story. I point no moral to it; I lift no finger to show any one way to salvation. Indeed, if you look well at our history—look between the eyes at our conquest of the land, once all the red man's, you find yourself, like me, falling silent. All we can say is that out of that murder and rapine, out of that courage and struggle, came this, our nation. And in its history there's one more paragraph I must relate, which adds an envoy to my ballad.

You remember the two little sons she had, out in the whirlwind wilderness? The eldest, Quanah, was in battle where she was captured, and he escaped with the remnant of his people. At

*Cynthia Ann's son, Quanah, marched in Teddy Roosevelt's Inaugural Parade.*

22 he became the chief of the Kwahadi band, still the most bitter and intractable of all Comanches. Most of them agreed, by the Medicine Lodge Treaty of 1867, to come onto the reservation. Not Quanah; he kept out on the Llano, leading the United States Army in circles after him. He is described as the most ferocious Indian ever encountered, by an officer who saw him lead a charge — a smoking six-shooter in his hand, bear-claw necklace at his throat, war bonnet streaming behind him, his face satanic with daubs of red and ochre.

And then — what gentling, south-wind spirit reached to him? What strangely prompted him, in 1875, suddenly to surrender? He brought his people down out of the plains, turned over all his arms, and settled with his band at the foot of the Wichita Mountains, in Indian Territory. He saw to it that every little Comanche went to school, to learn the white man's language and study in his books. Jovial, hospitable in the big house he built for his three wives and fifteen children, Quanah was fond of a good cigar and relished a fund of racy stories.

It's the last of the story, it's the end of the song — all the plaintive sorrow drowned in the sound of a big brass band. It's 1905, on Pennsylvania Avenue in Washington, and that's Teddy Roosevelt's Inaugural Parade swinging down through the cheering throng, the flags, the gaudy music of *Stars and Stripes Forever* and *Hail to the Chief*, the white man's chief, the Rough Rider President. And in the parade are great chiefs of his red brothers, Chief Joseph of the Nez Perces, Geronimo the Apache, and Quanah of the Comanches — Quanah, son of Cynthia Ann, her victory out of defeat.

*The Alamo under siege, in a canvas painted nearly fifty years after the event*

# THE STORMING OF THE ALAMO

## By CHARLES RAMSDELL

ew battles in our history have had more reverberations than the siege and assault of the Alamo, and yet no battle of consequence has been so skimpily reported.

In this action fewer than 200 men, most of them Americans, were besieged by 3,000 Mexican troops in a fortress built on the ruins of a Spanish mission at San Antonio, in Texas, then a part of Mexico, from February 23 to March 6, 1836, when the walls were stormed and the defenders slaughtered to the last man.

None of the Mexican officers who witnessed the shambles cared to give a full account. The only plausible version of the final assault was written by the Mexican second-in-command, General Vicente Filisola, but he did not arrive until three days after the last shot had been fired.

The evidence about what happened at the Alamo is scattered. There is no bristling array of fact to inhibit the armchair theorist's romping fancy, and consequently writers—even scholars—have felt free to draw their picture of the action any way they pleased.

But recent writings give proof that a well-defined picture or stereotype has now emerged from the chaos of conflicting tales.

According to this standard view, the Alamo was an indefensible ruin held, in defiance of superior orders, by a band of frontiersmen who were valiant but far from wise.

And yet, according to the evidence, the Alamo was "a strong place," and the defenders were in good part professional men; they disobeyed no orders, and their sacrifice was not without effect.

Let's look at the scattered evidence. Who were the men in the Alamo, and what were they doing there?

Few of the 150 "effective" men who went into the Alamo on February 23 at the approach of the Mexican army were Texans: most had been in the country less than a year. They had come singly or in small groups—a few had even walked—from the southwestern United States. But most of them were natives of the Atlantic seaboard. Some thirty-six were from the British Isles, including fourteen from Ireland. Two were Germans; one was a Dane.

But their officers, whose leadership they respected—or they would have chosen new ones—were well-known figures among the American colonists in Texas. Each had taken an active part, early or late, in the revolt. The men in the Alamo, therefore, were in sympathy with the Texas revolution, and had come to join it.

The revolution itself was not a conflict between "races" or peoples, nor between systems of government. Nor was it a conspiracy to steal Texas away from Mexico. To find the beginning —but not the meaning—of it, we must go back to the failure of Spain to take firm hold on Texas.

Even before the British fleet, Napoleon, and civil war had ripped the web of Spain's empire, there were not enough Spaniards in the Americas to hold down half a hemisphere. The wonder is that they were able to occupy Texas at all, considering the stark mountain ranges and grim deserts they had to cross coming northward from the opulent valleys of Mexico. Spain's hold on Texas was shaken in 1800, when Napoleon maneuvered a weak Spanish king out of Louisiana. When he sold his immense prize to the United States three years later, it was obvious that the Americans, as soon as they were settled in Louisiana itself, would begin to spill over into Texas, for it is attached by geography to the Mississippi Valley, with no natural barriers between.

Spain's policy for more than a century had been to keep Texas empty, a vast cushion of space to protect the rich mines of Mexico. An economical policy, it suited the king and worked fairly well for a time. Texas remained a vacuum.

But within the vacuum an unforeseen menace grew like a stormhead. The Comanche Indians, with 5,000 warriors, perhaps the most expert horsemen the world has known, roamed at will, lords of the prairie. In the whole reach of the province, counting the friendly Indians (who died off fast, inside and outside the missions, from the white man's diseases), there were scarcely 3,000 people who could be called subjects of Spain. Texas was at the mercy of the Comanche.

Forced to choose between the marauding Indians and the American frontiersmen who had begun trickling into Texas, the Spanish authorities chose the Americans. And in 1821 the commanding general of the frontier provinces, acting in the name of the king, granted to Moses Austin, a Connecticut Yankee turned Spanish subject, permission for an American colony.

In that same portentous year of 1821, Moses Austin died, leaving his Texas concession to his son, and Mexico declared its independence from Spain. Young Stephen F. Austin, in order to get clear title to his grant, had to petition each shaky new government as it arose, until the Mexican Republic, established in 1823 by men who admired the institutions of the United States, gave him full authority to settle American colonists in Texas.

He found some already there. Most of them scarcely hankered for annexation to the United States. Many had left·home between suns, and the government they preferred was the one that governed least. That was Mexico, which levied no taxes, required no military service, and gave them land for the asking. They held the formidable Comanches in check. And so long as the government left them alone, the colonists seldom gave it a thought.

The government, however, began to grow more and more alarmed about the Americans in Texas, who rapidly outnumbered, and by far, the native population. The trickle from the east had become a steady stream, and in 1830 further immigration was prohibited. This and other repressive measures caused some violence but did not produce outright revolt. Even when Stephen Austin was arrested for urging the separation of Texas

*Santa Anna, commander of the Mexican forces, in a daguerreotype of about 1850*

from Coahuila and confined in Mexico for a year and a half, there was no uproar. But when he reached home early in September of 1835, he found Texas in tumult.

In 1833, Antonio Lopez de Santa Anna, a bloody-minded royalist officer who had shifted with each political wind, had finally succeeded in seizing power in Mexico and subverting the high purpose of the republic's founders by establishing a military dictatorship. When he threatened to unleash an army of occupation on Texas, revolution flared. Mexican forces entered Texas from the coast in mid-September and occupied San Antonio—or Bexar, as it was called then—and Stephen Austin, usually a patient man, declared: "I will wear myself out inch by inch, rather than submit to the despotic rule of Santa Anna."

The revolution in Texas, as Austin made plain, was a stand against military dictatorship. The aim was not, in the beginning, independence from Mexico. The colonists, in a consultation at San Felipe de Austin on November 7, 1835, declared they had "taken up arms in defense of the federal constitution of Mexico of 1824." Only on March 2, 1836, while the Alamo was under bombardment, did a convention of colonists, held at Washington-on-Brazos, declare the independence of Texas.

The events of the preceding fall, when the colonists had begun their revolt, had gone badly for the forces of the Mexican government. On October 2, 1835, a detachment of Mexican troops from the garrison at San Antonio attempted to take a battered cannon from the colonists at Gonzales, the nearest American settlement, seventy miles to the east. The cannon belched defiance, and several soldiers were killed; the rest withdrew. Then colonists captured the fort at Goliad, near the coast, cutting the garrison at San Antonio off from the sea. From Gonzales a small motley army in buckskin, with Austin at its head, set out to capture San Antonio. On October 27 the advance guard led by James Bowie defeated an attacking force near Concepcion Mission, and the surviving Mexican troops took refuge behind the stone walls and palisades of the old Spanish town. The Americans' siege of San Antonio culminated in the house-to-house storming of the town from December 5 to 10 and in the surrender of the Mexican garrison, which was allowed to return across the Rio Grande with its arms.

While Austin's "army" was encamped outside the town, its numbers swelled to more than a thousand. And then, tired of inaction, most of the colonists went home. Austin himself, a sick man, resigned. Not more than 300 men took part in the storming.

Nearly half of those who were to become the defenders of the Alamo went through this ten-week campaign in the fall, then waited out the hard winter at San Antonio. They were abandoned, toward the last of December, by 200 victory-happy volunteers who headed south for the Gulf of Mexico, having been cajoled into an expedition aimed at seizing the port of Matamoros near the mouth of the Rio Grande — 300 desolate miles away.

This ill-conceived, ill-fated Matamoros venture was intended to be the first step in a scheme to detach from Mexico all the rich mining states north of a line drawn straight west from Tampico, including the pauper state of Texas. The aim: to make, in collusion with Mexican politicos, a great new empire. The backers of this scheme were, of course, opposed to independence for Texas. Working through the provisional council, they succeeded in shunting aside early in January, 1836, the provisional governor, Henry Smith, and the commander in chief, General Sam Houston, both of whom were in favor of independence. Houston was stripped of power when the council made his subaltern, James W. Fannin, its agent, giving him all funds and all available manpower for a march on Matamoros.

Meanwhile, at San Antonio, 104 men were left destitute under Colonel J. C. Neill, who wrote to Governor Smith that the stampede for Matamoros had carried off most of the food, clothing, medicines, and the horses. Smith, in his log-cabin capital of San Felipe, 150 miles to the east, was already irked at the deal with Fannin and now vented his wrath on the council. This was what it was waiting for: an excuse to "depose" him. He in turn "dissolved" the council. Henceforth, until the convention met in March, the government of Texas was divided against itself. The result was disaster, at the Alamo and elsewhere.

Some at the Alamo, "not even sufficiently clad for summer," endured the winter "with but one blanket and one shirt." They had no money. "If there has ever been a dollar here," wrote Neill, "I have no knowledge of it." This was early in January, and the story is the same to the end: the men were not paid. In mid-January Neill reported he had only eighty "effective" men. The rest, apparently colonists, had gone home.

These eighty men had to garrison two distinct fortresses. In the town of San Antonio were the remnants of the Spanish fortress (on what is now Military Plaza), and a block to the east, with the old parish church in between, was the Civil Plaza (now Main). These dusty squares, surrounded by stone houses with flat roofs, had been fortified by the Mexican army in December.

Half a mile away, across the San Antonio River, which here makes a large bend to the east, was the Alamo. This was a compound of stone walls, with huts of adobe and "little houses of mud and stone" ranged along their inner sides, enclosing a bare and dusty area the size of a city block. There was a gateway on the south, and facing west on the enclosed area was a two-story ˙stone building, the "long barracks." Behind this were two corrals walled with stone; and, south of these, a church — the "Alamo" of our day — facing west and making the southeast corner.

This drab enclosure comprised more than three acres. Built by Franciscan friars during the half-century after 1724 as a mission for Indians, it had been named San Antonio de Valero in honor of Saint Anthony of Padua and the reigning viceroy, the Marquis de Valero. It had long since been used as a barracks and cavalry yard, and renamed *El Alamo* for a military company from the town of Alamo de Parras (now Viesca), in Coahuila, which occupied it for decades. But during the fall of 1835 the Mexican Army had made the enclosure into a fort, with ditches and gun emplacements. The outer walls of stone, two feet thick and twelve feet high, were strengthened with palisades and tamped earth, until the thickness at crucial points was five feet. The Alamo, said an observer, was "a strong place."

To defend this sprawling compound, the Americans had about twenty captured cannon and a prized 18-pounder (for 18-pound balls) that had been dragged up from the coast, 150 miles away, by oxen. This gun was given the place of honor, on the southwest corner, pointed at the town. The rest of the guns were, in the main, 6-pounders, 9-pounders, and 12-pounders. This was a tremendous armament for that time and place. The Americans improved the fort, building ditches and redoubts.

"In case of an attack," wrote Green Jameson, the engineer at the Alamo, "we will whip 10 to 1 with our artillery."

A false report of invasion, in mid-January, was forwarded by Neill to General Houston, who was visiting the coast to put a damper on the "Matamoros fever." Houston, before leaving the field to Fannin, sent Colonel James Bowie to San Antonio with about thirty men and the suggestion to Neill that he remove the artillery and blow up the Alamo. Neill replied that he had no teams for the purpose. Then Bowie wrote: "Colonel Neill and I have come to the solemn resolution that we will rather die in these ditches than give it up to the enemy."

*James Bowie, who fought for Texas independence until his death at the Alamo*

An indignation meeting held by the officers at the Alamo on January 26 passed resolutions denouncing the council and its agent, Fannin, and upholding Houston, Governor Smith, and independence. Smith threatened to have the council arrested and sent to San Antonio for trial on a treason charge. The council, no doubt frightened, responded with an order for Neill: he was "required to put the place in the best possible state for defence, with assurances that every possible effort is making to strengthen, supply and provision the garrison, and in no case to abandon or surrender the place unless in the last extremity."

At the same time, an order was issued that no more men were to be sent to San Antonio. Nor were any supplies ever sent there.

*William Barret Travis of the Texas Army commanded the Alamo defenders.*

But Governor Smith had already ordered Colonel William Barret Travis to San Antonio, where he arrived about the second week of February with twenty-six men of the Regular Texas Army. On February 11, Neill took leave, on account of sickness in his family, asking Travis to accept the command. Some of the volunteers chose Bowie instead. Much has been made of the ensuing "quarrel," but it was over in twenty-four hours.

Bowie was a sick man, in the last stages of a disease later diagnosed as consumption. He was also a sad man. He had married Ursula Veramendi, daughter of the vice-governor of Coahuila-Texas, and she, together with their two children, had died of cholera in 1833. At San Antonio on one occasion he got "roaring

115

*David Crockett reinforced the Alamo garrison with his twelve "Tennessee boys."*

drunk," released prisoners from the calaboose, marched his men on Main Plaza, and generally raised a ruckus.

Travis was a handsome six-footer, ruddy and blond, hardly more than a boy. He had taken part in every vigorous action against "the despotic rule of the usurping military" (as he called it) since 1832, and now, from San Antonio, he too wrote the governor asking for money, clothing, provisions, and men. "We have not more than 150 men here, and they are in a very disorganized state. Yet we are determined to sustain this Frontier Post as long as there is a man left, because we consider death preferable to disgrace. Should we receive no reinforcements, I am determined to defend it to the last, and should Bexar fall, your friend will be buried beneath its ruins."

Among the 150, Travis counted David Crockett and his twelve "Tennessee boys," who arrived about February 10. Few if any of these were rude backwoodsmen. Among the twelve were several lawyers, while among the whole force who went into the Alamo there were at least four doctors. Most of the men were young, but it seems they were not unlettered.

Crockett climbed on a goods box in front of a store on Main Plaza and made a speech. He spun some yarns to warm up the crowd, then declared he had enlisted in the "common effort for the common cause," and wanted to be only "a kind of high private."

The ragged men at the Alamo had only beef and corn to eat — no coffee, sugar, or salt. The remnant of the council, adjourning in mid-February, denounced them as "insurgents to the government"; it had never sent them supplies of any kind.

Why, then, did they remain at their post?

There is an answer, given a little earlier in a sort of manifesto signed by a few of them:

We, the undersigned, have embarked on board the schooner Santiago, on December 9, 1835, at New Orleans, for Texas, to relieve our oppressed brethren who have emigrated thither by inducements held forth to them by the Mexican government, and rights guaranteed to settlers of that province, which that government now denies them; and in our opinion, their situation is assimilated to that of our fathers, who labored under tyrannical oppression. Resolved, that we have left every endearment, as our respective places of abode in the United States of America, to maintain and defend our brethren, at the peril of our lives, liberties and fortunes. . . . We declare these as our sentiments and determination.

Seldom in time of war has a garrison so tiny been so isolated.

To the north, as far as the Arctic ice, was Indian country. To the east the sparsely settled American colonies began at Gonzales, seventy miles away, with no habitation in between. To the southeast, one hundred miles away, near the Gulf of Mexico, the stalled Matamoros expedition waited for supplies that never came. Two-thirds of its members joined with groups just arrived from the United States, gathering, through February, at Goliad (an old Spanish fort) under the command of James Fannin, until their number passed 400. The remainder hunted wild horses at

San Patricio, an abandoned Irish colony fifty miles south of Goliad.

To the west and southwest of the Alamo stretched 150 miles of mesquite, prickly pear, rattlesnakes, and Indians. Then, along the Rio Grande, a few Mexican towns were scattered. South of the river, beyond deserts and rugged *sierras,* larger towns were widely separated, and in several of these Santa Anna was assembling, feverishly and not always by gentle persuasion, men, money, and supplies. Early in February he had more than 7,000 troops at points, including Matamoros on the coast, from which he could hurl them against Texas.

His darkening shadow in the west was not unperceived by any of the three officers who, in succession, had some charge of the tiny garrison at the Alamo. They were kept informed by certain friendly Mexican citizens of San Antonio who traded across the Rio Grande. In his first reports, early in January, Colonel Neill warned the governor of enemy troop concentrations. Bowie's warning was more ominous. Travis, in his report of February 12, pointed out accurately the size and progress of the threatening forces.

It has been said that the officers in the Alamo "allowed themselves to be surprised" by Santa Anna. But even with a much larger garrison and many more horses, it would have been impossible to guard all the trails from the Rio Grande.

They could not have known that Santa Anna would drive his troops through a snowstorm and searing heat, across deserts, without adequate rations and without any medicines, the sick being heaped on pack animals, dead men and mules left strewn along the way. They could not have known, yet, the full measure of his contempt for human life, except his own.

Relations had been friendly between the San Antonio Mexicans and the men of the Alamo. They attended fandangos and cockfights together. Travis, proud of his Spanish, wrote: "The citizens have every confidence in me, because they can communicate with me, & have shown every disposition to aid me with all they have." Some joined the Texas Army, and three more were to die in the Alamo. But the approach of Santa Anna's army brought with it a chill.

San Antonio was a town of some two thousand Spanish-speaking people, mainly herdsmen and horsemen, who loved dancing, gambling, racing, and religious festivals. They remembered the cruelties of a Spanish army (Santa Anna was with it as a young lieutenant) that had sacked the town in 1813. They did not wish to see a repetition.

By the middle of February, Bowie, as commander of the volunteers, and Travis, as commander of the Regulars and the cavalry, were signing a joint appeal for money, provisions, men.

On the evening of February 21, Santa Anna and the advance guard of his army reached the bank of the Medina River, some twenty miles southwest of San Antonio. Heavy rains kept him from crossing for two days. Then, about noon on February 23, a sentinel posted in the tower of the parish church on Main Plaza sounded the bell. He said he had seen a "glittering, as of lances" in the west. Two horsemen rode out and reported a company of Mexican cavalry in formation, "their polished armor glistening in the rays of the sun," an officer riding up and down in front of them waving his sword, as if giving orders.

About two o'clock in the afternoon Santa Anna's advance guard entered the town. Bowie, Travis, and their men were in the Alamo. With them were several friendly Mexicans, including women and children; also the wife and infant daughter of Alme-ron Dickinson, captain of artillery. On their way in, the men had rounded up a herd of beeves and found some corn stored in the houses. Within the enclosure they had opened up a well. They would not lack for food of a sort, nor water. There was a scene of wild confusion, with men clamoring for arms and no semblance of order; the swearing was phenomenal.

About three o'clock a blood-red flag, meaning NO QUARTER, was hoisted on the tower of the parish church. Travis replied from the Alamo with a cannon shot. The next day, February 24, he sent out his famous message "to the People of Texas and all the Americans in the World":

Fellow citizens & compatriots, I am besieged by a thousand or more of the Mexicans under Santa Anna — I have sustained a continual Bombardment & cannonade for 24 hours & have not lost a man — The enemy has demanded a Surrender at discretion, otherwise the garrison are to be put to the sword, if the fort is taken. . . . *I shall never surrender or retreat.*

Then, I call on you in the name of Liberty, of patriotism & everything dear to the American character to come to our aid, with all dispatch — The enemy is receiving reinforcements daily & will no doubt increase to three or four thousand in four or five days.

If this call is neglected, I am determined to sustain myself as long as possible & die like a soldier who never forgets what is due to his own honor or that of his country —

*Victory or Death.*

He meant every word of it.

A cold wind blew from the north on the night of February 25, chilling the blanketless men in the Alamo. Bowie, who had been hurt by a cannon ball that had rolled from a platform, was put to bed with pneumonia. Travis now had sole command.

On the twenty-fifth the enemy attempted to set up a battery in front of the Alamo's south gate. The defenders made a sally and killed some soldiers. After dark the enemy charged the north wall and were repulsed with musket shot and grape. A detachment of cavalry attempting to cross the river on a narrow bridge was blasted by the Alamo guns and a Mexican colonel, knocked into the water, nearly drowned.

During the first four days of the siege the defenders made sallies, burned huts near the walls, and fought the attackers hand to hand when necessary. But after February 26 they were hedged in by artillery; the bombardment let up at intervals, only to resume with increased fury.

Davy Crockett entertained the men with his fiddle; but he did not like to be penned up. "I think we had better march out of here and die in the open air," he would say.

But if the main body of defenders was pinned down, couriers could still go in and out. Travis sent a rider to Goliad, but there Fannin was in no position to help anyone; on February 27 and March 2 the remnants of the Matamoros expedition were killed or captured at and near San Patricio. Travis also appealed to the colonists at Gonzales, and he had some success. On March 1 a band of thirty-two volunteers, some of them boys, somehow found their way into the Alamo.

On March 3 Travis wrote his last letters and sent them out by couriers. He said the garrison had been "miraculously preserved"; he had not lost a man. But two 9-pounders near the town were tearing holes in the walls with every shot. He heard sounds of rejoicing in the town, where 2,000 reinforcements for Santa Anna had just arrived. When he heard the bell of the parish church ringing, he did not know it was for the annihilation of the Americans at San Patricio, but in any case he had given up

*Santa Anna's men were already on the ramparts when David Crockett fell fighting.*

hope of aid from Fannin: "I look to the colonies alone for aid; unless it arrives soon I shall have to fight the enemy on his terms. I feel confident that the determined valor and desperate courage of my men will not fail them in the last struggle; and although they may be sacrificed to the vengeance of a Gothic enemy, the victory will cost the enemy so dear, it will be worse for him than a defeat."

That same day, March 3, Travis is said to have drawn a line with his sword on the ground, and to have asked those who would stay in the Alamo to the end, even though the cause was hopeless, to step over the line and stand beside him. The story has been told separately by three alleged eyewitnesses, but historians have scorned it as "theatrical" and "improbable." Whatever the truth of it, the story goes on to relate that just one man stepped back, and later made his escape. Bowie asked his companions to carry his cot across the line so he could be with them.

On the same day, Santa Anna had heavy guns placed within musket range of the Alamo's north wall; despite the popular assumption that nobody was hurt in eleven days of shelling, skeletons in buckskin tatters dug up from the floor of the church years afterward should be proof that the Mexican artillery was effective. "Men died there, and women," said Enrique Esparza, the twelve-year-old son of one of the Alamo's gunners. "Even children died there."

In the dark of night the Mexican troops would feign assaults.

Sudden yells, cheers, and fusillades would keep the defenders off balance. Then, on the night of March 5, a roaring cannonade shook the Alamo, followed by a long spell of stillness to lull senses aching for sleep. At five the next morning, in the dark and the cold, a bugle shrilled from the north and suddenly, from four sides, came the tramping of massed feet, thousands of feet, advancing at a run.

The assault was intended to be a surprise, but raw recruits yelled "*Viva* Santa Anna!" and the cannon of the Alamo blazed. One Mexican soldier saw forty of his comrades fall around him. The mass surged against the walls and broke, screaming. From the rear, fusiliers who aimed too low shot their own storm troops in the back of the head. They toppled from the ladders. A wounded Mexican colonel, urging his men on, was trampled to death.

Again the columns were driven forward. The alcalde of San Antonio, whom Santa Anna had ordered to wait behind the Mexican lines to look after the dead and wounded, saw the second assault shattered by the "deadly fire of Travis' artillery, which resembled a constant thunder."

The slaughter had gone on for nearly two hours when Santa Anna pulled back and called up his reserves.

"At the third charge," said the alcalde, "the battalion of Toluca began to scale the walls and suffered severely: Out of 800 men only 130 were left alive." Then, according to the account written later by General Filisola, the columns attacking the east and west sides joined the force on the north "by a spontaneous movement," smashed over the cannon, and poured through the breach.

Travis fell on the gun there, "a single bullet wound in his forehead."

When the defenders turned "a small cannon on the high platform" to stem the breakthrough on the north, the Mexican column on the south side, "taking clever advantage of the protection offered by some little houses of mud and stone near the southwest angle, by a daring move seized the cannon [the 18-pounder] embrasured in that angle, and through the port entered the plaza." Other troops "poured over the walls like sheep."

Santa Anna now approached close enough to observe that "the brisk fire of musketry illuminated the interior of the fortress, its walls and ditches."

The men in the Alamo abandoned their artillery, useless now at such short range. In the vast, bare plaza, the size of a city block, they were few and scattered and utterly exposed. There was no chance to reload their rifles or muskets. So they clubbed their assailants with the stocks as they ran for the two-story stone building on the east side of the plaza.

Here preparation had been made for a final stand. Within each of the five arched doors opening west in the "long barracks" was a semicircular parapet of stakes shoring a double curtain of rawhide rammed with earth. The Mexican troops, said Filisola, turned the captured guns against this building, "in which the rebels had taken refuge, and from which they were firing on the troops that were climbing down into the plaza. And within these doors, by grapeshot, musketshot and the bayonet, they were all killed at last."

But not quite all, yet. The church in the southeast corner of the enclosure held a few defenders. There lay the stricken Bowie. The women and children were there: Mexicans of San Antonio except for Mrs. Dickinson, holding her child in her arms. She knelt and prayed, clutching the child, in the narrow, vaulted sacristy, now filled with smoke. Pursued by Mexican troops, two boys, eleven and twelve years old, ran into the room with their father, a gunner. The father begged for mercy, but the soldiers ran him through and carried the boys out of the room on their bloody bayonets. Another gunner ran in; they shot him "and four Mexican soldiers stuck their bayonets into his body and raised him up into the air like a farmer does a bundle of fodder when he loads it into a wagon."

In the small adjoining room, Bowie, from his cot, fired until his body, too, was riddled with bullets.

The father of twelve-year-old Enrique Esparza had been killed beside his cannon, which had been embrasured in the window of the south transept of the church. There was hand-to-hand fighting in the dark, the Mexicans rushing the defenders with bayonets. "It was pitch dark there," said young Esparza. "After the soldiers of Santa Anna had got all the women and children huddled in the southwest corner of the church, they stood still and fired into the darkness. They kept on firing at the men who had defended the Alamo. For fully a quarter of an hour, and until someone brought lanterns, they kept on firing on them, after all the defenders had been slain, and their corpses were lying still."

The Mexican women were taken to Santa Anna, questioned, and released. Mrs. Dickinson and her child were treated kindly.

Five "foreigners," found hiding, were brought before Santa Anna; he upbraided the officer who had spared them, then turned his back. Soldiers set on them with bayonets.

"After all the dead Mexicans were taken out of the Alamo," said the alcalde, "Santa Anna ordered wood to be brought to burn the bodies of the Texans. He sent a company of dragoons with me to bring wood and dry branches from the neighboring forest. About 3 o'clock in the afternoon they commenced laying the wood and dry branches, upon which a file of dead bodies was placed. More wood was piled on them and another file brought, and in this manner they were arranged in layers. Kindling wood was distributed throughout the pile, and about 5 o'clock in the evening it was lighted.

"The dead Mexicans of Santa Anna were taken to the grave-yard, but not having sufficient room for them, I ordered some of them to be thrown into the river, which was done on the same day. Santa Anna's loss was estimated at 1,600. These were the flower of his army." (This estimate is too high, even counting both dead and wounded.)

"The men burned numbered 182. I was an eyewitness, for as alcalde of San Antonio, I was with some of the neighbors collecting the dead bodies and placing them on the funeral pile."

Travis had said, three days before he died, "Victory will cost the enemy so dear, it will be worse for him than a defeat." Santa Anna's frightful losses did not deter him from driving his army on through Texas. But the slaughter of the men in the Alamo shocked the colonists out of their apathy.

On March 13 scouts from Gonzales met Mrs. Dickinson on the prairie. She had been given a horse and sent with an intimidating message for the colonists. That night the frontier town was a choir of grief.

Then Sam Houston, with less than 400 men, began a strategic retreat eastward, drawing Santa Anna after him. First Gonzales, then San Felipe, went up in smoke. Women, children, the old and infirm, struggled on foot or in creaking oxcarts through rain, slush, and mire across swollen rivers. Some reached the Trinity, some the Sabine. Bedsheets spread for tents dotted the Louisiana shore. At last, on April 21, Santa Anna, who had dashed on with a fraction of his army to Galveston Bay, hoping to catch (and hang) the officers of the upstart Texas Republic, was surprised by Houston's smaller force on the San Jacinto River, just east of the present city of Houston. The Mexican commander was captured, and more than half his men were killed. The cry was "Remember the Alamo!"

*By dawn on March 6, 1836, the Alamo garrison was putting up its last resistance.*

*Sir William Drummond Stewart (on a white horse near the Platte River Forks in 1837) hired Alfred J. Miller to record this and other moments of that trip.*

# FIRST "DUDE RANCH" TRIP TO THE UNTAMED WEST

By ALVIN M. JOSEPHY, JR.

In May, 1843, with the first greening of the prairie grass, a strange caravan, billed as a "Sporting Expedition to the West," rolled spiritedly out from the Missouri frontier past tight-lipped groups of emigrant families grimly preparing what history would call the first great migration to Oregon. It was three years before Parkman, five and more before the California gold rush, and what was still to gain popular calling as the Oregon Trail had never before seen the likes of this train.

Ahead of the carts and wagons rode a company of wealthy young American bloods in fancy and expensive trappings, greenhorns with high-powered European rifles, and whiskered sportsmen on high-headed buffalo runners, hung with burdensome equipment for the hunt. The outfit's long column of pack mules and vehicles groaned under mounds of gay-colored tenting, India-rubber boats that would hold fifteen men, and costly, imported wines, liquors, potted meats, jams and other delicacies for a luxury outing. In the lead rode a beak-nosed, mustachioed Scottish nobleman, Sir William Drummond Stewart, the nineteenth of Grandtully and seventh baronet, and beside him an ill and aging veteran mountain man, the famous trapper of Wash-

*A self-portrait of Alfred Jacob Miller*

ington Irving's celebrated book, *The Rocky Mountains,* Colonel William Sublette.

"Individual gentlemen," Sublette described the party in his journal, "Some of the armey, Some professional Gentlemen, Come on the trip for pleasure, Some for Health ... doctors, Lawyers, botanists, Bugg Ketchers, Hunters and men of nearly all professions." More than half of the 93 members of the group, he added, were "hired men Belonging to Sir William."

The expedition, bound in style for a summer holiday of pleasure and sport on the plains and in the Rocky Mountains, was of Sir William's making. A veteran of Waterloo and a former captain in the Fifteenth (The King's) Hussars, he had first come to the West in 1833 to hunt buffalo and to find high adventure. He had spent six straight years in the West, living dangerously with mountain men and trappers and falling in love with the wild beauty and freedom of the plains and mountains. In 1837, he had brought with him a Baltimore painter, Alfred Jacob Miller, to record grand views of the western wilderness to hang in his Scottish castle.

*Miller's drawings of Sir William Drummond Stewart and a Canadian guide*

Upon the death of his older brother in 1838, Stewart had had to return to Scotland to assume the duties of his estate, but the memories of his happy years in the American West tugged strongly upon him, and gradually, in correspondence with Bill Sublette, he evolved the idea of returning once more, this time to lead a grand expedition of paying guests back to his favorite lake in the Wind River Mountains.

Sublette was more than game to join the enterprise. One of the greatest of all the mountain men, he had explored and trapped great areas where no white man had ever been before. He had pioneered long sections of the Oregon Trail, he had taken the first wagons to the Rocky Mountains in 1830 and had built the post which men were now beginning to call Fort Laramie. Ill health—the initial stages of tuberculosis—had overtaken him, and he was now living quietly in Missouri. A trip to the high, dry land might benefit him.

In the autumn of 1842, Sir William returned to New York. He spent the winter in New Orleans, enlisting members for the adventurous excursion, and purchasing equipment and supplies. In

St. Louis, Sublette was similarly busy through the winter, signing up additional recruits, hiring hunters and servants, and buying pack animals, buffalo-running horses, carts and other necessities.

In May, the two parties rendezvoused on the Kansas River. The idea of a large group going to the mountains simply for pleasure was brand-new. To the average American, the West was still a wild and dangerous land. Even the first emigrants for Oregon, now also gathering near the Kansas for this year's great covered wagon trek, viewed the crossing that lay ahead of them as anything but a lark.

But to Stewart, Sublette and the sportsmen and hired hands of the pleasure excursion, the West was already taming. In the hands of the veteran guides and hunters, nothing was to be feared. The party would "rough it" in the greatest wilds of all, the Rocky Mountains, would hunt buffalo and antelope, trade with tribesmen, and fish and frolic in the streams and lakes where trappers had worked for beaver. It would be the first use of the Rockies as a "dude ranch" playland for thrill-seeking sportsmen.

In Sublette's group at the rendezvous camp was an assortment of mountain men, including his brother, Solomon Sublette, and the hunter, Joe Pourier. Also, from St. Louis to take the trip, came two U.S. Army officers, Lieutenants Sidney Smith and Richard Hill Graham, on leave from the service, but under orders to file a report on the country, inhabitants and conditions met by the expedition.

In Sir William's party were a French-Canadian hunter, Antoine Clement, who had served with the baronet during his earlier years on the plains, and an exuberant gathering of eager young sports from eastern cities and New Orleans. Among them were two botanists, a youthful doctor from Baltimore, and Matthew C. Field, who had tried the stage and newspaper work, and who would write heady letters of the trip back to the New Orleans *Picayune.*

Prior to setting off, the expedition accepted a company of traveling companions, two Belgian priests and their retinue, on their way to a Catholic mission among the newly converted Flathead Indians. The group would accompany the pleasure-seekers across the great South Pass, then turn north and continue alone across present-day Wyoming, Idaho and Montana to their charges in the Bitterroot Valley.

*During the 1837 expedition Sir William and his retinue explored the route the dudes would follow six years later. Here Miller sketched breakfast at sunrise.*

The caravan jumped off on May 22. Along the way, the excursionists reveled in every new impression and made adventures out of the commonplaces of the trail. One man was thrown from a horse and another dragged when he became entangled in his stirrup. The hunters served up exotic prairie dishes: turtle soup, antelope steak and, later, when they came on their first buffalo, sizzling hump ribs and marrow bones. The sports raced and cavorted across the prairie, riding to nearby hillocks to peer over them for first sight of buffalo, but careful not to go too far from the caravan, lest they come on Indians instead.

Fourteen days out, the party was treated to its first excitement with Plains Indians. First, they came on three blanketed Pawnees, afoot on the prairie, and apparently wandering around without any object in mind. The trio readily attached themselves to the caravan, plodding along behind the wagons with the hopeful look of scavengers patiently awaiting something to fall their way. Soon afterward, the expedition's advance riders topped a knoll and almost rode into a war party of 25 hideously painted Osages, Otos and Kaws who had been out fighting the Pawnees.

The three vagabond Pawnees saw their enemies and in terror tried to hide behind a large Pittsburgh wagon belonging to the priests. The warriors spied them, and in an instant rushed at them. The expedition might have been witness to a triple scalping on the spot, but the priests, assisted by some of the more experienced members of the party, interceded and secured the release of the Pawnees, who scurried back to the wagons and continued walking on with the camp. At nightfall the frustrated war party gave up and rode away.

The Pawnees, too, disappeared, as the expedition moved to the country of the Sioux and Cheyenne. Chimney Rock, Scott's Bluff and other landmarks of the route were passed, and the travelers continued to experience the usual occurrences of greenhorns on the trail. They imagined near-brushes with deadly rattlesnakes in the rocks, and were uneasy over the possibility of meeting a grizzly bear.

The party passed Sublette's old post on the Laramie, and in the foothills of the Laramie Mountains the veterans in the caravan had a reunion with a band of grizzled old mountain men, bringing a pack train of furs east from the Green River country. On the Fourth of July, they celebrated with a "munificent and magnificent jollification." The party sat down to a huge feast that included buffalo hump ribs, side ribs, tongues, marrow bones, sweetbreads, elk steaks, corn dodgers and plum pudding, washed down with juleps, milk punches and "excellent hock."

There were Sioux and Cheyenne all about the party as it proceeded now west of Fort Laramie, but the travelers were beginning to feel themselves rugged frontiersmen and professed not to be afraid. "Ahead are 1,000 Cheyenne warriors," Field wrote boldly in one of his letters to the *Picayune*. "We are 93 strong, well-armed and provisioned, and mean to march through them with all ease and confidence." The Cheyenne melted away somewhere and were never encountered, but one day eight strapping Brulé Sioux chiefs came riding breakneck into camp, angry as hornets.

"They were all in high dudgeon with Captain Stewart," Field wrote, "as they had understood that the white chief and his young men intended a visit to them at their village, some fifteen miles away, for which occasion they had prepared a grand feast, and none of us were there to eat it. Half the dogs in the village had been killed and cooked, robes had been spread for us in the big lodges, all the squaws had been busy with unusual culinary operations, and not one of us attended the feast. The Indians were very angry."

The day was saved by Sir William who calmed the chiefs by inviting them "to take a shock from an electrifying machine" that he had brought with him. "This," Field continued, "was about the newest 'medicine' that the Sioux had heard of. Bottled Lightning. One of the Sioux chiefs, 'The Man That Shades the Sun,' turned pale when he heard of it. A few of us stood around and received a shock before the Indians, that they might gain something of an understanding of the affair and witness what effect would be produced. But though they manifested great wonder at the clicking of the sparks and at our simultaneous start, they didn't understand it." When the Indians mustered courage, and allowed Sir William to touch them with the machine, "The Solitary Dog thought the White Bull struck him, and at once commenced pummeling him furiously. They shouted and jumped and tossed their arms in the air. When they calmed, they acknowledged that the dose of lightning was great medicine." The slighted dog feast was apparently forgotten.

*A detail from "Sioux on the Warpath," by the Baltimore artist Alfred J. Miller*

The most exciting events of the long journey to the mountains were the buffalo hunts under the expert guidance of Joe Pourier. The first sight of the shaggy game on the hills above the Platte had been the most memorable. Riding one day miles ahead of the caravan with Joe, they had seen two specks, like mice, way off on the rolling plains "at the very kissing of sky and land." The spots were moving quickly, and Joe casually informed them that when buffalo moved that rapidly, it must be because Indians were chasing them. The tourists immediately became frightened, and suggested a hasty retreat to the protection of the caravan, but Joe determinedly drew the cover off his rifle, dismounted to tighten the girth of the mule he was riding and muttered, "Sacre jeengo! Ze red rascal drive off all cow! By damn, we ess four—nuff for whole nation rascal savage. We must have meat zis day."

With that staunch pronouncement, the French-Canadian hunter hastened forward at a trot, the tourists gripping their rifles nervously and following fearfully in a little knot. Suddenly Joe stopped and pointed. The buffalo were rising into the air. As the men watched incredulously, the hunter started to laugh. The specks were crows. Relieved, the tourists started to laugh too. It had been a good joke.

Riding more easily now, they soon saw the real thing, a small group of bulls grazing quietly on a slope beneath a rocky eminence. They rode around the bluff, hobbled their mules and, while Joe circled back to the buffalo, the tourists climbed to the top to see the sport. From their vantage point, they watched

*This Miller painting shows Indians stampeding buffalo to their death in a ravine.*

while Joe fastened a coronet of shrubs on his head, then crawled on his hands and knees up a gully toward the unsuspecting bulls. When he was within range, he rose slowly to a sitting position, made a rest for his rifle by planting his ramrod in the ground, aimed at a fat bull and fired. He dropped flat right away, as the ounce ball hit the beast.

Field, like so many other Plains travelers before and after, could not resist describing in detail his first sight of a dying buffalo: "The bull was up in a moment, 'all standing'—the other two half-rose and glared about. The stricken animal lowered his head, then lifted it again and stared, turned and moved away a few steps, stopped and looked around again, ran, paused, ran again, walked slowly, stopped, trembled, stared piteously at his companions, his head dropped, his fore knees bent under him, his enormous head struck the ground heavily, and he rolled over on his side."

As the party approached its goal, the Wind River Mountains, Sir William dispatched three men to Jim Bridger's newly constructed fort on Black's Fork of the Green River, 200 miles away, to tell Bridger, the trappers and Indians in this area to meet with them for an old-time rendezvous at the little lake in the mountains. Early in August a group of Indians and whites set out from the fort for the festive reunion.

Meanwhile, the expedition reached the Little Sandy Creek, where the priests said good-bye and turned north to find the Flatheads. Sir William's party went on to the Green and up to the head of Piney Creek, the next to last fork of New Fork Creek near present-day Pinedale, Wyoming. They camped first on the creek, then moved five miles up into the Wind River Mountains to Stewart's favorite lake, a wild, crag-lined body of water, ten to twelve miles long and one and one-quarter miles across at its widest point, known today as Fremont Lake.

Now commenced two weeks of free and relaxed frolic and pleasure, the highlight of the trip. "Having pitched tents and formed camp," Field wrote, "one of the India-rubber boats was put together and launched, in which eight of us started, with two strong men to row, for the exploration of the lake. Our progress was slow, and having made about seven miles, we put into a lovely little sandy cove, bordered with pine and half hidden by enormous rocks. In this romantic little nook we disembarked, built a shanty of boughs, got our fishing arrangements to angle after a supper. The water was so clear that we could see the little finny people darting about among the rocks at the bottom, and we could drop our bits of bait almost into their very mouths.... We soon had a plentiful mess for supper, and after supper we disposed of half a dozen of 'Steinwein,' imported by E. Johns, of New Orleans, and put up in diminutive demijohns."

Fishing, hunting, exploring and lazing went on day after day. Then, as Field described it: "Jump, jump! Get your guns! Quick, for your lives! was the loud and alarming call heard suddenly in the stillness of the afternoon. Such a splashing and hurrying headlong out of the water, and up into camp as instantly followed, was probably never seen before in that section. Our ears were next cognizant of distant Indian screaming and almost the next moment a party of some thirty people appeared in view, dashing, with seeming frantic speed towards us. The alarm was soon over, however, the strangers proving to be trappers and Snake Indians, coming to visit us from the vicinity of Bridger's Fort...

"These Snakes, or Sho-sho-nees, threw up their lodges alongside of our camp, while the trappers did the same in close vicinity, and we did not part company again for nearly a fortnight. A busy trade time commenced, and after getting our skins from the trappers, we set the Sho-sho-nee girls to work tailoring up our mountain dresses for us."

The Snakes loved nothing better than horse racing and, moving downstream to a level plain, Field wrote, "We had three days' racing sport.... A straight mile had been laid off and marked upon a beautiful level meadow between Willow Creek and Green River, about half a mile from our encampment, and the stripes and stars floating upon an Indian lodge pole at one end marked the judges' stand." A tin pan, used as a drum by the Indians, served as starting signal, and during the races, the Snakes in the audience galloped around wildly, rolling about on their horses in mad tricks, yelling and screeching and flinging their arms in the air.

On August 17, after two weeks of holiday merriment, the time came to start back east. Sir William, for whom this U.S. visit was to be the last, and Bill Sublette, destined to die in two years, bade farewell to their old acquaintances of the mountains, and the dudes, no longer dudes, but hardened sportsmen of the West, made final trades for leather shirts and moccasins. The two par-

*Sir William bestows beads and baubles on the Indians in this Miller sketch.*

ties streamed down the Plains along Green River and took their separate ways for home, the trappers and Snake Indians to Fort Bridger, the others retracing their steps toward the settlements of civilization 1,100 miles away.

Two months later, as the emigrant covered wagon trains, now well up in the Northwest, straggled on their last lap to the Columbia River, the sporting excursion, bursting with tales of adventures they had had in a playground where only trappers and Indians had previously ventured, reached the first outposts of Missouri's frontier. Giving voice to the proud feelings of the young bloods, Matt Field wrote as dudes ever since have felt as they returned to civilization and their homes from a holiday in the Rockies: "We are the fattest, greasiest set of truant rogues your liveliest imagination can call up to view. We are the merriest, raggedest—perhaps you would add, the ugliest—set of buffalo butchers that ever cracked a rifle among the big hills of Wind River."

Waugh!

137

*Elisha Stevens led a wagon train from Iowa to California without loss of life.*

# THE SMART ONES GOT THROUGH

By GEORGE R. STEWART

he difference between "an historical event" and "a dramatic event" is well illustrated by the stories of the Stevens Party and the Donner Party. The former is historically important, and the pioneers who composed it brought the first wagons to California and discovered the pass across the Sierra Nevada that serves still as the chief route for railroad, highway, telephone, and airlines. The Donner Party, however, is of negligible importance historically, but the story has been told and retold, published and republished, because of its dramatic details of starvation, cannibalism, murder, heroism, and disaster. Against every American who knows of the one, a thousand must know of the other. As a kind of final irony, the pass discovered by the Stevens Party has come to be known as Donner Pass.

Yet actually the two parties had much in common. They were groups of Middle Westerners, native and foreign-born, migrating to California. Both included women and children, and traveled overland in ox-drawn covered wagons. Over much of the way they followed the same route. Both were overtaken by winter, and faced their chief difficulties because of snow. Some of the Donner Party spent the winter in a cabin built by three members of the Stevens Party. One individual, Caleb Green-wood, actually figures in both stories.

The difference in the significance, however, springs from two differences in actuality. First, the Stevens Party set out in 1844, two years before the Donner Party; they were the trail breakers. Second, the Stevens Party was efficiently run, used good sense, had fairly good luck—in a word, was so successful that it got through without the loss of a single life. The Donner Party, roughly speaking, was just the opposite, and the upshot was that the casualty list piled up to 42, almost half of the total roster and nearly equaling the whole number of persons in the Stevens Party. The latter, incidentally, arrived in California more numerous by two than at the start because of babies born on the road.

The contrast between the parties is shown even in the nature of the sources of material available on them. No one bothered to record much about the nondramatic Stevens Party, and we should have scarcely any details if it had not been for Moses Schallenberger, a lad of seventeen at the time of the actual events, who forty years later dictated to his schoolmarm daughter his memories of the journey. On the other hand, the story of the Donner Party is possibly the best documented incident of any in the early history of the West. Its dramatic quality was such that everyone and his brother rushed in to tell what he knew about it or thought he knew about it, either at first- or second-hand, and publishers took it all.

Of course, this is still the everyday tale. Drive efficiently about your business, and no one ever hears of you. Scatter broken glass and blood over the highway, and a picture of the twisted wreck makes the front page...

The Donner Party—to summarize briefly—was formed from family groups of other emigrant parties in July, 1846, and set out by themselves from Little Sandy Creek, in what is now Wyoming, to reach California by the so-called Hastings Route. They lost much time, found the gateway to California blocked by snow, built cabins to winter it out, and ran short of food. Soon they were snowed in deeply, and began to die of starvation. A few escaped across the mountains on improvised snowshoes. Others were saved by the heroic work of rescue parties from the settlements in California. As the result of hardships the morale of the party degenerated to the point of inhumanity, cannibalism, and possibly murder. Of 89 people—men, women, and children—involved with the misfortunes of the party, 47 survived, and 42 perished.

The Stevens Party left Council Bluffs on May 18, 1844. Before doing so, they performed what may well have been the act that contributed most to their final success—they elected Elisha Stevens to be their captain.

He was an unusual enough sort of fellow, that Stevens—about forty years old with a big hawk nose and a peaked head; strange-acting, too. He seemed friendly enough, but he was solitary, having his own wagon but neither chick nor child. Born in South Carolina, raised in Georgia, he had trapped in the Rockies for some years, then spent a while in Louisiana, and now finally he was off for California, though no one knows why.

How such a man came to be elected captain is more than can be easily figured out. How did he get more votes than big-talking Dr. John Townsend, the only member of the party with professional status and of some education? Or more than Martin Murphy, Jr., who could muster kinsmen and fellow Irishmen numerous enough to make up a majority of votes? Perhaps Stevens was a compromise candidate between the native American and the Irish contingents that split the party and might well have brought quarrels and disaster. He had good experience behind him, indeed. And perhaps there was something about him that marked him for the natural leader of men that he apparently was. His election seems to me one of those events giving rise to the exclamation, "It makes you believe in democracy!"

Yes, he took the wagons through. If there were justice in history, his name would stand on the pass he found and conquered, and not merely on a little creek that runs into San Francisco Bay.

So they pushed off from the Missouri River that spring day, numbering 26 men, eight women, and about seventeen children. During the first part of the journey they traveled in company with a larger party bound for Oregon. The swollen Elkhorn River blocked the way, but they emptied the wagons, ferried everything across in a waterproofed wagon bed, swam the cattle, and kept ahead. They chased buffalo, saw their first wild Indians at Fort Laramie. At Independence Rock they halted a week to rest the oxen, "make meat" by hunting buffalo, and allow Helen Independence Miller to be born. They were the first to take wagons across the Green River Desert by what was later known as Sublette's (or Greenwood's) cutoff. On the cutoff they suffered from thirst, had their cattle stampede (but got them back), were scared by a Sioux war party (but had no real trouble). All this, of course, is mere routine for a covered wagon journey, nothing to make copy of.

At Fort Hall they separated fom the Oregon party. At Raft River, eleven wagons in the line, they left the Oregon Trail, and headed south and west, following the wheel tracks of an emigrant party that Joe Walker, the famous mountain man, had tried to take to California the year before. Whether the people in

*Pioneers only copied the Indians by hunting the great buffalo herds of the West.*

the Stevens Party knew of his failure—the people got through, but the wagons were abandoned—is only one of the many details we do not know. Uneventfully and monotonously they followed his trail all the way to Humboldt Sink, a matter of 500 miles. Then, after careful scouting and on the advice of an intelligent Paiute chief, whom they called Truckee, they decided to quit following Walker and strike west.

From that point they were on their own, making history by breaking trail for the forty-niners, the Central Pacific, and U.S. 40. They made it across the Forty-Mile Desert with less trouble than might have been expected, considering that they were the first. Even so, the crossing took 48 hours, and the oxen were thirst-crazed by the time they approached the cottonwoods marking the line of a stream. The men of the party, with their usual good sense, unyoked the oxen some distance from the stream to prevent them from scenting water while still attached to the wagons and stampeding toward it. Thankful to their guide, the emigrants named the stream the Truckee, and prudently camped two days among its cottonwoods for rest and recuperation.

They knew no route, except to follow the river. The canyon got tighter and tighter until in places they merely took their wagons upstream like river boats. The oxen began to give out, hoofs softening because of being in the water so much. Now it came November, and a foot of snow fell. The oxen would have starved except for some tall rushes growing along the water.

Finally they came to where the river forked. Which way to go? They held "a consultation," which must have been close to a council of desperation. It was past the middle of November — snow two feet deep now, high mountain crags in view ahead, oxen footsore and gaunt, food low, womenfolk getting scared. But they were good men and staunch. They must have been — or we would have had the Donner story two years earlier.

Yes, there must have been some good men, and we know the names, if not much else about them. Old Caleb Greenwood the trapper was there, and he would have been heard with respect, though personally I do not cast him for the hero's part, as some do. Neither do I have much confidence in "Doc" Townsend, though his name is sometimes used to identify the whole party; he was full of wild ideas. But "Young" Martin Murphy, Irish as his name, was probably a good man, and so, I think, was Dennis Martin, Irish too. Then there was Hitchcock, whose Christian name has been lost because everyone has referred to him just as "Old Man" Hitchcock; he should have been valuable in the council, having been a mountain man in his day. But the one on whom I put my money is Stevens himself, who had taken them all the way, so far, without losing a man.

He or some other, or all of them together, worked out the plan, and it came out in the end as what we would call today a calculated risk, with a certain hedging of the bets. Leave five wagons below the pass at what is now called Donner Lake, and three young men with them, volunteers, to build a cabin and guard the wagons and goods through the winter. Take six wagons ahead over the pass, and with them the main body including all the mothers and children. Up the other fork of the river, send a party of two women and four men, all young, well-mounted and well-armed, prepared to travel light and fast and live off the country. Unencumbered they can certainly make it through somewhere; when they get to Sutter's Fort, they can have help sent back, if necessary.

So Captain Stevens and the main body took the six wagons ahead to the west, and with a heave and a ho, in spite of sheer granite ledges and ever-deepening snow, they hoisted those wagons up the pass, which is really not a pass so much as the face of a mountain. Even today, when you view those granite slopes, close to precipices, and imagine taking wagons up through the snow, it seems incredible.

Beyond the pass, some days' journey, they got snowed in, but by that time they were over the worst. On Yuba River they built a cabin to winter it out, and Elizabeth Yuba Murphy was born there. Eventually all of them, including E. Y. M., together with the wagons, got safely through to Sutter's.

As for the light-cavalry unit that took the other fork, they went up the stream, were the first white people of record to stand on the shore of Lake Tahoe, then turned west across the mountains. They suffered hardship, but got through.

That brings everybody in except the three young men who were with the wagons at the lake. They had built themselves a cabin, and were just settling down to enjoy a pleasant winter of hunting in the woods when snow started falling. Before long, the cabin was up to the eaves, all game had disappeared, no man could walk. The three were left with two starving cows that they slaughtered, but they themselves were soon close to starving. They decided to get out of there fast, and so manufactured themselves crude snowshoes of the hickory strips that held up the canvases on the covered wagons.

One morning they set out—each with ten pounds of dried beef, rifle and ammunition, and two blankets. The snow was light and powdery, ten feet deep. The improvised snowshoes were heavy and clumsy, and exhausting to use. By evening the three had reached the summit of the pass, but young Moses Schallenberger, a mere gawky lad of seventeen, was sick and exhausted.

In the morning he realized that he could not make it through. Rather than impede his companions, he said good-by and turned back—with no expectation but death. The two others went on, and reached Sutter's Fort.

All in now but Moses Schallenberger! He had barely managed to make it back, collapsing at the very cabin and having to drag himself over the doorsill. He felt a little better the next day, forced himself to go out hunting on his snowshoes, saw nothing except fox tracks. Back at the cabin, "discouraged and sick at

*Letting a wagon down a steep slope required the combined efforts of oxen and men.*

heart," he happened to notice some traps that Captain Stevens had left behind.

Next day he set traps, and during the night caught a coyote. He tried eating it, but found the flesh revolting, no matter how cooked. Still, he managed to live on that meat for three days, and then found two foxes in the traps. To his delight, the fox meat was delicious. This was about the middle of December. From then on, he managed to trap foxes and coyotes. He lived on the former, and hung the latter up to freeze, always fearing that he would have to eat another one, but keeping them as a reserve.

Alone in the snow-buried cabin, through the dim days and long nights of midwinter, week after week, assailed by fierce storms, often despairing of his life, he suffered from deep depression. As he put it later, "My life was more miserable than I can describe," but he never lost the will to live. Fortunately he found some books that "Doc" Townsend had been taking to California, and reading became his solace. The two works that he later mentioned as having pored over were the poems of Byron, and (God save the Mark!) the letters of Lord Chesterfield.

Thus the boy lived on, despondent but resolute, eating his foxes and hanging up his coyotes until he had a line of eleven of them. The weeks dragged along until it was the end of February, and still the snow was deep and the mountain winter showed no sign of breaking. Then, one evening a little before sunset, he was standing near the cabin, and suddenly saw someone approaching. At first he imagined it to be an Indian, but then he recognized his old comrade Dennis Martin!

Martin had traveled a long road since he went over the pass with the main body, in the middle of November. He had been picked up in the swirl of a California revolution and marched south almost to Los Angeles. Returning, he had heard of Schallenberger's being left behind, and had come across the pass on snowshoes to see if he were still alive to be rescued.

Martin had lived for some years in Canada, and was an expert on snowshoes. He made a good pair for Schallenberger, and taught him their use. Thus aided, the lad made it over the pass without great difficulty. The last one was through!

The men of the party even went back the next summer, and brought out the wagons that had been left east of the pass. The only loss was their contents, taken by wandering Indians, except for the firearms, which the Indians considered bad medicine . . .

If we return to the story that offers natural comparison with that of the Stevens Party, we must admit that the historical significance of the Donner Party is negligible. The road that the Donners cut through the Wasatch Mountains was useful to the Mormons when they settled by Great Salt Lake, but they would have got through without it. The Donners served as a kind of horrible example to later emigrants, and so may have helped to prevent other such covered wagon disasters. That is about all that can be totaled up.

There is, of course, no use arguing. The Donner Party has what it takes for a good story, even a dog—everything, you might say, except young love. So, when I drive past the massive bronze statue of the Donner Memorial and up over the pass, I think of these folk who endured and struggled, and died or lived, to produce what may be called the story of stories of the American frontier.

But as I drive over the pass, fighting the summer traffic of U.S. 40 or the winter blizzard, I also like to remember those earlier ones, to think of hawk-nosed Elisha Stevens; of Caleb Greenwood and "Old Man" Hitchcock; or gawky Moses Schallenberger, letting his comrades go on and facing death; of Mrs. Townsend, Moses' sister, riding her Indian pony with the horseback party; of Martin Murphy and fantastic "Doc" Townsend; of Dennis Martin who knew about snowshoes.

These are the ones who discovered the pass and took the wagons over, who kept out of emergencies or had the wit and strength to overcome them, who did not make a good story by getting into trouble, but made history by keeping out of trouble.

*A view of Sutter's Fort in 1847, three years after the Stevens party arrived*

*Dr. Marcus Whitman's assassins, Tamahas (top) and Tilaukait. To the artist, Paul Kane, Tamahas' face was "the most savage I ever beheld."*

# MURDER AT THE PLACE OF RYE GRASS

By NANCY WILSON ROSS

*I*n July of the year 1847, only four months before their murder at the hands of the Indians they had crossed the American continent to Christianize, Dr. Marcus Whitman and his high-minded, high-spirited wife, Narcissa, entertained a wandering Canadian artist at their little mission in the wilds of the Oregon territory, just west of present-day Walla Walla, Washington. The artist was a painter from Toronto named Paul Kane, who aspired—like the American George Catlin—to leave a record of Indian physiological types and Indian ways of life before alcohol, gunpowder, white men's diseases, and white men's customs forever altered them. It was through this chance visit that portraits have been preserved of the two men who killed Marcus Whitman, and incited their fellow tribesmen to the heartless massacre of his wife and other innocent residents in the lonely settlement at Waiilatpu, "the place of rye grass."

In Kane's journal, *Wanderings of an Artist*, we learn that it was Whitman himself who suggested the Cayuse braves, Tilaukait and Tamahas, as subjects for the artist's sketch book. Few uglier or more ominous visages were ever put on canvas. Certainly Kane, in his years of wandering among primitive tribes, painted

149

no other portraits of aborigines that convey quite the same expression of brooding cruelty. Their long black hair, parted in the middle and hanging lankly down over naked shoulders, frames high, protuberant cheekbones, narrow, suspicious eyes, outjutting chins, and mouths shut in a tight, vicious line. Both Indians look exactly what they proved to be — in spite of all the Whitmans' long-enduring optimism — dangerous, confused, and

*Immediately after their marriage in 1836, Narcissa and Marcus Whitman began*

irrationally violent men.

The Whitmans' long journey to their tragic fate had begun back in the year 1834, when a persuasive Congregational pastor named Samuel Parker came riding through the back roads of western New York State with an inspiring message about far distant red men and their fervent wish to be saved. Marcus Whitman, 32 years of age, a doctor in the village of Wheeler, heard

*the long trek across the continent to Oregon to bring Christianity to the Indian.*

Dr. Parker's appeal and was fired by it. So also was Narcissa Prentiss of Amity, an unusually gifted and attractive woman not yet married—mysteriously enough—though 26 years old.

Narcissa, the daughter of Stephen Prentiss, an eminent judge and housebuilder, had been fired to "go to the heathen" as early as her sixteenth year. Perhaps it was her dream of missionary life that had kept her single until she was 26, an advanced age that in those times classified her as a spinster. Apparently, however, there was little that was spinsterish about her. Friends have left descriptions in glowing terms. She had golden hair and a golden voice, "sweet and musical as a chime of bells." She was also "symmetrically formed, very graceful in her voice and carriage," and the possessor of a "brilliant sparkling eye—peculiarly so when engaged in animated conversation." In addition to these attributes, she had received an exceptional education for a girl of her day and, as a school-teacher herself, had the ability and audacity to give a class in "natural philosophy"—which we know today as physics—and even to attempt the teaching of chemistry.

That such a formidable array of charms and talents should be sacrificed in some rough, dangerous, and remote outpost of the Lord's vineyard did not seem as tragic to her friends and family as it did to some of the worldly gentlemen she was later to meet, for a great wave of Christian conversion was then sweeping rural America. There was no shame attached to rising, flooded with tears, in a respectable congregation and crying out in anguish of spirit, "What shall I do to be saved?" Narcissa had been "saved" at the age of eleven, and after she heard the Reverend Dr. Parker's inspirational appeal in the spring of 1834, she had made her first formal try at becoming a missionary. Among Parker's papers is a letter to the mission board asking, "Are females wanted? A Miss Narcissa Prentiss of Amity is very anxious to go to the heathen. Her education is good—piety conspicuous. . . ."

To Dr. Parker's cautious question the board replied with a polite but firm No. Female missionary teachers could not, it was believed, be "employed tactfully except at boarding schools." Narcissa's only chance lay, therefore, in the unlikely event that she would find a husband with the same burning zeal to go west and with qualifications as exceptional as her own. By a most extraordinary turn of fate just such a young man appeared.

Marcus Whitman too was well past the usual marrying age. He had had to make his way alone against frequent financial difficulties and recurrent bouts of ill health — a combination of misfortunes that also accounted for his being a doctor not of divinity but of medicine, a status considerably lower in the prevailing social scale of the period. Marcus was not even a Reverend. He had, to his deep regret, been unable to finance the seven years required for earning a minister's degree, though he had fulfilled more than the usual period of training then expected of doctors.

While the special circumstances surrounding the fateful meeting of Narcissa Prentiss and Marcus Whitman are not known, it can be assumed that the persuasive Dr. Parker had a hand in the romance. As soon as their troth was plighted, Marcus — over Narcissa's protests, for she wanted to be married at once and accompany him — set off with Parker on an exploratory trip to the western side of the Rockies. But he cut short his journey and came back to claim his bride long before he was expected, bringing with him two Indian boys picked up at the mountain rendezvous of the fur companies, as living proof of the red man's need for salvation. And so on a day in February, 1836 — almost two years after Parker's first stirring "Macedonian appeals" — Narcissa and Marcus stood up together in the little church at Angelica, New York, where the Prentisses were then living, and made their solemn marriage vows.

Certain details of the ceremony lend themselves to a macabre and prophetic symbolism. All Narcissa's female relatives were garbed in black, and even the bride had chosen black bombazine, the hue and material of formal mourning, for her wedding dress. Throughout the entire ceremony people could be heard weeping, and when it came to the last hymn — chosen by Narcissa herself — the little church was filled with sobbing. Familiar voices joined Narcissa's flawless soprano in the first stanza:

> *Yes, my native land I love thee*
> *All thy scenes I love them well:*
> *Friends, connections, happy country,*
> *Can I bid you all farewell?*
> *Can I leave you,*
> *Far in heathen lands to dwell?*

As the singing progressed, these poignant sentiments overcame the assembled guests. "Home — thy joys are passing lovely — Happy home! — 'tis sure I love thee! . . . Scenes of sacred peace and pleasure, Holy days and Sabbath bell. . . ." One by one the voices grew muffled and died out. When it came to the last stanza, brave Narcissa was singing solo:

*In the deserts let me labor*
*On the mountains let me tell,*
*How he died—the blessed Saviour—*
*To release a world from hell!*
*Let me hasten,*
*Far in heathen lands to dwell.*

One of the most baffling details of the story is the selection of Henry and Eliza Spalding to accompany the Whitmans and share their evangelical tasks. Those two fervent toilers in the early mission field were equally fitted for the high demands of their vocation—with one vital exception. Henry was a rejected suitor of Narcissa's. A man of touchy pride and smoldering resentments, overquick to place blame on others, Henry Spalding had never forgiven Narcissa Prentiss for rejecting his suit. Did Narcissa underestimate the full extent of his resentment? Was Marcus not acquainted at the time with all the facts? Or did they both decide, with true Christian spirit, to let bygones be bygones? We will never know.

Narcissa's detailed and informative letters describing the trip across the continent reveal, however, that on the whole she enjoyed the great adventure. For one thing, she was in love, and though the decorum of the period, and her own natural modesty, prevented her from writing any garrulous confidences, it is clear that she was happy. To her austere but affectionate mother, quite straightforwardly she writes, "I think I should like to whisper in mother's ear many things which I cannot write. If I could only see her in her room for one half hour. This much I can [say], I have one of the kindest husbands and the very best every way."

Narcissa was extremely fortunate on the western trip, for she was in good health at the time. Although before the journey ended she had become pregnant—like countless women who were to follow her westward in the years ahead—she was able to continue riding her horse and to keep up with the stiff time-schedule the travelers had to set themselves in their race against the weather. By the greatest good fortune she could also "take hold of" buffalo meat with "good relish," and since this was the staple of their diet on the plains, her plight would have been serious had buffalo flesh repelled her. Poor Eliza, who literally could not stomach the fresh meat or the "jerky" either, nearly died of malnutrition.

Through the intervention of what the missionaries devoutly took for the hand of Providence, they had been able to catch up with the annual fur caravan from St. Louis, bound for the summer rendezvous at the Green River in the foothills of the Rockies, carrying supplies for the beaver-trapping mountain men. Otherwise they might never have made it to Oregon. What is more, had not Marcus already taken that earlier trip across the plains with Dr. Parker in this same rough company, it is quite likely that the missionaries would have been rudely refused the privilege of accompanying the caravan. For the men of this annual expedition were, in the main, wild and rough adventurers, many of them voluntary exiles from civilization, in revolt against cramping association with pious men and women.

Whitman, on that earlier trip, had had the good fortune to encounter one of the most famous of the mountain men, Jim Bridger, who had heard that a doctor was traveling with the caravan and came to ask Marcus to remove an arrowhead lodged in his back. Marcus agreed to try, and Bridger, after generously belting himself with whiskey, lay down in the midst of an interested audience of trappers and Indians while Marcus, with the crude instruments at hand, removed the arrowhead. (Some years later, when the Whitmans were established at Waiilatpu, Jim Bridger sent his half-breed daughter to live with them.) After this successful operation, other mountain men and even Indians with embedded arrowheads had come to seek Whitman's help, and therefore when he reappeared among them a year later with a wife and two missionary companions, the fur caravan was ready to accept his presence.

It was by no means easy for the Whitmans and the Spaldings to associate with men of this caliber. The cursing and drinking, the unsanctified bonds with Indian women, the general filth and corruption, were very hard to tolerate. Mrs. Whitman was later to suffer greatly from the lack of her own kind of society. As the Reverend H. K. W. Perkins, a missionary acquaintance of Narcissa's, was to write to her sister Jane, Narcissa should never have gone to the Far West in the first place. It was plainly a kind of "suicide," for she belonged by nature in a "polished and exalted sphere."

Yet some degree of admiration for her must surely have stirred in the breasts of the rough men she met along the way. Her fine carriage, her animation, above all her glorious singing voice, were the wonder of many who encountered her. Joe Meek, a mountain man of Bridger's fame and stature, often recalled in later years the radiant vision that had come riding toward him across the wild land. Like Bridger, Meek too was to send his little half-breed daughter to the Whitman mission to be cared for by Narcissa, and her small body was among the other mutilated ones which Meek had to find and bury after the massacre.

When the party arrived at Fort Vancouver, Marcus and Henry went on up the Columbia River, to locate land for their missions, while Narcissa and Eliza stayed behind and were royally pampered by the Hudson's Bay Company's famous factor, John McLoughlin. Gentlemen insisted nightly on toasting them in wine — over their blushing protests as members of the "Tetotal Society." Narcissa dwelt at some length in her letters home on the food they enjoyed at Vancouver — a not-surprising emphasis after the diet they had tolerated for so many months. Roast duck was an everyday dish, also salmon, sturgeon, boiled pork, and tripe, every diner to make his choice — and "at every new dish a clean plate." It was all very high style indeed, and a memory on which Narcissa must often have dwelt in the years to come when she became virtually a slave to domestic drudgery, with hardly a single moment of peace in her own kitchen, due to the constant presence of the curious — and dirty — Cayuses, and later of exhausted, travel-weary emigrants.

When Marcus came back down the Columbia to say that he and Spalding had selected their home sites — a very injudicious 120 miles apart, at Henry's insistence — Narcissa, though now in her fourth month of pregnancy, refused McLoughlin's pressing invitation to remain at least through the winter. With reluctance and obvious apprehension, this "most sympathetic man" saw both women set off with Marcus in a pouring rain in a small open boat.

Though Marcus did not realize it at the time, he had invited bad luck when he chose to settle among the Cayuses. To begin with, when there had been competition between the various tribes over the honor of having on their own land these strange white people who did not come to trade but to teach, the Cayuses had begged hard for the privilege of being their hosts. Yet only a short time has passed before we find Narcissa writing about a Chief Umtippe, "full of all manner of hypocracy, deceit and guile," who had decided that the missionaries must pay the Indians for the privilege of learning to speak the Cayuse tongue!

The Cayuses' initial eagerness to learn about the white man's God and the teachings in the sacred "Black Book" was not long-

*A fanciful painting of Jim Bridger by the famous artist Alfred Jacob Miller*

lived. Unlike the more intelligent and devout Nez Perces, whom Henry Spalding had chosen, the Cayuses were soon angered by Whitman's demands for a "change of heart." Narcissa's own words convey a very good idea of what soon began to go on in the Indian mind:

Some feel almost to blame us for telling them about eternal realities. One said it was good when they knew nothing but to hunt, eat, drink and sleep; now it was bad. . . . Of late my heart yearns over them more than usual. They feel so bad, disappointed, and some of them angry, because husband tells them that none of them are Christians; that they are all of them in the broad road to destruction, and that worshipping will not save them. They try to persuade him not to talk such bad talk to them, as they say, but talk good talk, or tell some story, or history, so that they may have some Scripture names to learn. Some threaten to whip him and to destroy our crops, and for a long time their cattle were turned into our potato field every night to see if they could compel him to change his course of instruction with them.

These ominous difficulties sank into at least temporary insignificance for Narcissa with the arrival, on her own twenty-ninth birthday, of a little blonde, blue-eyed girl whom they named Alice Clarissa after her Prentiss and Whitman grandmothers. Narcissa did not have a difficult labor and — greatest of all blessings for a frontier woman — she had abundant milk with which to nurse the infant. The appearance of this first white child seemed for a time a hopeful augury of better relations with the Indians, for her birth was an event of great excitement and pride to the Cayuses. None among them was more delighted than Tilaukait, the eventual murderer, who told the Whitmans that they should call the child "Cayuse *te-mi*" (girl) because she was born on "Cayuse *wai-tis*" (ground).

The child was an indescribable joy to lonely Narcissa, left so much in solitude while Marcus went off among the Indians. It is difficult to account for the neglect of Narcissa at this time by her apparently devoted family. Even allowing for the slowness and general chanciness of mail delivery in the Far West — where letters came addressed simply to "So and so, west of the Rocky Mountains" — how could two years and five months have passed before a single word from loved ones reached Marcus and Narcissa? Yet she, though so singularly neglected, went right on generously sending detailed accounts of her strange new life — something for which all historians of the Pacific Northwest should forever offer their grateful thanks. Early in the Waiilatpu days we find her writing in desperation, "Who will come over and help us? Weak, frail nature cannot endure excessive care and anxiety any great length of time, without falling under it. I refer more particularly to my husband. His labor this spring has affected his health considerably. His old complaint in his side affects him occasionally."

And in truth there was no end to the sheer drudgery. First off, there was their own house to make, from the simplest of materials and with the crudest of implements. Domestic stock had to be purchased from the Hudson's Bay Company, and the Indians instructed in the feeding and care of pigs, chickens, and cows. They must also be taught, for the first time, the most elementary principles of agriculture; for instance, how to employ such a simple tool as a hoe. The Whitmans had also to set about learning the Cayuse language to ease the problem of their personal relations. They must immediately set up a school — without books or a building — and they must, above all, establish a pattern of divine service for the Indians. All this they must do against an increasingly resistant wall of laziness, abysmal ignorance, and indifference, hardening slowly into active antipathy.

At the end of two years, to the great surprise and joy of the Whitmans, nine missionaries arrived at Waiilatpu, coming on from the East to establish other teaching centers among the various Indian tribes. Their arrival swelled to thirteen the number of Presbyterian workers in the Oregon mission field. It was never to grow any larger. However, although they had prayed for this reinforcement, the arrival of so many people to crowd the inadequate living quarters at Waiilatpu became a source of strain and irritation — particularly to overburdened Narcissa, already beginning to show the first evidence of the frayed nerves that the hard life and unbroken strain were to produce in her delicate and sensitive nature.

While the somewhat ill-assorted missionary brothers went scouting for their separate mission sites, guided by Whitman and Spalding, the sisters, left behind at crowded Waiilatpu, failed to steer an unvaryingly serene course in their dealings with one another. Mary Richardson Walker, from Maine, waiting in natural anxiety for her first child to be born, was irked by her living quarters — a little lean-to room with no heat in it. Without any opportunity whatsoever for "collecting herself" among the six

white families and the eternal presence of the inquisitive Cayuses, Mary characteristically took to her journal and has left us
some pithy comment, not only on her own shortcomings but on
those of Narcissa as well: of the latter . . . "in a worry about
something, cross with everyone; went out and blustered around
and succeeded in melting over her tallow. . . . Mrs. W. has dealt
. . . largely in powder and balls of late."

There is touching evidence that poor, beset Narcissa was often
repentant and tried to make amends. So much did she deplore
her own faults that on one occasion she wrote a letter home that
seems excessive in its self-condemnation: "Perhaps never in my
whole life have I been led to see so distinctly the hidden iniquity
and secret evils of my heart. . . . Of all persons I see myself to be
the most unfit for the place I occupy on heathen ground." Narcissa, alas, was quite right in this statement of her essential unfit-
ness for the life she had chosen, but entirely wrong in her diag-
nosis of the reasons for her small daily failures. She was already
asking of her nature something that it could not supply.

To anyone who reads Narcissa's intimate, revealing letters and
journal, it becomes almost unbearable to face the great tragedy
that now visited her—the loss of her only child, the one bright
and shining spot in a deprived and burdensome existence.

The day of Alice Clarissa's death was the Sabbath, which to
one of Narcissa's faith must have seemed a special grace, helping
her to bear the agony. On that Sunday, Alice had been playing
in and out of the open door, but when it came time for dinner
and she was not around, Narcissa sent Margaret, the young Indian housemaid, to get her ready for the meal. The little Indian
did not find her but, without coming back to say so, went on into
the garden to get vegetables for dinner. While she was gone,
Mungo, a Hawaiian servant at the mission, came into the kitchen
to report the odd fact that he had seen two cups floating in the
river. Marcus, intent on his Bible-reading, said only: "Let them
be and get them out to-morrow because of the Sabbath." But
Narcissa suddenly remembered her child taking two cups from
the kitchen some time that morning. She cried out in terror.
Where was Alice? Where was the Indian girl who had been sent
to find her? So great was Narcissa's sudden fear that everyone
ran from the house at once in a frantic search. Finally an old
Indian entered the stream and found the child's body under a
root. Narcissa, in a letter to the grandparents, re-created the full

horror of the moment:

I ran to grasp her to my breast, but husband outran me and took her up from the river, and in taking her into his arms and pulling her dress from her face we thought she struggled for breath, but found afterwards that it was only the effect of the atmosphere upon her after being in the water.

Narcissa made the child's shroud herself. Some have it that she made it from her wedding dress, but the truth seems to be that it was made from the same gray dress she wore for the long journey west. Narcissa confessed to her parents that they kept the child for four days before burial.

She did not begin to change in her appearance much for the three first days. This proved to be a great comfort to me, for so long as she looked natural and was so sweet and I could caress her, I could not bear to have her out of my sight.

Narcissa was never to bear another child, and it is clear that some heart for the evangelical enterprise went out of her after she sustained this loss. True to their unquestioning faith, however, both Whitmans accepted the inscrutable will of God. They even found ways to justify it, in believing that their loss had "softened" them so that they could take into their lives unwanted children born to others, a little Indian boy and two neglected half-breed daughters of the mountain men, Bridger and Joe Meek. Later they adopted seven orphaned emigrant children who had lost both father and mother en route to Oregon.

After Alice Clarissa's death, eight difficult years were to pass before the end at Waiilatpu. Within the mission frequent disagreements arose, born of divergent viewpoints on policy and procedure toward the Indians. Some of the missionaries wanted more prayer and formal worship, longer seasons of soul-saving. Others felt that it would be wiser to emphasize practical matters: growing crops, weaving cloth, milling grain, raising sheep and cattle, teaching the English tongue. Throughout this time there is little doubt that Henry Spalding was getting in his licks at the Whitmans. In a letter to her father in 1840 Narcissa wrote to say of Henry, "Every mind in the mission that he has had access to, he has tried to prejudice against us."

Trouble with the moody and insolent Cayuses was constantly increasing—a situation quite unlike that of the Spaldings among the intelligent Nez Perces, or the Walkers and Eells among the

more tractable Spokanes. Marcus' patience and Christian for-
bearance often seem remarkable. He has left a description of
one encounter that shows the length to which he was prepared
to go in demonstrating a humble and Christ-like spirit:

He [the Cayuse] then took hold of my ear and pulled it and struck me
on the breast ordering me to hear—as much as to say, we must let them
do as they pleased. . . . When he let go I turned the other to him and he
pulled that, and in this way I let him pull first one and then the other
until he gave over and took my hat and threw it into the mud. I called
on the Indians who were at work . . . to give it to me and I put it on my
head—when he took it off again . . . and threw it in the mud and water,
of which it dipped plentifully. Once more the Indians gave it back to
me and I put it on all mud as it was, and said to him "Perhaps you are
playing."

To be sure, the Whitmans were not always so forbearing. That
invaluable and analytical Mr. Perkins, who appraised Narcissa's
character so shrewdly for her sister, did not feel that either of
the two Whitmans was a natural "missionary" to the Indians.
They were, he thought, too civilized, too proud, too aware of
their own superiority. The Reverend Mr. Perkins, in his long letter to Jane Prentiss, used an interesting modern word to explain
the Whitmans' failure and final tragedy. They did not "identify"
themselves with their Indian charges.

Within Marcus Whitman there was a constant conflict between
his vision of an Americanized Far West and his Christian duty to
the original inhabitants of this lovely land; Narcissa too was forever torn between her natural yearnings for the companionship
of her equals—for "something exalted—communion with *mind*,"
as Perkins put it—and her earnest, fervent wish to start an ignorant race on its long, slow climb to the civilization she so greatly
valued. Parson Perkins summed her up quite adequately and
honestly when he wrote that she "was not a missionary but a
woman, a highly gifted, polished American lady."

Eventually the recurrent internecine strife among the missionaries died out, thanks to earnest sessions of repentance and for-
giveness among the persons most concerned, with renewed
pledges of better behavior on Henry Spalding's part. What was
more, the first emigrants had begun to trickle past the Whitmans' door, and Marcus rightly judged this to be a hopeful sign
of that great flood of settlers he had for so long anticipated. By
this time, however, so many divergent reports of trouble among

the isolated missions had reached the mission board in Boston that one day, out of the blue, to the dismay of them all—the Whitmans and Spaldings in particular—an official letter was received, ordering Henry and Marcus to dissolve their missions, Spalding to return at once to the States, and Whitman to join the Walkers and Eells at Tshimakain. Marcus bravely volunteered to go back across America in the dead of winter to plead the mission cause, to save Henry Spalding from expulsion, and to set the board straight on the real state of affairs in distant Oregon.

While he was gone, ailing, distraught Narcissa, now rapidly declining in strength, though only in her thirty-fifth year, was able to enjoy another brief period of comparative comfort and peace—her last. After an attempted assault on her by an Indian who tried to enter her bedroom at night, every white "neighbor" at Fort Walla Walla 25 miles away and at the scattered missions insisted that she leave Waiilatpu for the duration of her husband's absence. She finally agreed to spend the winter at The Dalles with a congenial family of Methodist missionaries.

Narcissa herself, in her letters, begins to admit to increasingly poor health: "My eyes are almost gone ... writing is very injurious to me." She had an internal growth of some kind. Though she had stoutly urged on Marcus the necessity of the journey, she missed him cruelly. It was impossible for her to keep from vivid imaginings of the dangers of a wintertime journey overland and the final outcome of his conference with the mission board in Boston.

She began to suffer at this time too from melancholy fears of the future: "I am restless and uneasy, numbering the past, anxiously looking forward, struggling between hope and fear." She lived in the vain hope that her adored sister Jane and her husband would accompany Marcus back to Waiilatpu.

Marcus, after an exhausting journey, succeeded in persuading the board to extend the western mission venture until it had more time to prove its worth. He returned safely—and in comparatively good health—in the spring of 1843, having hastened his departure in order to join, and thereby lend valuable aid and counsel to, the first great train of emigrants crossing the plains to Oregon. This was the Great Migration of 1843, an important signpost on the widening road of western expansion.

Sister Jane and her husband did not come to Oregon with the doctor. We do not know why. Together, thankful to be reunited once more, the Whitmans returned to their mission. Although everything seemed peaceful, the charred ruins of their gristmill, which had been burned before Narcissa had left for The Dalles, must have spoken to them both of the turbulent, unplumbed depths of Indian suspicion and malice.

The Cayuses were, in fact, further than ever from a state of grace. Disturbed and agitated by the increasing number of white people, they were quite ready to listen to the propaganda of one or two "eastern educated" half-breeds who circulated among them telling them what was, in fact, the bitter truth—that their days as free men were numbered.

The measles epidemic was the fuse that lit the powder keg. Not only did Dr. Whitman *not* cure the sick—virtually an impossibility, no matter how he wore himself out in the attempt, since the Indians had no immunity to this white man's disease—but also an ugly rumor had begun to circulate among the Cayuses that he was actually causing deaths by administering poison instead of medicine.

Whitman had been away from home tending the sick in his own parish and outside it, visiting Spalding, even calling on some Catholic missionaries to discuss the growing tensions, not only between white and red but also between Protestants and Catholics, both contending for the souls of the aborigines in their respective ways.

The twenty-ninth of November, 1847, dawned cold and foggy. It began like every other normal day among the regular mission group, grown somewhat larger now with volunteers and hired hands and swollen besides with emigrants stopping over at this welcome oasis on the long, exhausting trail to the gentle valleys of lower Oregon. (So strategically located was the Waiilatpu mission that it had, in fact, become almost a hospital for sick and weary travelers, thus adding immeasurably to the Whitmans' already heavy burden.) On this gray early-winter morning people were coming down with measles or slowly recovering from them, just as were the Indians in their nearby lodges. Men were at work as usual in the rebuilt gristmill. John Sager, one of the seven emigrant orphans adopted by the Whitmans, was winding twine in the kitchen to be made into brooms. Others were studying, sewing, cooking, caring for the sick.

The school had just reopened after an enforced vacation due to the measles epidemic. A tailor was making a much-needed suit of clothes for Dr. Whitman. A floor was being laid. They were preparing to butcher beef. Mrs. Whitman had not appeared for breakfast that morning, and when one of the young girls took her meal to her room, she found her weeping terribly with a handkerchief pressed against her face. In silence she motioned the girl to leave. She did not touch the food. Word had come at dawn that another child had died the night before in the lodge of Tilaukait. The doctor had already gone to perform the burial service. Did Narcissa sense the impending doom?

The midday meal came and went. It was in the afternoon that Tilaukait and Tamahas appeared at the mission house. On a pretext of securing medicine, they tomahawked the doctor without warning. As always with firsthand accounts of shocking experiences, the stories vary, but it seems likely that Marcus tried to escape—at least he managed to get outdoors—perhaps hoping thus to save the others from harm. After striking him several deadly, mutilating blows that he vainly tried to dodge, and after having killed the only male witness, the two Cayuses fled. Mrs. Whitman, who had been bathing one of the convalescent children in another part of the mission, rushed to her husband at the news of the assault, and with the aid of two women managed to drag the doctor indoors, where they lifted him to a settee and tried vainly to stanch his bleeding.

Almost at once, from all sides, the Indians began to attack. One mission worker, who had been shot and tomahawked near the river, managed to make the house to give warning, but by the time he burst into the room where the doctor already lay bleeding to death, the massacre had begun. Mrs. Whitman went to the door to look out. She was immediately shot in the side under her left arm, and though she fell to the floor with a scream, she managed at once to stagger to her feet and take charge of the terrified group that by now had gathered in the sitting room. Forced to leave Marcus behind—still breathing but now unconscious and plainly beyond hope—she herded them all up the stairs to a second-story bedroom.

They had hardly reached this room when the Indians burst in below. The broken end of an empty gun, held strategically at the top of the narrow stairwell at Mrs. Whitman's suggestion, held them temporarily at bay. And then a friendly Indian named Tamsucky appeared and urged them all to come down, offering them full protection and safe guidance to the nearest fort. Mrs.

Whitman was not immediately reassured. She urged Tamsucky to come upstairs and after some hesitation, for fear that he might be shot, Tamsucky mounted the stairs. He was able then to persuade her of his good intentions; so much so that she cried, "God has raised us up a friend!" It was arranged that the adults would leave first, while some of the children, promised

*This drawing of Tamahas' attack on Dr. Marcus Whitman is dramatic but*

full protection by Tamsucky, remained behind for the time being, perhaps to spare them exposure in the wintry fields.

Mrs. Whitman, by now too weak to walk from loss of blood, was carried from the house on a settee. Hardly had she appeared in the open than the shooting began again. Tamsucky had been a traitor. The men carrying Narcissa were shot at once,

*incorrect in detail: Narcissa was actually in another part of the mission at the time.*

and a number of bullets entered her body as the settee dropped to the ground. An Indian rushed up, overturned it, and thrust her down into the thick November mud, while another Indian lifted her head by its long, pale hair and struck her face viciously with his leather quirt. No one knows how long it took her to die. For her, however, death came sooner than for Marcus. Some of the terrified occupants of the mission house, still in hiding, heard the doctor's groans far on into the night.

When the Indians had fully satisfied their thirst for revenge — and apparently the murder of the Whitmans served as some appeasement, since Narcissa was the only woman they killed — they withdrew to their own lodges. The next day and on days thereafter they returned, however, to feast on the mission stores, forcing the remaining white women to cook for them. To what other indignities these women were subjected the record is not clear. Altogether, fourteen people had been killed at the mission; 47 were taken captive and later had to be ransomed.

The first outsider to reach this hideous scene was a Catholic priest named Brouillet. On November 30 he visited Tilaukait's camp and heard of the massacre at Waiilatpu. He went at once to the mission and helped one of the few survivors wash and bury the dead, still lying in the open in all their ghastly mutilation; he read the burial service with quaking knees, the Indians standing at a little distance, painted and armed. It was Brouillet also, on his way back from Waiilatpu, who probably saved Spalding's life, for he encountered Henry en route to the Whitmans to pick up his little daughter, Eliza, and warned him to return with all speed to the friendly Nez Perces. Although Eliza Spalding's life had been spared by the Cayuses, Henry, uncertain of his daughter's fate, did go a little later to Waiilatpu, and it was there that he sat down and wrote in its full horror a detailed description for Narcissa's parents of her last hours on earth.

The anxious settlers in lower Oregon were quick to pursue the murderers. The Cayuses, who had looted all they could loot and seemed now to be intent on running the mission plant for their own use, fled into the mountains at the coming of fifty avenging riflemen. After two years of desperate wandering, five of them voluntarily gave themselves up to justice, among them Tilaukait and Tamahas. It is reported that Tilaukait, when asked why he had surrendered, answered: "Did not your missionaries teach us that Christ died to save his people? So we die to save our people." Perhaps he hoped to save himself death by hanging—the most terrible of all deaths for an Indian. If so, the hope was vain. He, Tamahas, and three others went to the scaffold. In the end the fate they had feared overtook the Cayuses. They not only lost their land and their freedom, but they lost standing with other Indians like the Spokanes and Nez Perces and were for a long time thereafter anathema to all far western whites.

It was following the flight of the Cayuses from Waiilatpu that Joseph Meek, along with other riflemen from the Willamette Valley, undertook the task of removing the dead from their shallow grave, where wolves had already been making their grisly meals, and reburying them. Shortly after, Meek set off for Washington as a one-man embassy from Oregon to plead with his cousin, President James K. Polk, for government protection for the settlers and for the admission of Oregon as a territory.

The massacre of the Whitmans, when made public through Meek's mission, horrified the nation. Polk determined to settle the matter of Oregon while he was still President. This was not too easy, for England still had certain claims. Moreover, Southern interests in Congress had long been blocking the territorial admission of this distant land, hoping to delay until Oregon would enter the Union with the status of another "slave state." It was not until the very day before Polk's term expired that Oregon was officially proclaimed a territory.

Undoubtedly the martyrdom of the Whitmans helped settle the fate of this portion of the American West. Today, historical museums treasure not only Narcissa's remarkable letters, and other documents from early mission days, but even locks of her bright hair, cut from the mangled body that poor Joe Meek had to help rebury. The mission precincts have been made a national monument supervised by the National Park Service.

The site of the ruins has been carefully excavated and plainly marked for all to see, and there is even a small museum that houses artifacts excavated from the site. Every year thousands of visitors come out from Walla Walla to climb the hill of the rye grass and gaze down at the shaft that marks the grave of the victims. Perhaps they wonder, as they stand there in the clear bright light, where on the green plains below lie the bones of little Alice Clarissa Whitman, that "treasure invaluable" who briefly gladdened the daily cares of the first white woman to cross the Rocky Mountains.

*Expelled from their settlement at Nauvoo, Illinois, the Mormons start west.*

# "HERE IS MY HOME AT LAST!"

## By CARL CARMER

After Joseph and Hyrum Smith were murdered by an anti-Mormon mob at Carthage, Illinois, on June 27, 1844, great contention arose among the Latter-day Saints as to who would succeed Joseph as head of the Church. At a vast meeting beside the unfinished temple on August 8, Sidney Rigdon urged that he be made Church guardian, claiming that he had received a revelation from on high that this should be his office. A little later a sturdy figure rose from the audience and spoke for himself. Not as tall as Joseph Smith, Brigham Young was nevertheless of commanding presence. He proclaimed himself a dedicated follower of the Prophet, and he spoke with a sincerity and practicality which made Rigdon seem both small and pretentious. He was overwhelmingly sustained as president of the Twelve Apostles, on whom the power of the Church now rested.

Brigham Young had been born four years earlier than Joseph Smith, and in the same state of Vermont. His family had moved to western New York when he was two. As he grew older Brigham devoted his energies to becoming a carpenter and joiner. There are fine houses still standing in New York State (including the home of Lincoln's Secretary of State, William Henry Seward, at Auburn) that are testimonials to the thoroughness and quality of his craftsmanship.

The young builder was converted to the Church of Jesus Christ of Latter-day Saints by Mormon neighbors. He did not meet the founder of the faith until 1832, after Joseph had moved to Kirtland, Ohio. At that time Brigham made a pilgrimage for the express purpose of declaring his loyalty and found Joseph in the forest, back of the house where he was living, "chopping and hauling wood." Thus the originator of the Mormon Church and the man who was to do more than any other member in perpetuating it, both Yankee-born, became known to each other.

The new head of the Latter-day Saints was to prove himself not only an effective administrator but one of the greatest leaders of men in all American history. He spoke the vernacular of his time with exactness of meaning, yet with a touch of poetry. He had an intuitive knowledge of his fellows. He had common sense. He had a kind of down-to-earth spirituality. And he bristled with authority.

Though President Young was aware of the gathering tempest of hatred which was soon to result in the Mormons being driven out of Nauvoo by armed mobs, he insisted that the magnificent temple of which Joseph Smith had dreamed be completed. Before it was finished, however, the decision had been made that the whole body of the Nauvoo Saints would move westward. The first wagons left Nauvoo in February, 1846.

By autumn twelve to fifteen thousand of the Saints had reached the west bank of the Missouri, where they built a temporary city called Winter Quarters. While they waited at this place (the site of Florence, Nebraska, now a residential section of Omaha), they received word that the few remaining Mormons left at Nauvoo had in September been attacked by mobs and after a gallant defense had been driven from the city. A month later, on October 9, vandals burned the temple to the ground. As the winter of 1846 set in, President Young and his advisers planned an exploratory expedition which would set out to find a home for the Mormons somewhere in the Far West.

All through the early days of April, 1847, Brigham Young busied himself at Winter Quarters with getting under way an expedition to find a land in the West where all members of the Church might live safely and in peace.

His first plan had been to enlist twelve groups of twelve men each, but the number fluctuated as the time for departure neared. At the Church conference on April 6 he was upheld as president of the Church, and a dozen of the most important Saints were continued as members of the Quorum of the Twelve Apostles—among them both Willard Richards and John Taylor, who had been eyewitnesses of the lynching of Prophet Joseph Smith and his brother Hyrum in 1844. There were a few delays as the wagons gathered and the members of the pioneer group reported. By Saturday, April 10, sixty-four wagons were rolling toward the banks of the little Elkhorn River thirty-four miles from Winter Quarters. They crossed Papillion Creek, and as one of the Pioneers, Norton Jacobs, recorded their journey, "Towards evening we hove into sight of the Elk Horn River and the valley of the great Platte, affording a full view of the river as it stretched away for many miles to the west."

On Sunday morning all wagons were ferried across the Elkhorn and were counted as sixty-nine. Still there were delays caused by necessary rides back to Winter Quarters for conferences, for more good-bys to families, for brothers who were hurrying from eastern places.

At eight o'clock on the morning of Friday the sixteenth President Young had the camp called together at his wagon and ordered a count of those going on the journey. There were 143 men, three women, and two children. The three women were Clarissa Decker Young, a wife of Brigham Young; Harriet Page Wheeler Young, a wife of Brigham's brother Lorenzo; and Ellen Sanders Kimball, a wife of Heber C. Kimball, one of the Council of the Twelve. The two children were Isaac Perry Decker, son of Lorenzo's wife by a former marriage, and Zobriski Young, son of the same woman by Lorenzo. Three of the men were listed as "colored"—Oscar Crosby, Green Flake, and Hark Lay. Inventory of property made at this time showed seventy-two wagons and carriages of many types—some small, some large and covered— (besides a wagon on which a large leather boat served as the wagon box) and a cannon brought along as protection against Indians (who were notoriously afraid of the sound of artillery). Ninety-three horses, fifty-two mules, sixty-six oxen, nineteen cows, and assorted dogs, cats, and chickens went along.

To avoid contact with non-Mormon parties going west, President Young chose to travel on the north side of the Platte in-

*Brigham Young at forty-three*

stead of on the Oregon Trail along the south bank, which was more distinct and more heavily used. Their road led through Pawnee Indian country.

On Sunday, April 18, the weather was still cold and spring not far advanced. At five o'clock that day the officers met with President Young, who gave them the daily routine. A bugle would sound at five in the morning. Each Pioneer would arise and attend to his prayers before leaving his wagon. Cooking, eating, and feeding the stock would fill the time till seven, when the camp would move. Each teamster was to stay beside his team with loaded gun in hand. The order of encampment was to be a circle, with the mouth of each wagon to the outside and the horses and cattle tied inside. At 8:30 P.M. the bugle would sound again. At this time all were to have prayers in their wagons and go to bed by nine.

The next day was warm, and the Pioneers followed the President's orders implicitly. William Clayton, suffering from a toothache, walked beside his wagon and thought of "fixing up a set of wooden cog-wheels to the hub of a wagon wheel in such order as to tell the exact number of miles we travel each day." The next day the tooth still ached, and Clayton asked Luke Johnson to pull it. "He only got half of the original tooth, the balance being left in the jaw. After this my head and face pained me more than before."

A week went by—a week of hard pulling in soft and sandy loam—day after day of monotonous plodding on a trackless prairie not yet awakened by spring. The brethren nooned one day on the bank of Loup Fork opposite a Pawnee village, and the Indians ran into the water to cross and ask for presents. Young ordered powder, lead, salt, and flour given to them, but they continued to beg. Hastily he ordered the wagons to move. At six o'clock they encamped where Looking Glass Creek flows into Loup Fork. More days followed on the same pattern, and then came a day of rest, Sunday, April 25, with services at four o'clock. "This Earth Was Once a Garden Place" sang the newly formed choir lustily. Then on. The wagons took their own way west across the prairie wasteland. Suddenly April was over. On the last evening of the month the brothers camped beside marshy ground. They were cold and bored and disconsolate. Brother Brigham urged them to dance to warm up, and they did so.

On May 1 the Pioneers caught their first glimpse of buffalo. At once the wagons halted, and those brothers appointed as buffalo hunters raced their horses toward a herd of over seventy. Wilford Woodruff wrote of the chase: "I then saw that Orrin P. (Porter) Rockwell had three bulls at bay on the prairie . . . Brother Kimball came up at the same time. We surrounded them and commenced firing upon them . . ." "The meat is very sweet and as tender as veal," wrote William Clayton. After that the brothers were so often at the kill that President Young forbade them to continue, although both sides of the Platte River were black with buffalo for miles, and as Wilford Woodruff wrote, "It looked as though the whole face of the earth was alive and moving like the waves of the sea." There were days when Porter Rockwell or Luke Johnson would capture buffalo calves and bring them into the camp for the two little boy Pioneers to romp with.

On some mornings when the bugle blared, the brethren would wake to see flames on the horizon and to feel smoke stinging their eyes. The earth would be black over measureless acres, and ashes blown by prairie winds would make their faces as dark as those of their fellow travelers, Green Flake and Hark Lay.

On May 12 the monotony of their day-after-day marching was lessened by Clayton, who, with the aid of mechanic Appleton Harmon, had put into practice the idea evolved when he had a toothache. He had invented what he called a "roadometer" and attached it to the axle of the carriage in which he rode. Now its wooden cogs ticked off the miles relentlessly, and at the end of every day he could report how much nearer the brethren were to the Rocky Mountains.

Spring finally came to the wagon train in the last week of May. On Monday the twenty-fourth the brethren saw across the river a band of about thirty-five Indians, also riding west. After the Mormons had made camp, some of the savages rode across the river toward them, one of those in the lead carrying a United States flag. They were well-dressed and impressive people, handsomely adorned. President Young fed them and entertained the chief and his wife overnight. The chief was fascinated by the camp telescope. Through it he looked long at the moon. He may well have been puzzled by a wild dance in which the brethren indulged themselves later.

Now the wagons were rolling into the land of western wonder. For three whole days the high thin tower of Chimney Rock was constantly in sight, and beyond it rose Scotts Bluff like the tumbled walls of a ruined temple. They were almost at the present-day Nebraska-Wyoming line.

Life in the camp had become lax in the springtime. The Pioneers played cards and checkers and dominoes in their wagons. Some of them played musical instruments, and their hearers cavorted to fiddle tunes, the men dancing with each other and cutting pigeonwings and other figures in the joy of the warming

*Some Mormons, too poor to afford wagons, emigrated to Utah pulling handcarts.*

spring season. On the cold, rainy morning of May 29 after the bugle sounded at ten, President Young summoned the camp to gather about the boat-wagon and there spoke his mind. His speech was emphatic and earnest, and it ended in burning words of rebuke:

Joking, nonsense, profane language, trifling conversation and loud laughter do not belong to us. Suppose the angels were witnessing the hoe-down the other evening, and listening to the haw haws the other evening, would not they be ashamed of it? I am ashamed of it. . . . Now let every man repent of his weakness, of his follies, of his meanness, and every kind of wickedness, and stop your swearing and profane language, for it is in this camp and I know it, and have known it. I have said nothing about it, but I now tell you, if you don't stop it you shall be cursed by the Almighty and shall dwindle away and be damned . . .

Here are the Elders of Israel, who have the priesthood, who have got to preach the Gospel, who have to gather the nations of the earth, who have to build up the kingdom so that the nations can come to it, they will stop to dance as niggers. I don't mean this as debasing the negroes by any means. They will hoe down all, turn summersets, dance on their knees, and haw, haw, out loud; they will play cards, they will play checkers and dominoes, they will use profane language, they will swear! . . . If we don't repent and quit our wickedness we will have more hindrances than we have had, and worse storms to encounter. I want the brethren to be ready, for meeting to-morrow at the time appointed, instead of rambling off, and hiding in their waggons at play cards, etc. I think it will be good for us to have a fast meeting to-morrow and a prayer meeting to humble ourselves and turn to the Lord and He will forgive us.

The Sunday morning of May 30 on the Platte River bottoms was still, but high above the circle of Mormon wagons clouds were scattering in a windy sky. Wakened by the early bugle, the travelers could still see Chimney Rock, forty miles behind them, lifting an admonitory finger. The Black Hills northwest of the encampment had turned a deep blue, laying grotesque and portentous patterns on the horizon.

At eight o'clock the whole camp gathered near their leader's wagon and raised their voices in Brother William Phelps' hymn. "The Spirit of God like a fire is burning," they sang. "The latter-day glory begins to come forth."

Brother Brigham's rebuke had accomplished its purpose. Wilford Woodruff later wrote of this day: "In the morning I shaved, cleansed my body, put on clean clothing, read a chapter in the

Book of Mormon, humbled myself before the Lord . . ."

Soon Woodruff and other chosen leaders followed President Young into a little valley where they "clothed themselves after the manner of the Priesthood." That afternoon they trudged in picturesque procession across the plain for more than two miles to climb a high, sandy point. From this they could see to the west a long aisle of bluffs towering on both sides of the river. As they knelt in prayer upon the highest ground they had yet stood upon, Thomas Bullock, who had expected to join them, made note in his journal that he had not been asked to do so. Feeling rejected and sick at heart, he wrote: "I have been deprived of my greatest and most sacred privileges. O my God look down upon my tears and suffering and have mercy on me; wherein I have offended thee, make it manifest to me, that I may repent, whatever it may be."

When the robed priests again entered the circle of their wagons, campfires were spotting the dusk. Somewhere out on the plains a drift of cloud loosed a shower, and light from the moon, quick-risen on the eastern rim of the valley, penetrated the falling drops to arch a rainbow above the westward road they would travel on the morrow. Many who had that day promised themselves a holier life saw the gleaming, many-colored gateway as a sign of welcome to the country they were seeking.

For all its promise, however, the brethren found the last day of May none the easier. Wagon wheels sank almost to their hubs in sand. Horses and mules strained against the hames. Men bruised their shoulders against the ungiving spokes. Nine miles before nooning — seven and a half more before sunset — and then there was Brother Brigham barking them into a circle beside the straggling cottonwoods and willows of Rawhide Creek.

The morning horn of June 1 wakened Brigham Young to his forty-sixth birthday. Though his body had thickened and the lines of his face had deepened in the years since Joseph Smith's death, he did not yet resemble in appearance the image which in his later years all of America came to know. He moved with authority, and his duties had kept him so much in the saddle through storm and sunshine that none of his companions on the long and wearisome journey resented his leadership.

In the early afternoon came a shout from the lead wagons — "Laramie!" Repeated again and again down the long line, the cry brought a quicker rhythm and the happiness of achievement. By

*A decade after the establishment of the Salt Lake City settlement, four thousand*

six o'clock the train had covered twelve miles and, rounding a wooded point, trotted into night camp along the River Platte, here more than a hundred yards wide. On the low bottoms, ash and cottonwood trees lined the water. On the high bluffs beyond, twisted cedars reached into the sky.

"The scene is romantic," wrote Lorenzo Young, sitting in his tent beside the pair of sleeping small boys in his charge. Nearly all of the Mormon travelers who kept journals noted that in the center of the camp, tied between two of the highest limbs of a towering ash, hung the tiny dead body of an Indian baby, wrapped snugly in animal skins. The bark of the tree had been peeled off to prevent wild animals from climbing up to eat the high-buried child. Truly they were in the land of the Lamanites with their strange un-Christian and decadent customs.

On the next day Erastus Snow wrote into his journal: "Today a coal pit is on fire within our circle, and three portable blacksmith shops are in operation; smiths are shoeing horses, repairing wagons, etc."

About ten in the morning Brother Brigham led a delegation across the river to visit Fort Laramie. There they found a small, gay settlement mostly of French husbands and Indian wives, all under the paternal direction of the agent of the American Fur Company, Mr. Bordeaux. He received them in an upstairs room which Appleton Harmon (who now had begun to look upon him-

*handcart emigrants braved blizzards and other dangers in the long walk to Utah.*

self as the inventor of the roadometer as well as its maker) described as "much like a bar room of an eastern hotel . . . ornamented with several drawings, Portraits, etc., a long desk, a settee and some chairs." There was much bargaining at the company store, where the French, knowing well that their customers could buy nowhere else in the area, profited well. Superintendent Bordeaux liked the solemn Mormons, who, after the dressing-down given them by their leader in the previous week, were well-behaved and co-operative, not at all like the wild lot he governed or the roistering wayfarers who had passed the fort in previous months.

Bordeaux told them their passage on the north side of the Platte would be blocked by the Black Hills, which slanted steeply down to the water, and urged them to cross the river at once to take the Oregon Trail. The Mormons accepted his advice and for fifteen dollars rented his flatboat to ferry their wagons over the stream.

The crossing began the next morning but was interrupted by a thunderstorm accompanied by hail. Since Bordeaux had told them there had been no rain in the area for two years before their arrival, the travelers regarded this as a further evidence of God's favor. All wagons had crossed before the next noon, and at once the expedition set out on the Oregon Trail, which was to lead them up the Sweetwater River and across the Great Divide.

Before he left, Brother Clayton, true inventor of the roadometer, consulted the records he had taken with its aid and proudly set up a guideboard on the north side of the Platte; "543¼ miles from Winter Quarters," it read, "227½ miles from the junction of the Platte" (north and south branches), "142½ miles from Ash Hollow, 70¼ miles from Chimney Rock, 50½ miles from Scott's Bluffs."

The rainy spell continued as the wagon train in the next few days rolled through a narrow ravine, strained up a steep slope, and came out on a rolling prairie gay in the June colors of red, blue, and yellow *Artemisia* (sagebrush of the aster family and known throughout the West by many names—absinthe, wormwood, wild sage, greasewood, mugwort, Southernwood). An eagle sailed above the caravan as a light shower from the west caught a moment of sun to set up answering colors in the sky—twin rainbows arching below snow-covered Laramie Peak.

On the rain-washed Sunday morning that followed, the bugle called the brethren to assemble at nine o'clock. While thunder rolled along the horizon, they raised their voices in the hymn, "With All the Power of Heart and Tongue." Loudly they proclaimed, "Angels shall hear the notes I'll raise" and "To God I cried when troubles rose, He heard me and subdued my foes." Wilford Woodruff's journal reads, "The spirit of the Lord was with us."

In the week that followed, the Mormons rolled out of the colored prairie into country so wild and grotesque that they were amazed. Between Horse Shoe Creek and the stream called La Bonte they came upon earth so red that William Clayton wrote, "It affected my eyes much from its brightness." Here the travelers saw a toad with a tail and with horns on its head. "It did not jump like a toad but crawled like a mouse." Big black crickets lay so thick on the red soil that it was almost impossible to keep from stepping on them.

Within two weeks after the brethren had left Fort Laramie they had covered 125 miles and reached a second crossing of the winding Platte. Here with Yankee common sense Brigham Young himself worked prodigiously at constructing two raft ferries, and he ordered eight men and a blacksmith left behind to float the many "gentile" trains behind them across the river at charges sufficient to make a "reasonable profit."

On they went in a routine saved from monotony by the grotesquerie of a landscape growing ever more barren—a horn in the morning and a breakfast made over fires built of sagebrush and dried buffalo dung ("buffalo chips"); then a glimpse of members of the Twelve standing on a high place and sometimes clad in the robes of priesthood, their President kneeling in prayer and the others dropping to their knees beside him, their faces turned upward to the sky; the cries of the scouts and outriders leading off; the lonely carriage of Brother Brigham leading the train; the squeal of wagon wheels that grease from slain wolves failed to silence; the divisions falling into the procession in the order of accustomed place; the galloping of the teams, when the road was wide enough, to bring the wagons five abreast and lessen the danger of Indian attack.

On June 21 Wilford Woodruff wrote:

I arose early this morning and took breakfast and in company with Brother John we rode clear around Independence Rock. I should judge the distance to be about three-quarters of a mile. We examined the many names and lists of names of the trappers, traders, travellers and emigrants which are painted upon these rocks. Nearly all the names were put on with red, black and yellow paint; some had washed out and were defaced. The greatest number were put on within a few years. Some of the names were quite plain after about 30 years. Nearly all the companies that pass by put some of their names on the rock.* After going around and examining it we staked our horses and mounted the rock. I went forward and gained the highest point at the south end of the rock which contained the names. After examining it I then went to the north end which is the highest part of the rock. Here is an opening or cavern which could contain thirty or forty persons, and a rock stands on the highest peak of about three tons weight. We got upon this rock and offered up our prayers according to the order of the Priesthood; we prayed earnestly for the blessings of God to rest upon President Young, his brethren, the Twelve, and all of the Pioneer camp and the whole camp of Israel and house of Israel; our wives and children and relatives; that the Lord would hasten the time of fulfillment of his promises to Abraham, Isaac, Jacob, Joseph, Lehi, Nephi, Alma and Moroni, and all the sayings of the Lord concerning the building up of Zion in the last days and avenging the blood of the Prophets and while offering up our prayers the spirit of the Lord descended upon us, and we truly felt to rejoice. . . . I was the first Latter Day Saint that ever went onto that rock or offered up prayers according to the Priesthood.

* With their usual acumen the Mormons soon stationed two of their members at the rock to chisel the initials of "gentile" travelers into its surface, and charge them for it.

Five miles beyond Independence Rock the Mormons stopped again to see Devil's Gate and hear the roar of the water dashing through perpendicular stone cliffs four hundred feet high. A mile beyond, they camped beside the wild current of the Sweetwater. The Pioneers could see then, almost obscured by the twilight mists, the distant, snowy peaks of the Wind River Mountains, and they knew that their long journey would soon be at an end. They had traveled, according to the guide-board they erected there, 175¼ miles from Fort Laramie.

June 24 began with exasperation for Brigham Young. His team ran away with a wagon but was caught ("by the bit") at the very edge of the river. His best horse, the finest in the expedition, died when a herdsman named Holman nudged the animal forward with his rifle and the trigger caught in his clothing, causing the weapon to fire. Known as the leader's "John" horse, it was the third killed during the trek and caused strong recommendations that the brothers no longer carry loaded guns "with caps upon their tubes." As the day ended, Thomas Bullock wrote, "The Sweetwater Mountains are disappearing and the Rocky Mountains are coming into plainer view." Devout Norton Jacobs bethought himself of the words of "Old Nephi" as reported in the Book of Mormon: "When upon the cross the Savior died for man's sin and wickedness, darkness covered the earth. She trembled and her bosom heaved mightily. . . . here upborn from their lowermost foundations these mighty piles of granite . . . —despite the efforts of summer's suns—have held aloft the ensign of peace."

In the last week of June, cold winds from the ice-white slopes of the Rocky Mountains froze milk and water in their pails. Little Isaac Decker and Zobriski Young snowballed each other, their missiles gathered from the ten-foot drifts along the way. Dandelions, strawberries, and wild onions bloomed in the sharp, dry air of the Sweetwater Valley. On luxuriant grass Wilford Woodruff saw carnelian stones "from the size of a goose egg to a pound"— more in one hour than he had ever seen "in the rude state or polished and set in breastpins." Red willows stood deep in snow that fringed the river. And on Sunday, June 27, all the Mormons remembered that this day was the fourth anniversary of the murder of the founder of their faith, Joseph Smith, and of his brother, Hyrum. Fittingly on this morning, the expedition crossed the Great Divide through the South Pass, and all knew that another of the mystic leader's prophecies, that the true Zion would be settled in the Rockies, would soon be fulfilled.

As June gentled into July the weather was warmer, and the brethren were visited on the trail by strangers who spoke the dialect of the mountain men and raised it to an intensity that held them spellbound. Brother Brigham and the members of the Twelve felt the historic importance of these meetings with interpreters of the land they were about to enter, and so in turn did the mountain men.

One of these was old Moses Harris, trader and trapper in the Rocky Mountains for a quarter of a century. "He spoke unfavorable of the Salt Lake country for a settlement," wrote Wilford Woodruff, and William Clayton was depressed by his saying there was "little chance to hope for even a moderate good country anywhere in those regions." The whole countryside was sandy, barren, and treeless, the old man said. The Salt Lake Valley was a wasteland of the wild sage.

Heavy of heart, the Mormon Pioneers pushed on until Brother Brigham at their head heard the jingle of spurs, the hoofbeats of approaching horses. Suddenly out of a hollow appeared three eastbound riders. The leader was forty-two-year-old Jim Bridger, most famous of all mountain men, and he had hardly dismounted before he began to talk, asking that he might be heard not only by their official leader but by his principal advisers. By the Little Sandy, where they nooned, he told all these about their promised land.

Beside the swift Green River, he said, the mountains stand so close that horsemen cannot pass. On the far side lie level plains that end in hard black rock. It shines in the sun, and its edges are so sharp they will cut a horse's feet to pieces. From Bridger's Fort, his home, to Great Salt Lake is about a hundred miles. Along the trail stand sugar trees and cottonwoods. The outlet of Utah Lake runs into Salt Lake. It runs muddy and it runs low but its banks are red and white with clover. There is timber all around the Utah Lake and plenty of blue grass. Great Salt Lake is so big it takes a man in a canoe three months to go all the way round.

Jim Bridger went on to speak of mines of gold, of copper and of lead. He knew of lodes of silver and of iron, of sulphur and saltpeter. He said at the end of Great Salt Lake a bubbling spring spurted hot and cold fresh water, hot and cold salt water, and at the same time manufactured scads of verdigris which the Indians used for green paint with which to daub their bodies. And, speaking of Indians, they raised in this area as good corn, wheat, and pumpkins as were ever raised in old Kentucky. Wild flax grew in all the valleys. So did grapes and cherries, berries and persimmons. Bridger described mountains with snow melting on their peaks and streams striping all the slopes, and, on the level, frequent saleratus deserts and lakes surrounded by white salt flats. Nevertheless, said Jim Bridger simply and with a bit of pathos, "This country is my paradise and if this people settles in it I want to settle with them." But when some of the brethren said they would plant corn there, and potatoes, and wheat, Jim laughed and said the winter cold would freeze all such plants.

"I'll give you a thousand dollars for the first bushel of corn you grow in the Great Salt Basin," he said, and Brother Brigham said quietly, "Wait and we will show you." Obviously, he had made his decision as to the journey's end.

That night while Bridger was dining with President Young in private, Wilford Woodruff set down in his daily journal his estimate of the famous mountain man and his report: "We found him to have been a great traveler and possessed a great knowledge . . . if what he told us was true."

As he wrote, a plague was attacking the camp. "Mountain fever," characterized by headaches, high temperatures, and resultant delirium, had disabled several of the Pioneers, and in the following weeks it affected many of the men and Clarissa Decker Young (wife of Lorenzo), one of the three women, as well. Fortunately its victims recovered in a few days, but they remained weak and listless for varying lengths of time. Some of the brothers attributed the disease to "mineral saleratus" picked up on the shores of small lakes they passed.

On the last day of June Samuel Brannan, commander of a group of Mormons who had taken ship for San Francisco by way of the Horn, appeared in camp with news of the brethren he had led and of the Mormon Battalion (500 volunteers who had fought with the Army in Mexico), many of whom were at Pueblo de Los Angeles. He urged President Young to lead the party to the west coast and described with lyric fervor the climate and fertility of California. Barley there had no hull on it. There was no necessity to cultivate oats, for they grew wild. Clover reached as high as a horse's belly. Wild horses were scattered over the

*Joseph Smith, founder of the sect, receives the gold plates of the Book of Mormon.*

plains. Salmon caught in the San Joaquin River weighed ten or twelve pounds. To all this talk the brethren turned deaf ears. They already mistrusted the shifty Brannan (who was eventually excommunicated), and they were still enchanted by the spell Jim Bridger had cast upon them.

Now that they were within striking distance of their goal, the Mormons were in fine fettle and even inclined to regard with humor the hardships they were enduring. On July 3 Thomas Bullock wrote: "We passed a mosquito manufactory, immense swarms of them," and Wilford Woodruff wrote, "The mosquitoes have filled my carriage like a cloud."

Shortly after noon on Sunday, July 4, a detachment of twelve soldiers under command of Sergeant Thomas Williams crossed the Green River (where the expedition had stopped for the night) and rode into camp in strict formation. Williams said with dry humor that they were in pursuit of horse thieves, as indeed they were, but they were immediately recognized as members of the Mormon Battalion. While they were still in line President Young spoke a few words. Cheer after cheer rose from the brethren. Then, according to Thomas Bullock's account, the President proposed "Glory to God for their safe return," and all who heard him responded, crying out: "Hosanna! Hosanna! Hosanna! Give Glory to God and the Lamb!"

More soberly Norton Jacobs wrote: "This is Uncle Sam's day of Independence. Well, we are independent of all the powers of the Gentiles; that is enough for us."

The next day was hot, the road was dusty. The Pioneers saw a hard shower descending near the mountains and felt a little wind from it. "In this country," wrote Brother Woodruff, "it rains about the mountains but not much in the valleys and plains." The units of the train stayed farther apart to avoid the dust. They traveled twenty miles to Black's Ford, twenty miles of a trail lined by the blossoms of prickly pears, some red, some yellow, and found at the end nine wickiups in a beautiful vale, and horses grazing peacefully beside them. Now each day the country grew richer. Cedars flourished in the woods, pines were tall on the mountains, cottonwood roots dug deep into the shallows of the rivers. That night they halted beside a wide-mouthed cave lined with soft sandstone (Redding Cave) and many of the Pioneers, boylike, cut their names into its walls. The next day they forded Bear River, nooned at Needle Cliff, and as they made their camp at sunsetting, came a few drops of rain "sufficient [wrote Brother George A. Smith] to cause a full-arched rainbow." The brothers were happy.

But in the wagon of Wilford Woodruff there was worry, even fear. President Young had been stricken by mountain fever. His temperature was so high that those who tended him were concerned for his life. Stops became more frequent. On July 13, after consultation among the leaders, it was decided that Orson Pratt should take twenty-three wagons and forty-two of the most able-bodied men as an advance party to explore and make ready the road through the mountains for the rest of the Pioneers to follow. Among the advance party were many men famous in the history of the church—and also the three Negroes of the lot—Oscar Crosby, Hark Lay, and Green Flake. Three days later the main camp had inched slowly down a steep gulch and stopped for the noon rest, when the long-haired scout Porter Rockwell arrived from the advance band to assure them that their party was nearing the canyons that would lead into the Great Basin.

On either side of the lurching wagons that afternoon the red rock walls towered hundreds of feet. "There is a very singular echo in this ravine," wrote William Clayton. "The rattling of wagons resembles carpenters hammering at boards inside the highest rocks. The report of a rifle resembles a sharp crack of thunder and echoes from rock to rock for some time. The lowing of cattle and braying of mules seem to be answered behind the mountains." The playing of band instruments by some of his companions, he added, bounced back from the gulch's walls in exact duplication. (Today the ravine is called Echo Canyon.)

On the seventeenth President Young's illness was much worse, and the party moved only three miles. From their campsite at Weber River they could see a group of small towers, "Witches Rocks," resembling "old factory or furnace chimneys."

The sun had passed above the amazingly deep defile in which the wagons waited, when a band of the camp elders led by Heber C. Kimball, Willard Richards, and Ezra T. Benson* presented themselves in their priestly garments "before the Lord." To Him they offered up their united prayers for their stricken President to be healed, the camp to be prospered, the Saints to be blessed. On their precarious way back to the camp "the brethren amused themselves by rolling big rocks down the hill," wrote Thomas Bullock, and William Clayton wrote his own description of this curious scene.

The bugle sounded at ten in the morning and the brethren met at a cool bower made in a little grove near the wagon of Willard Richards. Heber C. Kimball then spoke very earnestly. He recommended that the whole camp, except President Young and enough men to care for him, set out on the following day to find fertile ground in which to plant potatoes, buckwheat, turnips, and other crops. The project was unanimously adopted, and on July 20 the major division of the camp was moving in the wake of the advance party, though Heber Kimball, Wilford Woodruff, and Ezra Benson stayed with President Young, who now was improving rapidly.

Erastus Snow left the main camp in the morning and by strenuous riding overtook Orson Pratt's advance group during the day. He bore messages, one of which was a letter to Pratt from Willard Richards and George A. Smith detailing President Young's advice. The general happiness of the expedition was apparent in a humorous passage dictated by Brother Brigham: "... prosecute the route as you have hitherto done until you ar-

---

* Benson's great grandson and namesake, the Secretary of Agriculture under President Eisenhower, is a member of the present Council of Twelve of the Mormon Church.

189

rive at some point in the Basin where you could hear the potatoes grow, if they had only happened to be there."

On July 22 historic events came with a rush. The main camp rattled down the roughest section of the long road it had covered, with clownish black-and-white magpies tumbling about before them on stumps the travelers had cut to facilitate the advance. Sandhill cranes gazed solemnly at them from the banks of steaming hot springs. A hawk sailed above them. The ground "seemed literally alive with very large black crickets crawling around up grass and bushes." Thomas Bullock, camp historian, wrote in his journal,

We succeeded in getting through the narrow part of the canyon about 4 o'clock p.m. when we turned around the hill to the right and came in full view of the Salt Lake in the distance; its islands with their lofty hills towering up in bold relief behind the silvery lake . . . I could not help shouting hurrah, hurrah, hurrah, here is my home at last!

That night the camp bivouacked beside a little stream almost hidden by tall grasses. Several of the advance party joined them for excited talks. So happy were they all that when hot springs were reported only a few miles away, the brethren suggested that one would do for a barber shop and that the largest, pouring out of a large rock having a big stone in the middle, "would make a first rate . . . steam house."

On the morning of the twenty-third the Pioneers set up a campground on the banks of the stream today called City Creek, and exactly at noon Seth Taft turned the first furrow. The plow broke! It was soon repaired, and there were other plows.

At two o'clock the brethren began work on building a dam and cutting trenches to carry water into the land. Word came, welcome word indeed, that Brigham Young was much better and would enter the Great Basin on the morrow.

On that morrow the President, still weak but gaining strength, asked Wilford Woodruff, in whose carriage he was riding, to turn the vehicle so that he might look out over the valley. From his seat, then, the tired commander surveyed the long sea of grass over which only one cedar lifted crooked limbs. Below him, but out of sight, he knew that those whom he had brought to this Canaan were already enthusiastically at work making the flat acres bordering the wide blue lake a garden spot. "This is the right place," he said to Wilford Woodruff. "Drive on."

"This is the first Sunday that the Latter-day Saints ever spent in the Great Salt Lake Valley," wrote Woodruff on July 25. "We washed, shaved and cleaned up and met in the circle of the encampment. . . . George A. Smith preached an interesting discourse, standing upon the cannon." Other speakers followed, and at noon the program was interrupted until the afternoon. At two it began again. At its close President Young, though feeble, spoke. Brother Woodruff entered his memories of the President's speech in his journal later on in the day. The brethren must not work on Sunday, said Brigham Young, and if they did they would lose five times as much as they gain by it, and they must not hunt or fish on that day, ". . . and there should not one man dwell among us who would not obey these rules; they might go and dwell where they pleased but should not dwell with us."

After a few remarks on the distribution of land, the speaker "warned the Saints against keeping anything that did not belong to them, that if they followed such a course it would leak out and they would stink in the nostrils of Jehovah, the Angels, and the Saints, and though they might live with the Saints and die with them, they would be damned at last and go to hell, for they were thieves and nothing but burning through hell would cleanse them."

Brother Brigham was obviously and audibly himself again.

*The journey's end: Mormons enter the Great Salt Lake Valley on July 24, 1847.*

*Gold miners in California pose for a daguerreotype by an unknown photographer.*

# GOLD!

## By RALPH K. ANDRIST

he California Gold Rush was the biggest and the richest of them all, but it was no different from any of those that followed in providing the majority of its participants with much rushing and little gold. When forty-niners reminisced through beards grown longer and whiter, the strikes of the past became richer and the nuggets bigger, but the mournful truth is that most gold hunters would have done better financially staying at home — and been considerably more comfortable.

Let there be no misunderstanding, though; the gold across the Sierra Nevada was rich beyond belief, and many miners made strikes that deserve the adjective "fabulous." It was just that there was not enough gold in the streams to make everyone rich. Hubert Howe Bancroft, historian of the West, estimated that during the peak years of 1849 and 1850 the gold taken out averaged about $600 per miner. Averages are usually misleading: this one, on examination, can mean only that for every miner who struck it rich, there must have been a platoon who hardly got to see what gold looked like.

It all began, as every schoolchild is taught, at the sawmill of John Sutter one January day in 1848. A Swiss immigrant, Sutter at the time ruled, benevolently and graciously, over an estate of

49,000 acres which he had received from the Mexican government and had built into what amounted to a self-sustaining kingdom. It lay in the valley of the Sacramento, still almost empty of
settlers, and his settlement, called Sutter's Fort, was situated
where Sacramento now stands.

In the summer of 1847 he sent a carpenter named James Marshall, in charge of a crew of men, up the South Branch of the
American River to build a sawmill. Work proceeded through the
next several months until January, when Marshall turned water
into the millrace for the first time. He let it run all night to wash
the race clean of debris; the next morning, January 24, 1848, he
saw yellow specks glinting through the running water, and the
famous discovery was made.

Sutter was deeply disturbed by the finding of the metal; gold
and the pastoral serenity of his pleasant empire were incompati-
ble, and he had a foreboding of things to come—although the
results were to be more devastating than he could possibly have
imagined: his cattle butchered, his fields trampled and un-
tended, his land taken by squatters, until he had not a thing left.
At the moment all he could do was ask the men at the mill to keep
the secret for another six weeks, so that his ranch workers would
not desert him to dig gold before spring planting was done. The
men at the mill did not leave but continued to work as before,
panning for gold only on Sunday, until the sawmill was finished
in March.

So far, the discovery had produced no gold fever at the scene,
nor did it do so farther afield. The news began trickling into San
Francisco within two or three weeks (Sutter's request for six
weeks of secrecy had been ignored), carried by letter and by
word of mouth. Both of the town's two newspapers duly reported the discovery, but no one became excited. The people of
San Francisco—there were 850 or 900 of them—were still not
convinced that this amounted to anything.

But the reports kept coming in, and with them, samples of
gold. Several Mormons were discovered quietly digging about
twenty-five miles from the sawmill; their site, which inevitably
became known as Mormon Diggings, turned out to be richer
than the first. San Francisco was impressed; the gold was more
plentiful and widespread than anyone had thought. By the end
of April, men who had gone up the American River to see for
themselves were returning with fat pouches of gold, replenishing

their supplies, and then hurrying back. Now, at last, the town was filled with excitement, though restraint still prevailed. Men talked about gold, but went about their business as usual. It needed a little more to turn the excitement into roaring gold fever, however, and a man named Sam Brannan supplied the extra bit of frenzy.

Brannan was a ubiquitous figure in early California, always on hand when there was a dollar to be made, and shrewd enough to make it. He was in turn a storekeeper, a hotel owner in Sacramento when miners were willing to pay anything for a bed and meal, a merchant in San Francisco so respected that he was elected to head the first Vigilante organization, a newspaper publisher, and a wealthy landowner. A man of formidable talents, Sam Brannan.

In 1848, he was operating a store in Sutterville, a small settlement near Sutter's Fort. He was an elder in the Mormon Church and had gone up to Mormon Diggings to look the situation over

*James Marshall at Sutter's Mill, where he found the first gold of the gold rush*

and talk to his brethren there. Some of the excitement had begun to stir in his own veins, and he felt moved to get his share of the wealth—but not by digging, an activity which had no charm for him. His approach, at first glance, appears completely irrelevant. During the second week of May, he traveled by boat to San Francisco with a bottle of gold dust. It has become folklore that he spent the day walking the streets, waving the vial of gold and shouting, "Gold! Gold! Gold from the American River!" It is more likely that he collected groups on corners and in stores and saloons, passing the gold around and telling how he had seen plenty like it being panned out up at Mormon Diggings. Whatever he did, he left them burning with gold fever.

Brannan came to town about May 12; fleets of boats left on the fourteenth and fifteenth for Sutter's Fort, where all passengers had to disembark and set out on foot for the diggings. Sam Brannan's store was right at hand as they left the boats, and Brannan had thoughtfully laid in a large stock of provisions and mining supplies. He was one of the first to demonstrate something that would be proved again and again during the gold rush: the surest way to prosper was to leave the mining to others, and concern oneself with selling the miners what they needed.

San Francisco became almost hysterical. More gold arrived, this time from the Fort, about a week after the first exodus, and

*Prospectors making their way west cook their meal over a fire of buffalo chips.*

another large group of citizens dropped everything and left. It is usually estimated that less than one hundred people remained by the end of June. Doctors, lawyers, bakers, blacksmiths, laborers, schoolteachers—all went. There was no government left; the first and second alcaldes were gone (the Americans had adopted from the recently dispossessed Mexicans the alcalde system, a kind of hybrid mayor-magistrate), and so was the sheriff. Women and children also departed; this first gold-rush year was different in many ways from those that followed.

Now the fever spread to other California settlements: Monterey, San Diego, Sonoma, Benicia, San Jose, Santa Cruz, Santa Barbara, Los Angeles. Walter Colton, alcalde at Monterey, wrote of the way the people of his village disappeared when the first proof of the gold strike reached them in June, leaving little more than women and soldiers at the army post. A crew of carpenters who were at work on a schoolhouse "threw down their saws and planes, shouldered their picks, and are off for the Yuba. Three seamen ran off from the *Warren,* forfeiting their four years' pay; and a whole platoon of soldiers left only their colors behind."

Ranches were deserted or left with only women to tend them, grain went unharvested, cattle and horses roamed wild. Sailors deserted from the U.S. Pacific Squadron in San Francisco Bay and at Monterey, and the Army lost 716 enlisted men in the eighteen months beginning July 1, 1848. Said one soldier: "The struggle between *right* and six dollars a month and *wrong* and seventy-five dollars a day is rather a severe one."

By early June ships had carried the news to the Sandwich Islands (Hawaii); by July it reached Oregon; and in August, the neighboring Mexican state of Sonora. In each case there was skepticism at first, then wild-eyed gold mania. In less than four months, nineteen ships left Honolulu with 300 foreigners, most of the Islands' white colony, and an unknown number of Kanakas, or natives. An estimated 5,000 to 6,000 Mexicans headed north. In Oregon many settlers had very recently refused to do military duty against the Indians because they did not want to leave their families without protection; now, as the gold fever seized them, they said a hasty good-by to families, possibly added a few brief words of caution about locking the doors at night, and were off.

Young Mormons returning home carried news of the discovery east across the mountains to Salt Lake City. Once again the first reaction was tepid, but when a second group of young men came, carrying considerable gold, "the cry was raised, 'To California — To the Gold of Ophir our brethren have discovered! To California!'" (Men gave voice to more rousing cries in those days than now.) Brigham Young tried to hold them, without success; gold had more appeal for many of the young Saints than did building the Mormon garden in the desert.

Sometime between August and September the news got back to the Atlantic states and the Mississippi Valley — and once again was ignored. But as later ships brought increasingly sensational accounts, interest mounted. There were tales of men who had dug out thousands of dollars' worth of gold in a matter of days. Walter Colton, the alcalde of Monterey, and Thomas Larkin, Navy agent in the same town, laid it on with a heavy trowel in their letters and reports, talking of streams "paved with gold," and claiming that the mines exceeded "all the dreams of romance and all the golden marvels of the wand of Midas." That sort of thing made pretty heady reading for a New England farm boy after a day of building rock walls. Once again excitement gradually built up to a point where it needed only a spark to touch it off, and that came on December 5 when President James K. Polk, in his annual message, gave official recognition to the stories. They were, he said, of such an extraordinary character as "would scarcely command belief" were they not corroborated by the authentic reports of officers in the public services.

Almost literally overnight, tens of thousands of men were on their way. The overland route, of course, was closed until spring. The Argonauts, as the gold seekers inevitably came to be called, had a choice of two sea routes. One was the all-water route around Cape Horn. The other took the traveler by ship to the Isthmus of Panama, which he crossed; then he boarded another ship on the Pacific side (a small proportion crossed at Nicaragua). In 1849, the Cape Horn passage was by far the most popular; the ratio swung the other way in subsequent years.

The trip around South America was long and expensive, but it was passably comfortable for a man on a good ship with an able skipper and a fair break in the weather. One Franklin Buck who left New York on January 18, 1849, did not reach San Francisco until August 6; but he passed the time without undue tedium: he had included in his baggage a backgammon board, a library of 250 volumes, and a good supply of wine. As the demand for ships grew, all possible vessels were diverted to carrying California-bound passengers. The New England whaling fleet was taken over almost in its entirety. Merchant vessels were, for the most part, only minimally converted for passenger comfort (but this was not vital if these ships were sound and well-handled). What was criminal was the way in which get-rich-quick operators dragged rotten-bottomed ships out of retirement, patched the worst of their leaks, and, as often as not, gave command of them to incompetents or drunks who could no longer hold a berth under normal conditions.

But it made no difference to the clamoring crowds of Argonauts: they would board anything headed for California. Many ships went down, especially in the stormy passage around Cape Horn — how many no one knows — and gold-rush diaries frequently record sighting the wreckage of some unfortunate craft, and speak of the chilling effect it had on those who saw it.

The Panama route was much shorter and, in terms of actual traveling time, faster: six to eight months via Cape Horn, six weeks by way of Panama. The only trouble was that there were often months of waiting mixed in with the six weeks of traveling. The Argonaut landed at Chagres on the Isthmus, crossed the seventy-five-mile stretch of jungle, partly by native boat on the swirling, treacherous Chagres River and partly by mule train

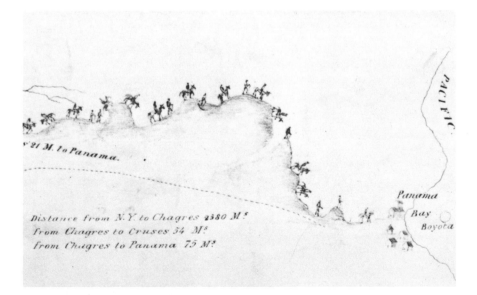

*The last lap of the journey across the Isthmus of Panama was made on muleback.*

along narrow, dripping, insect-infested trails fetid from the rotting carcasses of mules, and finally reached the moribund city of Panama on the Pacific, whence another ship could be had to take him on to California. But there were few ships on the Pacific, especially in 1849, and as fast as they arrived in San Francisco, their crews deserted them to go mining. Argonauts found themselves stranded in Panama for weeks and months while the floating population of the town continued to swell—for passenger agents back East went on selling tickets with bland assurances of

*A self-sufficient gold prospector on his way to the elusive riches of California*

connections at Panama. Hundreds died of malaria, cholera, and other diseases as a result of the inevitably unsanitary conditions. Some men, as foolhardy as they were impatient, started up the coast in various small craft. Most were never heard of again.

When a ship did come, four or five times as many men crowded aboard as the vessel was meant to carry. As a result, the passage was usually miserable. Hiram Pierce, a dour, middle-aged blacksmith from Troy, New York, who left a wife and seven children to go after gold, described mealtime as an al-fresco affair on deck with sailors carrying food between a double row of passengers while everyone grabbed: "Many behave so swineish that I prefer to stay a way unless driven to it by hunger." The ship's doctor was a drunk; one night he got himself entangled in his hammock and was suspended with his head dangling. Another time, "The same worthy took a dose of mede-cine to a patient & haveing a bone in his hand knawing, he took the medecine & gave the bone to the patient."

Most of those who came by sea arrived at San Francisco. The town had gained back all the population it had lost to the mines, and thousands more. It was an ephemeral place of tents and wooden walls with canvas roofs, changing so fast that the diary-keeping Argonaut, passing through and then returning three or four months later, invariably noted that nothing was as it had been. San Francisco was the great warehouse of the gold fields, the port of debarkation for gold seekers, the place where a miner down from the hills could purchase various pleasures more titillating than anything he had dreamed of back home.

The strange hysteria that gripped men, many of them sober, levelheaded citizens until that moment, was variously known as gold fever, yellow fever, California fever, California mania, and gold mania. The term "fever" seems to fit it best because, like a real fever, its peak or crisis could almost be pinpointed and the period of recovery charted. In the Atlantic coast states it raged at its height from December of 1848 into the following March and then began a slow decline through the rest of 1849. In the Mississippi Valley it was a little later getting started, reaching its peak from February through May of 1849.

To those living in the Mississippi Valley, the natural route was overland (although many gold seekers from seaboard states also joined the wagon companies). A number took various southern routes, such as the Sonora Trail, which swings down into Mexico, and the Sante Fe Trail and its westward extensions. But by far the overwhelming majority followed the Oregon and Mormon trails, which parallel each other on opposite sides of the Platte River over the Great Plains; once through the Rockies they swung down toward the California passes along various routes and cutoffs, none of them easy.

Travelers began gathering in March at the three Missouri River towns that became the outfitting places for the overland trip: Independence and St. Joseph, Missouri, and Kanesville (now Council Bluffs), Iowa. Accommodations in the towns were quickly filled and tent cities grew up on the outskirts. Steamboats arrived almost daily with men, mules, and supplies to add to the growing chaos; the river front was a continual jam of wagons, herds of oxen and mules, and cursing teamsters. Almost every man wore a gun and a bowie knife, but more as a sort of California Ho! uniform than because he had any thought of using them. This was not a gun-fighting crowd, and there was remarkably little shooting or stabbing.

The trip had a rigid timetable. The wagons could not start before late April, when the grass on the prairie was green and high enough to provide food for teams, and they had to be over the Sierra Nevada in California before snow began to fall in the high passes, which meant the last wagon had to be on its way before June was over.

A great many men on the trail never should have been there. There were carts pulled by a single mule or ox, wagons with a mule and oxen hitched together, and various other makeshift evidences of shoestring ventures. A man with a rifle and bulldog was in Independence in 1849, planning to walk all the way to California; he very well might have, because he had already walked from Maine. Another man was planning to push a wheelbarrow to the gold fields.

The first part of the trip presented no undue difficulties or dangers. The grass was new and plentiful, the ground solid, animals and men fresh, and equipment still new. But the picnic atmosphere soon began to evaporate. The wagons formed an almost continuous line at times, and all but those in the lead drove in a cloud of choking dust. In the western part of present-day Nebraska, sandier ground and the upward-trending trail made pulling difficult, and animals began to show the effects; breakdowns occurred more often as equipment became worn, and more and more of the faint-hearted turned back.

Now the Argonauts began divesting themselves of excess baggage until the trail looked like the line of retreat of a routed army. Alonzo Delano, a forty-niner, wrote on June 3,

We were compelled to throw away a quantity of iron, steel, trunks, valises, old clothes, and boots, of little value and I may observe here that we subsequently found the road lined with cast-off articles, piles of bacon, flour, wagons, groceries, clothing, and various other articles which had been left, and the waste and destruction of property was enormous. In this the selfish nature of man was plainly exhibited. In many instances the property thus left was rendered useless. We afterwards found sugar on which turpentine had been poured, flour in which salt and dirt had been thrown, and wagons broken in pieces or partially burned, clothing torn to pieces, so that they could not be worn, and a wanton waste made of valuable property, simply because the owners could not use it themselves and were determined that nobody else should.

Besides being marked with debris, wrecked wagons, and animal carcasses, the trail was soon lined with graves, mainly those of cholera victims. The disease had come to New Orleans from Europe late in 1848, had been spread by steamboat up the Mississippi Valley, and was carried onto the plains by the wagon trains. It is a disease spread by human filth, and with the travelers' lack of concern for sanitation, it rampaged among the gold seekers. Their comrades buried the victims and hurried on – though there were dark stories of stricken men carried out of sight of the trail and left to die.

Travel through the mountains was hard going; there were places where wagons had to be eased down some of the steeper slopes with ropes, and spots on one or two of the cutoffs where they were actually lowered down cliffs. But beyond the Rockies the way really got difficult. In Utah and Nevada water and grass, scarce enough anyhow, were very often bitter, and even poisonous, from the alkali, salt, and sulphur they contained. The worst part of this dry stretch was the final drive over a searing, lifeless desert that had to be crossed in one single stage, requiring usually about twenty-four hours. Here, a traveler had the option of two routes. One took him to the life-giving water of the Truckee River with Boiling Springs at the midpoint, where unappetizing but drinkable water for the animals could be had by pouring it from the hot springs into troughs and allowing it to cool. The other way led to the Carson River across the Forty-Mile

Desert, where there was no water of any kind.

Animals already in poor condition collapsed and were left to die. In many cases, companies tried to save weakened animals by leaving their wagons with a guard and driving their mules or oxen without loads on to the river, hoping that two or three days of rest, water, and good grass would revive them so that they could go back into the desert and haul the wagons the rest of the way. Forty-niner Joshua Breyfogle spent more than three days on the Forty-Mile Desert guarding his company's wagons while waiting for the mule teams to be brought back. "From twelve o'-clock till sunrise the emigrants are passing in crowds, nearly perishing for water," he wrote in his diary while he waited, "and are leaving mules, horses and oxen to starve on the plains for they can't drive them on. I don't know what will become of the back trains." At the end of his last night on the desert he noted: "This is the most horrid night I ever passed. The road was strewd with the carcasses of dead mules, horses and cattle, and most of them with pieces of flesh cut out by the Indians. . . ." And two days later, after safely crossing the desert: "There is about four thousand wagons behind that will have to pass about three hundred miles without any grass and very little water. There must hundreds perish on the plains. The forty-five mile stretch is now almost impassable because of the stench of the dead animals along the road which is literally lined with them and there is scarcely a single train or wagon but leaves one or more dead animal, so that it must be getting worse every day."

That, too, was part of rushing for gold. And having got through the desert, they had the Sierra Nevada to cross, once again a land of ups and downs, where wagons had to be worked through boulder-strewn canyons and eased down steep slopes with ropes. Some of the gold seekers no longer had any wagons. After the crossing of the desert, there were groups that salvaged so few animals that they had to give up their wagons and use their remaining beasts as pack animals. Some lost all, and slung packs on their backs, and went on foot with what few miserable possessions they could carry.

And so, finally, they crossed the last mountain barrier and came down the American River to Sutter's Fort and the new boom town of Sacramento, where potatoes and onions were selling for a dollar each. But what did it matter?—prices meant nothing to a man who would soon be up in the hills where there was gold waiting to be picked up from the ground.

How many miners came to California in 1849 is not known, and estimates differ widely. By the overland trails, at least 35,000 is a plausible guess. The ships around Cape Horn brought 15,000 more; another 6,000 arrived by way of Panama. How many died on the plains or in the jungles or left their bones at the bottom of the sea cannot even be guessed, but it reached tens of thousands before the gold rush ended, late in the 1850's. The tide of gold seekers continued as high during the next three or four years, but there never was another year quite like 1849, when the gold fever still raged, when hills and streams still lay untouched and waiting, and no disillusion had yet thrown the slightest shadow over the most fantastic visions of great and sudden wealth.

What happened to these gold-fevered men when they finally reached California? Most of them worked harder than they had ever worked before, and suffered a large variety of ailments and injuries which youth and clean living usually helped them to survive. A few found enough gold to make themselves wealthy, but most probably just managed to break even.

For mining involved more than swishing a little gravel and water around in a basin; it was hard, back-straining work. Placer

*Wagon trains faced countless hazards, among them the Nevada canyons.*

gold, the only kind really known during the gold rush, consists of gold dust and occasional nuggets scattered thinly through sand and gravel (a miner never called it anything but "dirt"). To obtain the gold, it was necessary to wash a great deal of dirt, taking advantage of the fact that gold is about eight times as heavy as sand and will settle to the bottom while the sand is being carried off by the water. The gold pan, traditional symbol of the miner, was used only in very rich claims or for testing samples of dirt to see whether they were worth working further. In ordinary circumstances, a hopper-like device of wood and perforated sheet iron called a cradle, or rocker, was employed in a two-man operation: while one shoveled in the dirt, the other rocked the device and poured water with a dipper. The dirt was washed through, and the gold was caught in settling pockets.

After 1849, an invention called the long tom was used wherever there was a good supply of running water. It was simply a wooden flume with water running through it; dirt was shoveled in and sluiced through while the gold caught on a slatted bottom. A long tom was worked by several men and could handle four or five times as much dirt per man per day as could a cradle. That meant, of course, that a miner had to shovel four or five times as much dirt into it as he would into a cradle to keep it operating at full efficiency. A man usually had to pay for what he got, even in the gold fields.

The terrain on which the prospectors worked did little to make things easier for them; it was usually difficult. The diggings were chiefly along the tributaries of the Sacramento and San Joaquin rivers, which flowed out of the Sierra Nevada; each river, fork, branch, and creek was eventually followed by prospectors to its source. In the lower foothills the land might be only moderately rocky and hilly at best; near the headwaters rushing streams flowed in the clefts of deep, precipitous gorges whose bottoms were often cluttered with boulders and fallen rocks and choked with jackstraw tangles of dead trees. Even under these conditions, miners persevered at the ever-absorbing task of separating a small amount of gold from a mountain of gravel, and with amazing energy and ingenuity constructed hydraulic works to enable them to move the stream here or there or otherwise exploit it in their search for wealth.

Sometimes these constructions reached the proportions of major engineering works—and were often complete wastes of time and talent. Louise Clappe—"Dame Shirley" she called her-self in her letters—who lived with her doctor husband in the mining camps of Indian Bar and Rich Bar on a high fork of the Feather River for a year, wrote of a company of thirteen men who worked from February almost through September on a project to divert a section of the stream so they could mine the bed. It involved building a dam six feet high and three hundred feet long, as well as a flume and other supporting works. Lumber had cost $1,000 and thirty laborers had been hired for nine and a half days; in all, the dam cost $2,000. When the company

*A California miner hunkers down in a stream bed to pan the gravel for gold.*

totaled its take in gold dust at the end of the venture, it amounted to $41.70.

While such experiences were frequent, they were very far from universal, or else a crowd of amateurs would not have been able to take out, between 1848 and 1852, a quarter of a billion dollars' worth of gold, more or less—no one knows exactly how much—before the rich placer deposits began to give out. For a great many men, the gold fields yielded up a very good day's wage for a day's work. But a day's wage was not what started the gold rush and kept it going; the Argonauts came expecting nothing less than a strike that would make them rich overnight. And there were places where the new Eldorado was almost as rich as the wildest stories ever told about it—locations like those at Auburn, where four cart loads of dirt yielded $16,000, and where, during the first delirious days, it was not at all unusual for a man to dig $1,000 to $1,500 worth of gold between dawn and dusk. Even the stories about gold being found at the roots of bushes turned out to be true: a man hunting rabbits near Angel's Camp jammed his ramrod into the roots of a manzanita bush and turned up a piece of gold-bearing quartz; he scratched out $700 worth of gold the rest of the day using the rod, but with better implements gathered $2,000 the next day and $7,000 the third.

There were stories of men digging gold flakes out of cracks in the rock in stream beds with spoons. Three German prospectors taking a short cut home through unexplored country found just such a situation on a high tributary of the Feather River and were reported to have taken out $36,000 in four days without even having to wash any gravel. The story of the find leaked out

—miners seemed able to smell a gold strike—and the location, named Rich Bar, was quickly swarming with men. It was so rich that it was agreed that claims should be limited to ten square feet. Single panfuls of dirt here often contained $1,500 to $2,000 in gold; the record for one panful reportedly was $2,900. One company of four men took out $50,000 in a single day.

Such strikes were largely phenomena of the early part of the gold rush, however, when men were prospecting virgin ground. Even as early as 1850 such surprises had become quite rare, and by the end of 1852 the gold rush was just about over. By that time all the rivers had been prospected, almost all the big strikes made. The gold fields no longer had much place for a man operating on only a dream and a shoestring. Hard-rock mining, beginning to become common, involved tunneling into rock and crushing and treating gold-bearing quartz, and so necessitated tremendous capital outlays. Hydraulic mining, a new development, was making it possible to recover gold from very low-grade placer deposits, but it required tremendous amounts of water under very high pressures, which were obtained from the high Sierra by complex canal and flume systems far too costly for an independent prospector.

But the gold seekers kept coming, though in rapidly diminishing numbers, until 1859. That was the year the great Comstock Lode was discovered in what is now Nevada. Virtually every miner in California dropped what he was doing and headed through the passes of the Sierra Nevada to the new Eldorado. It was a great rush, but it was anticlimax after the one in California. But then, so has been every other gold rush since.

*Fortune hunter's routine: back to the mine; a deep, wet hole; damming the stream*

*A lithograph of about 1860 showing Butterfield's Overland Mail in California*

# GREAT DAYS OF THE OVERLAND STAGE

By W. EUGENE HOLLON

For a town which had been sur-
veyed only a few months earlier, Tipton, Missouri, began life
with a creditable little bang on October 9, 1858. That was the
day the first Overland Mail stage arrived, twenty-three days and
four hours out of San Francisco — a day that marked the beginning
of regular mail service across the continent. Tipton was 160 miles
west of St. Louis at the end of the Missouri Pacific Railroad, and
from this tiny dot on the map, mail and passengers from the West
were put aboard the trains to St. Louis, Cincinnati, and New York,
completing a transcontinental journey in approximately four
weeks. What had once been a fantastic dream was now a reality,
and the occasion did not go unnoticed in the press.

*Harper's Weekly* observed that California was no longer "a colony of the East," and the London *Times* described the opening
of the Overland Mail route to California as "a matter of greatest
importance to Europe, inasmuch as it will open up a vast country
to European emigration, will be the precursor of the railroad
and land telegraphic communication from New York to San
Francisco, and will greatly facilitate intercourse with British Columbia."

The man who made much of this possible was John Butterfield, a gentleman of 57 years, comfortable fortune, and enormous energies. Born in Berne, New York, Butterfield acquired an abiding love of horses and was known in his youth as one of the best drivers in Albany. A broad-shouldered man with prominent nose, heavy brows, and dark hair, he left his mark on the West's costumes as well as its transportation. For years stores in that area sold long yellow linen dusters, high leather boots, and flat-crowned "wide-awake" hats patterned after those that Butterfield wore.

Actually, it was the contract John Butterfield and his New York associates made with the Post Office Department that made possible the first semiweekly mail service to and from California. When Butterfield guaranteed to deliver the mail between St. Louis and San Francisco in 25 days or less, he was awarded a $600,000 annual Post Office subsidy. As in the case of so many transportation developments in America—land, sea, and air— carrying the mail was the decisive factor. Passenger freight, even at full capacity, would not defray operating expenses over Butterfield's 2,800-mile route.

Soon after the Mexican Cession of 1848, pressure had been exerted from both ends of the country for transcontinental communications. The safest route to California was by water, and before the end of the year contracts were awarded for semimonthly service by sea between New York and San Francisco. In this way letters were carried to Panama by the United States Steamship Company, carted across the isthmus, loaded on vessels of the Pacific Mail Steamship Company, and then forwarded northward. The trip took thirty days, but the cost of a single letter varied from twelve to eighty cents per ounce.

The discovery of gold brought a virtual flood of settlers to California, and before long the people of the newly admitted state demanded faster and cheaper overland mail service. Pressure reached a climax in 1856 when 75,000 Californians signed a petition to Congress, requesting daily mails over a road through South Pass.

This action had the effect of the proverbial egg tossed into a whirling fan, injecting the sectional issue into the discussion. Southerners wanted the proposed overland route to terminate at some southern city, instead of Chicago or St. Louis, since the overland stage route would undoubtedly be followed soon afterward by a railroad. Congress dodged the sectional jealousies by authorizing the Post Office Department to call for bids on carrying the mail semiweekly from "a point on the Mississippi to San Francisco." The route was to be "selected by the contractor."

Since the postmaster general, Aaron Brown, was a southerner, it surprised no one to learn that the successful contractors—John Butterfield, William G. Fargo, and other New York expressmen —had proposed a southern route. Actually, the postmaster general threw out all bids from companies advocating routes that bypassed the South. Therefore, before Butterfield signed the contract, he reluctantly agreed to a route nearly 600 miles south of his original proposal.

The route approved by Aaron Brown was a compromise. Starting at St. Louis and proceeding west on the railroad to Tipton, Missouri, it ran southwest to Springfield, Missouri, and Fort Smith, Arkansas, then along Randolph B. Marcy's old road to El Paso. Passing through Tucson, it went on to Fort Yuma, California, and to San Francisco via Los Angeles.

On September 16, 1857, the contract was signed, and exactly one year later stages left simultaneously from Tipton, headed west, and from San Francisco, headed east. Operating regularly until the southern route was abandoned at the outbreak of the Civil War, the Butterfield stages nearly always completed the journey within the stipulated 25 days.

The route was a semicircular one which the northern press derisively dubbed the oxbow, and most of the eastern papers predicted that the venture would be a total failure. There was no doubt that Postmaster General Brown's sympathies were bound up in the South. His choice of the southern route, although touching both North and South in its semicircular trail, was aimed particularly at the latter region. It did have certain advantages over more northerly routes: grass and water were available for the livestock, the trail was passable any day in the year, and at this period there was no trouble anticipated from the southwestern Indian tribes. Four other overland mail routes were in operation by 1859, but the Butterfield coaches were the only ones never halted by weather or mountain passes.

At first John Butterfield's company carried letter mail exclusively, but newspapers and small packages were transported later. A strict rule by the stock holders prevented shipments of gold or silver, thus practically eliminating holdups by highwaymen, and on only one occasion was there any interference by the

Indians. From the outset, passenger service was available; but few people took advantage of the opportunity until the coaches had been in operation for several months. Twenty-five days of constant jolting over washboard roads, mudholes, deserts, and swollen streams were not likely to be anticipated pleasantly by even the most experienced traveler, and the available food was something to curdle a goat's stomach. From St. Louis to San

*On rough stretches of road the elegant Massachusetts-built Concord coaches*

Francisco the throughfare was $200. Local or wayfare was ten cents per mile for the distance traveled. Passengers were allowed forty pounds of luggage—the same, incidentally, as that allowed by modern airline companies. But food, such as it was, came out of the traveler's own pocketbook.

There were crude stations approximately twenty miles apart along the 2,800-mile route, each outpost being under the charge

*(right) were changed for the solider celerity wagons (center) made in New York.*

of an agent who, with four or five helpers, cared for the stock, changed relays, and prepared meals for the dusty passengers, drivers, and conductors. A New York *Herald* reporter, William L. Ormsby, accompanied the first westbound coach for its entire journey and facetiously remarked that "the fare could hardly be compared to that of the Astor House in New York." Generally it consisted of bacon, beans, bread, onions, and what passed for coffee; but milk, butter, and vegetables could sometimes be had toward each end of the line. In addition, some writers referred to a strange and mysterious concoction known as slumgullion. Mark Twain described this drink as "a pretense of tea, but there was too much sand and old bacon rind in it to deceive the intelligent traveler."

An ancient tale still makes the rounds describing a New York dude who took the Overland stage through Texas in 1858. At a particular station he found the food less than appetizing, consisting of stale sourdough biscuits and rancid bacon, floating in its own grease. Timidly the traveler pushed back his plate as he cast a glance at the burly proprietor, the corners of his mouth revealing what his tongue dared not utter. "All right, dammit," growled the short-tempered host, "help yourself to the mustard."

After the contract was awarded, the Butterfield Company had a tremendous task ahead of it. The route had to be surveyed, roads built or improved, grades leveled, ferries and bridges constructed, wells dug, and the stations erected. Butterfield personally inspected much of the route, while 1,800 horses and mules were purchased and distributed over the trail, test runs made, a regular schedule planned, and forage and food deposited at the various stations. Orders were placed for 250 regular coaches, special mail wagons, water wagons, harness sets, and accessories.

These preliminary expenses alone amounted to nearly a million dollars, and one thousand or more employees were hired before the start of the first mail. They included divisional superintendents, conductors, drivers, station keepers, blacksmiths, veterinarians, wheelwrights, mechanics, helpers, and herders.

Two types of coaches were used, the Concord coach made at Concord, New Hampshire, and the "celerity" wagon manufactured at Troy, New York. The former, a regular full-bodied coach, weighed 3,000 pounds, had a capacity of about two tons, cost approximately $1,400, and could accommodate six to nine passengers inside and an unlimited number on top. These stages were made of the finest white ash, oak, elm, and prime basswood grown in New England forests. Fashioned by the famous Abbott-Downing Company, makers of horse-drawn carriages and buggies for more than a century, the light, elegant, and durable vehicles revolutionized western travel. Along with the Colt revolver, another New England export to the frontier, the stage so permeated the Old West that no horse opera is complete without it.

The Abbot-Downing coaches made for the Butterfield Company were painted in bright colors, usually red, green, or canary yellow. The wheels were heavy, with broad iron tires that would not sink in soft sand, and set wide enough apart—five feet two inches—to keep the coach from tipping. The body, reinforced with iron, was swung on leather straps or thorough braces stitched three and one-half inches wide. The cab rocked back and forth as the coach bowled forward, the thorough braces serving as shock absorbers. The more elegant Concord coaches were used only at each end of the route, but on the rougher sections of the road, from Fort Smith to Los Angeles, passengers and mail were shifted to carriages, or the specially built celerity wagons.

These were much like the regular coaches in appearance except for smaller wheels and a frame top structure covered with heavy duck. Also, they had three seats inside which could be adjusted to form a bed where passengers could sleep in relays. Heavy leather or duck curtains protected the occupants from rain and cold. The interiors of both types were lined with russet leather, with cushions of the same material. Illumination was furnished by wire-pattern candle lamps.

Eventually, nearly 200 stations were erected along the route, some at a minimum of nine miles and others at a maximum of sixty miles. The stations were built of log, adobe, or stone, depending upon the locality. Four or five well-armed men tenanted each station, but in Indian country the personnel might be increased to as many as eight or ten, since the isolated outposts tempted raiding bands of Indians and Mexicans. In 1858 three of the four men at work on Dragoon station in Apache country were hacked to death by Mexicans. The only survivor, whose arm had been cut off by an ax, endured four awful days, during which he was attacked by buzzards and wolves, before help arrived. Because of the constant danger, Texas and Arizona sta-

*Dwarfed by giant cacti, the Overland Mail coach races toward Tucson, Arizona.*

tions were fort-like stone and adobe structures, similar to the inns built in Mexico by the Spanish. Eleven-foot walls formed a rectangular corral, and small rooms were attached to the interior of the stockade. The single entrance was wide enough to admit a coach and team.

Ormsby wrote that the employees without exception were courteous, civil, and attentive. A few years later Mark Twain took the Central Overland stage to Carson City, Nevada. His observation of the drivers, conductors, and station keepers, most of whom had worked for Butterfield on the southern route before it was shifted north, was anything but flattering. The driver he acidly described as a contemptible, swaggering bully, "the only one they bowed down to and worshipped"; the station agent, a profane cutthroat, was wanted by half a dozen vigilante committees. And the district agent or superintendent, who supervised the various stations along his 250-mile division, differed from his subordinates in that he was quicker on the draw: "It was not absolutely necessary that he be a gentleman, and occasionally he wasn't."

The conductor's beat was the same as that of the divisional agent, and frequently he rode the fearful distance night and day without rest or sleep. He had absolute charge of the mail, express matters, passengers, and stagecoach until he delivered them to the next conductor and got his receipt.

The vehicles were pulled by four to six horses or mules and rolled day and night except for brief stops for meals and a change of relays. Their speed varied from four miles in rough country to spurts of twelve miles per hour over level stretches of prairies or down long straight slopes. The drivers were proud of the time they made, and Ormsby wrote feelingly of "the heavy mail wagon whizzing and whirling over the jagged rock ... in comparative darkness." Inside, "to feel oneself bouncing—now on the hard seat, now against the roof, and now against the side ... was no joke." Each driver drove a sixty-mile run, stopped for a few hours' rest before taking the next opposite-bound coach back over the same stretch of road.

Except for the meal stops twice each day, the coaches lingered only ten minutes at each station to obtain a fresh relay of horses or mules and to pick up and discharge mail sacks. The conductors sounded a bugle two or three miles from the station, announcing the coach's arrival, so that everything was in readiness for a quick change. In 24 hours the stage covered approximately 120 miles, and after the first three or four days the passengers became inured to the discomfort of the hard seat, jolting road, and insufferable dust—catching a few winks of sleep when they could.

There is a record of only one attack by Indians which halted the mail along the southern route. It happened at Apache Pass, or Puerto del Dado, Arizona, early in February, 1861. At nearby Fort Buchanan, the commander had received word that Apaches had raided a beef contractor's cattle and had also abducted a young boy. Lieutenant George Bascom and sixty men of the 7th Infantry were sent in pursuit, and in the Dragoon Mountains met Chief Cochise of the Chiricahua tribe, who insisted his tribe did not have the boy. Apparently Bascom did not believe the Chief, and there was a brief fracas in which one Indian was killed and four taken prisoner.

After Bascom and his men went on to Apache Pass, the Indians on February 5 planned a mass attack on the station. The Butterfield mail from the east was due the next evening; but luckily it arrived two hours early, left shortly after changing teams, and reached the west end of the pass while it was still light. Here, about a mile and a half from the station, dried grass was piled in heaps across the road to form a fire ambush. The Butterfield men cleared the road, and had proceeded for another half mile when they came on what was left of an emigrant train. Amid the smoldering embers of the wagons were the mutilated bodies of the victims. Eight of them, who had not been fortunate enough to be shot, had been chained to the wagon wheels and burned alive.

By this time it was too dark to go back through the dangerous pass to inform the station about the massacre, so the stage pushed on to the west. About halfway to the next station, they met the eastbound stage and warned them of what lay ahead. Aboard were nine passengers, including a superintendent inspecting the line; the conductor, A. B. Culver, brother of the station keeper at Apache Pass; and the driver. All were armed, and they decided to risk an attack and proceed.

Entering the pass after dark, the driver whipped the mules to greater speed, and as the stage clattered down the eastern grade shots rang out from ambush. Two mules went down, and the driver was wounded, but the passengers kept up a steady fire in the direction of the shots while the superintendent and Culver cut the two mules out of the traces. With the animals that remained, they fought their way to Apache Pass Station, where they spent the night.

Knowing they were outnumbered by at least 5 to 1, the station agent, C. W. Culver, decided to make terms with the enemy. Next morning he and his helper Welch and the driver, J. F. Wallace, went out of the little fort under a flag of truce. Some distance from the station the Indians rushed them, managing to capture Wallace.

The other two men turned and ran; Welch was shot down, but Culver, although badly wounded, made it to the station. Several days later Wallace's body and the corpses of five prisoners from the luckless wagon train were found staked out on the plains west of the pass, half-eaten by vultures and coyotes.

After John Butterfield stepped down as president of the Overland Stage Company in 1860, the morale and discipline of the employees declined. On March 12, 1861, Congress ordered the route permanently discontinued and the service transferred to the central section of the country by way of South Pass and Salt Lake City.

A year later Ben Holladay took over the company, selling it

in 1866 to Wells, Fargo and Company. It continued in operation from the Missouri River to Sacramento, California, until completion of the Union Pacific Railroad in 1869. From then until the close of the century, overland staging was relegated to a secondary place in frontier life. Eventually even the local stage disappeared completely from the American scene, to be revived only by Hollywood and the commercial rodeo.

After being practically abandoned for a quarter of a century, the southern overland road laid out by John Butterfield soon became crisscrossed and paralleled by highways, railroads, and airlines, each of which profited from the labors of those early road builders.

In many places the railroad grade follows the very ruts of the old trail, and trains take on water today from wells dug by the Butterfield men. Even now the best all-weather highway from St. Louis to San Francisco approximates the thin line across prairies and mountain passes over which the Concord and Troy coaches once kicked up dust, and the best year-round air route follows the same low passes over which the Butterfield stages "flew" a century ago.

*Perhaps because Butterfield made it a firm rule never to carry gold or silver, his coaches were rarely stopped by bandits, and only one was attacked by Indians.*

*Daring miners in a homemade boat shoot down a flume bringing water to the mine.*

# "GO IT, WASHOE!"

## By REMI NADEAU

*I*nto the mountain-bound mining camp of Grass Valley, California, rode a weary traveler late in June, 1859. He had jogged more than 150 miles over the massive Sierra Nevada from the Washoe country in western Utah Territory. With him, mostly as a curiosity, he carried some odd-looking chunks of gold-bearing ore.

Next day Melville Atwood, the local assayer, tested the rock. What he discovered made him doubt his own calculations. For besides the gold content, which ran about $1,000 to the ton, the specimens contained a much higher value in silver — over $3,000 per ton!

What was more, the stranger confided, over in Washoe the discoverers were extracting the gold and throwing the rest away! Since California's big strike more than a decade earlier, prospectors had not even thought of looking for anything but gold!

Those queer-looking rock samples launched a human stampede that created the state of Nevada, transformed the financial structure of the Far West, and set the pattern of settlement for the vast basin between Great Salt Lake and the Sierra.

Within hours of Atwood's assay, the neighboring towns of Grass Valley and Nevada City were boiling with excitement. First to learn the news was Judge James Walsh, an old hand in California mining and a friend of the ore-bearing stranger from Washoe. Near midnight he banged frantically on the door of another friend. Quickly they piled provisions on a mule, mounted their horses, and spurred out of Grass Valley. Not far behind them clambered a desperate party in pursuit, some traveling on borrowed money, others on borrowed horses. Within two days a clattering column was surging through the pine-forested Sierra, some on horseback, some afoot, all bent forward like hounds on the scent. Riding in the van was the tall, muscular figure of George Hearst, then a rising young mining man of Nevada City. With him was Atwood the assayer, who had confided the news and joined the rush.

When this vanguard arrived in the barren hills of Washoe, the original miners still knew nothing of their ore's silver content. The two discoverers, Peter O'Riley and Pat McLaughlin, were washing out the gold with their "rocker," letting the rest of the rock roll down the side of Sun Mountain. One of them sold his share for $3,500 to George Hearst, who was so anxious to buy that he rode his mule back over the mountains to Nevada City to raise the money. Judge James Walsh paid $11,000 for the interests of one Henry Comstock, a local prospector who had fast-talked the two discoverers into giving him a share. To seal his bargain with Walsh, Comstock took ten dollars as a down payment for what would later be worth millions. Then he bragged

*Staking the first claim in the Comstock Lode. The pensive Henry Comstock (far left) sold out too soon, vainly sought another rich lode, and died a suicide.*

to his fellow miners that he had fooled "the California rock shark!"

He thought enough of the discovery, however, to call it Comstock's Lode wherever he went. And so talkative was he that his name became permanently attached to the greatest single deposit of precious metal ever discovered in the United States.

By the summer of 1859 Walsh and Hearst were shipping ore over the Sierra—ore so rich that it could be carried 160 miles by muleback and another 80 by steamer, and could still be smelted in San Francisco at a fantastic profit. By October the growing shipments were attracting attention as they passed through California's mining region. Early arrivals in Washoe were writing back that the mines were the richest in the country. California newspapers were quoting assay figures of thousands of dollars per ton. Before long, bars of Washoe silver were hauled through the streets of San Francisco and displayed in bank windows before the eyes of gathering crowds. All at once California rang with a new cry: Silver in Washoe!

In fact, only silver could have excited the Californians in 1859. For too long they had followed the call of gold. As the placers had declined in the mid-fifties, they had been quick to heed each rumored strike. Only the previous year some 20,000 had swarmed aboard ship for Fraser River in British Columbia, only to find the gold excitement fading: the glittering prize lay out of reach beneath flood waters. California had sent money to help them return, and they vowed never to be stampeded again by that golden call.

But against the cry of silver these stalwarts had no immunity. When it burst upon them in the fall of 1859, they were especially vulnerable. It had been a long summer, and in Sierra canyons the placer and hydraulic mines were idle for lack of water. At the end of September one Sacramento man estimated that a thousand unemployed men were roaming the town. "Never before," he wrote, "have I seen so many people looking for work and can't get it."

To this restless crew the silver call was like a trumpet blast. All at once mules, horses, flour, picks, and shovels were in fevered demand. "From the crack of day to the shades of night," exclaimed one San Franciscan, "nothing is heard but Washoe." It made no difference that the new strike was located in the very desert through which most of them had suffered on their way west to California. All they knew was that it was "Forty-nine all over again!"

With "Washoe!" thundering like a battle cry, the rabble army converged on Sierra passes. From San Francisco they swarmed onto the decks of river steamboats, sprawling wherever they could find room between bales and boxes, jabbering about Washoe in a dozen languages. At Sacramento they took the puffing Iron Horse—first on the West Coast—a few miles farther, then staged onward in six-horse wagons. With a dozen people crammed into each stage, they were so tightly packed that when one overturned nobody was hurt. The passengers crawled bravely out, helped to right the wagon, and lurched merrily onward.

At Placerville, snugly tucked in the Sierra foothills, they came to an abrupt halt. This depot for the Washoe mines had suddenly been so overwhelmed with business that there were not enough wagons or mules in the countryside to keep the stampede moving. The hills above town were piled with boxes of merchandise while their owners vainly offered fantastic freight fees for hauling them over the Sierra. Stagecoaches and mule trains were booked up days in advance. Streets and hotels, saloons and restaurants, were thronged with a noisy crowd of expectant millionaires. One of them was a writer named J. Ross Browne, who later described his attempt to get a night's sleep in a hotel room. People were rushing through the corridors all night, he wrote, "in and out of every room, banging the doors after them, calling for boots, carpet-sacks, cards, cock-tails, and toddies; while amidst the ceaseless din arose ever and anon that potent cry of 'Washoe!' . . ." In the midst of the pandemonium his door burst open.

"I say, Cap!" cried a disheveled intruder wearing a wide-brimmed hat and long underwear. "Are you the man that can't get an animal for Washoe?"

"Yes, have you got one to sell or hire?"

"No I hain't got one myself, but me and my pardner is going to walk there, and if you like you can jine our party."

When Browne agreed, the door was closed, only to be opened again.

"I say, Cap!"

"What now?"

"Do you believe in Washoe?"

"Of course; why not?"

In this breathless spirit California marched to the Comstock Lode. And as the line of glory-hunters moved through Placerville's streets each morning, clattering along with shovels, picks, and washpans, there rose from the throats of bystanders the inevitable shout, "Go it, Washoe!"

Up into the pines the adventurers thronged, making an unbroken line of men, mules, and wagons from Sacramento Valley over the mountains to Carson Valley. As the stagecoaches whirled around blind bends, the passengers found themselves looking hundreds of feet downward to the churning American River while the wheels dusted the brink. In the steepest stretches they walked and sometimes pushed as the teams struggled upward. Those who hiked or rode muleback suffered worse—slogging in the ruts of freight wagons, jumping out of the trail to avoid being knocked down when a pack train brushed relentlessly past.

Among the worst hazards on the trail were the wayside taverns, where the travelers piled in on one another in frantic quest for board and bed. Typical was Dirty Mike's, where one paid for the privilege of sleeping on the floor in company with numerous other flea-bitten vagabonds, in a room whose only fixtures were a piece of looking glass fastened to the window casing and a common comb and toothbrush dangling by strings nearby. The best stopping place on the route was Strawberry Flat, where hundreds of travelers congregated each night, flooding the barroom and jostling each other for a place near the dining-room door. J. Ross Browne thus described the evening meal:

At the first tinkle of the bell the door was burst open with a tremendous crash, and for a moment no battle-scene in Waterloo . . . could have equalled the terrific onslaught of the gallant troops of Strawberry. The whole house actually tottered and trembled at the concussion, as if shaken by an earthquake. Long before the main body had assaulted the table the din of arms was heard above the general uproar; the deafening clatter of plates, knives, and forks, and the dreadful battle-cry of "Waiter! Waiter! Pork and beans! Coffee, waiter! Beefsteak! . . . quick, waiter, for God's sake!"

Next morning, after a night's sleep in a room with 250 companions and a bracing wash at the horse trough, the silver-hunter was on his way. At Genoa, first settlement reached on the east side of the Sierra, accommodations were even more formidable.

Lodgers were packed like stowaways—two and three in a bunk, the unfortunate ones curling up on saloon floors, behind store counters, between packing boxes, and even on the tops of nail kegs. At the booming new town of Carson City, last stop before the mines, one weary arrival ate a hearty meal and then told the hotel-keeper he was ready to be shown to his room. "Just imagine my surprise," he wrote, "when the landlord informed me that he had no place for me to sleep but on the floor, that is, if I had blankets . . ."

Early in November a storm struck the Sierra, covering it with snow and ice such as had already brought tragedy to many California-bound emigrants in previous years. But this deterred only the faint-hearted and the sane. While commerical traffic was halted, the most frantic rainbow-hunters floundered upward in the snow, resting at the highest outposts until the weather cleared enough for them to push over the summit. One storm after another raked the Sierra in one of the fiercest winters on record. Snow drifted as deep as sixty feet in the upper canyons. Numberless animals and a few men met death in blizzards and avalanches, but still the most daring pressed on, driven by visions of Washoe silver.

As the spring thaw approached, all of California seemed to rally at the foot of the Sierra. The winter's isolation had left the Comstock so short of supplies that prices were soaring, and between rival freight-packers there was a breakneck race to be first across with whiskey and other "necessities." As early as February they were laying blankets in the snow for their animals to walk on, taking them up behind the train as it advanced and spreading them on the path ahead. Imaginative freighters tried sleighs, but these were stalled at the frequent patches of wind-swept granite. Mule trains were the only resort—taking not only merchandise, but offering to deliver passengers in Washoe at thirty dollars per head. By early March even the stages were running again, but passengers had to walk much of the way, holding the coach to keep it from rolling down the mountainside. Above Strawberry Flat they trudged onward on foot, braving fierce winds and shoveling a path before them across the summit.

With the first days of spring the Washoe trail was a continuous scar of slush and mud through the Sierra snow. A traveler called it "nothing but one trough of mire from two to three feet deep . . ." Adding further obstructions were the broken wagons, aban-

*These contemporary sketches suggest that whiskey fueled the rush to Washoe. It fortifies passengers on the stage and helps wash down a meal at Strawberry Flat.*

doned boxes, and dead animals that literally lined the trail for the entire hundred miles across the mountains.

Worse hazards stalked the other Sierra routes opened to accommodate the tide. From California's Northern Mines the adventurers stormed up the tempestuous Yuba River, joined a mule train at Downieville, and bent onward along narrow trails that hung hundreds of feet above the foaming river. From the Southern Mines they ventured through giant redwood groves, over Ebbet Pass, to the Carson River. Near the summit of this remote passage the stampeders encountered more than rough trail. Two of them stayed up all night waving firebrands to protect a load of bacon from three grizzly bears that, as one man recalled, "were grumbling and gnashing their teeth."

By April, 1860, some 150 Californians were arriving in the Washoe country every day. Estimates of its population reached as high as 10,000 that spring, with thousands more on the way. Those remaining in California were investing every spare cent in Washoe mining stocks. "The Washoe mania has operated very much against us here," wrote one San Francisco merchant, "diverting men and money from the legitimate channels."

The Mormon settlement at Salt Lake sent its own contingent, despite an apparent effort by the church elders to silence the news from Washoe lest their colonists go packing off in quest of silver. The city's *Deseret News* ran scarcely a line on the subject through the height of the frenzy. But there were others in the Great Basin who were unprotected from Washoe's call. In 1859 the gold rush to Pike's Peak, in what was then western Kansas, proved a disappointment to many stampeders. Swinging farther westward, they swelled the annual tide of emigration to California. But having arrived in Carson Valley by late summer of '59, many families were caught in the rising silver fever. Forgetting California, they cast their lot with Washoe.

But most of the rush came from California—not only its drifters and schemers, who were ready to join each new excitement, but the very flower of its population. Nevada would soon boast that the best of America came to California, and the best of California came to Washoe.

First to arrive were the mining men—the Walshes and the Hearsts—who knew ore and who hoped to buy promising leads with their own or someone else's money. Marching after them was the whole lusty crew that made up frontier society: promoters and speculators, traders and gamblers. Among them were followers of the oldest profession, for not even Sierra snow-storms could bar Washoe to the fair but frail. Usually dressed in men's clothing, they suffered exposure and hunger with the rest. One was Julia Bulette, said to be the second woman to reach the Comstock. She brought to the Lode a subtle refinement compounded of French descent and a New Orleans past. In her parlor the rough manners of the mining camp were taboo. And when an epidemic of influenza struck the Lode, Julia ministered to the stricken. No wonder the boys would soon be toasting her as queen of Washoe.

Others tramped over the mountain passes with even less visible means of support—the thieves and cutthroats who customarily joined new stampedes. Of this ilk was "Fighting" Sam Brown—he of the bull voice and the clanking Spanish spurs. Sam was a "bad man," glorying in the name, working hard to keep it. Before his Washoe debut he had spilled the blood of several Californians. On his way he shot a man in Carson City; arriving at the Comstock, he got into a fight with a monte dealer and wounded two bystanders. He would become "chief" of the new camp, or stretch his bones at the feet of a better man.

But the backbone of the stampeders was the common miner— the same who for ten years had been pouring into California from the East, and had been rushing to every new strike on the coast. Honest, hard-working, hail-fellow, he was the sinew of frontier society. Shovel on shoulder, he walked or rode over icy Sierra passes to Washoe, eager to possess a new country. At the least he would gain a better wage as a miner there than in the declining California fields. At most he would strike his own vein of silver and return to the States a millionaire.

One of these was young John W. Mackay, Irish immigrant and hardrock miner. In California's Yuba diggings he heard the news of Washoe and loaded his back-pack. With another young Irishman for a companion, he trudged up through the timber, past shimmering Lake Tahoe, and descended on Washoe. As they stood at the gates of the Comstock, his sidekick took the last half dollar they had between them and threw it far down the canyon.

"What are you doing?" cried Mackay. "That's my last."

His pal had a reasonable answer: "Let us inter the city loike gintlemen."

When the first Californians reached Washoe they found only a handful of disreputable shacks, inhabited by an equally disreputable collection of sourdoughs. The center of society was the boarding house of Eilley Orrum, first woman on the Comstock. Having already shed two husbands, this stouthearted female had her eyes on a third in the person of her most eligible boarder, Sandy Bowers. Still another guest, in addition to Henry Comstock and the discoverers of the Lode, was a whiskey-soaked character named "Old Virginny" Fennimore. The grizzled old-timer had held a small interest in the discovery claim, but Comstock had bought him out for a bobtailed, half-blind horse.

Cheated of his chance for fortune, Old Virginny got back at Comstock in his own way. During a drunken spree on the site of the Lode, he solemnly christened the new community — with appropriate drops from a broken whiskey bottle — "Virginia Town." And so it immediately became, overshadowing in popular use the name of Comstock's Lode. Within a few months, after the grotesque humor of the miners insisted on a grander title, it became Virginia City — goal of every Washoe-bound traveler and eventually the most famous mining town in the West.

By the fall of '59 tents and shanties were sprawling up the sterile slope of Sun Mountain. There was only one miserable restaurant, and hotels were practically nonexistent. Newcomers were invited to find a soft spot for their blankets on the hillside,

*These would have been regarded as luxurious accommodations in Washoe.*

while the more fastidious slept in the beds of wagons. The drinking water was abominable, being strongly impregnated with arsenic. But the boys found a way of "correcting" it by diluting each teaspoon with half a glass of whiskey.

When winter settled upon Washoe it covered the hills with snow and sent thermometers below zero. What was worse, it virtually cut off supplies from California. But whiskey always seemed to make its way through Sierra passes when nothing else could. With scarcely enough food to maintain body heat, the resourceful Washoeites were said to "draw largely on the resources of the bar."

As the main body of stampeders arrived in early spring, they found Washoe the most dismal place on earth. One newcomer thus described it: "Imagine a flood in hell, succeeded by a snowstorm ..." Another wayfarer drew a more detailed picture of Virginia Town:

Frame shanties, pitched together as if by accident; tents of canvas, of blankets, of brush, of potato-sacks and old shirts, with empty whisky-barrels for chimneys; smoky hovels of mud and stone; coyote holes in the mountain side forcibly seized and held by men; pits and shafts with smoke issuing from every crevice ...

Night and day the saloons and gambling houses filled the air with a constant din of oaths and laughter, rattling dice, and clinking coins. Inside these foul dens, as one witness put it, "clouds of tobacco smoke filled the air and blackened the roof timbers, modifying the stench rising from the stained and greasy floors, soiled clothes, and hot flesh of the unwashed company." A San Francisco author and correspondent, Frank Soulé, wrote: "I have been through one hundred degrees of latitude, north and south, but never before have found so inhospitable, miserable, God-forsaken a spot as this same Virginia City ..."

Washoe's redeeming feature was that it was never dull. Through the spring of 1860 it was teeming with would-be tycoons—all talking "lodes," "dips," "angles," "indications," and trying to sell one another shares in a claim. New arrivals first encountered the frenzy at Carson City, where, as one of them warned, "Every man you meet has, or expects to have, something to sell, and can in no wise be trusted." It increased in fury at Silver City, in the canyon approaching the Comstock; there, according to another traveler, nobody estimated himself to be worth less than $50,000. It reached its zenith in Virginia City, where the riches of Monte Cristo were apparently changing hands by the minute.

"Nobody had any money," observed a newcomer, "yet everybody was a millionaire in silver claims. Nobody had any credit, yet everybody bought thousands of feet of glittering ore."

Adding fuel to this blaze of excitement were new mining discoveries in the very streets. One man digging a cellar discovered mineral "indications," claimed a whole streetful of houses for his lead, and set hundreds to turning up the earth under their tents. Title disputes over such valuable lots were usually settled on the spot, the parties using empty bottles or other instruments to emphasize the justice of their case.

Still greater panic was caused by frequent announcements that a new strike had been made in a nearby canyon. At first those who knew the secret would disappear, quietly packing a mule and making off. By the time their absence was noticed the rumor was on every tongue and the stampede began. For a day or two Virginia City would be nearly deserted while every able-bodied man scurried over the new ground staking claims. To get around local mining laws he would hang notices on the sagebrush in the name of every friend he had left behind in California, until the landscape fairly fluttered with the claims of strangers who would never see Washoe and never knew of the lodes and ledges taken up in their names. After a few days the new ground would be found far less promising than the main Comstock lead. The rushers would straggle back into Virginia City, waving ore samples and offering their fabulous bonanzas to every stranger they met.

By April, 1860, the Comstock mania reached its height. One visitor estimated that only one inhabitant in fifty was actually mining the earth. A few more were out prospecting for new leads, while the largest proportion was engaged in buying and selling shares. When two friends met on the street the customary salutation, rather than a handshake, was to thrust ore samples at each other; and instead of asking after one's health, they would inquire about assays, claims, and outcroppings. One man bunking with twenty roommates in a crowded Virginia City hotel complained that the others spent most of the night trading claims, displaying rock samples, and shouting: "Struck it rich!" — "Miller on the rise!" — "A thousand feet more!"

Providing a real basis for the excitement was the actual discovery of rich new extensions in the Lode. The main deposit ran lengthwise along the mountainside, each mine owner tunneling inward to strike it.

As a mine approached the lead, its stock took on new interest. The whole population kept alert to its progress, achieving new heights of hysteria whenever a messenger would come hurrying down the street with a handful of promising "indications." This was the signal for a flourish of magnifying glasses, which every Washoeite carried in his pocket; the verdict would be heatedly discussed with wild flailing of arms, and the price of the stock would rise $10 to $20 per running foot. Finally, with the whole town on edge, word would come that the mine in question had reached the Lode! In a single moment its chief owners became frantically rich, and the mine's shares were valued at $500 to $1,000 per foot.

So intense was the furor that as a tunnel approached the vein, speculators would keep a list of the owners, retaining messengers at the mine to report instantly upon its success. With his advance information, the operator would then scurry through town to buy up shares before the news was generally known. Many sent wires via the new telegraph line over the mountains to their San Francisco agents, who would then seek out every uninformed owner and buy his stock.

As early as April such speculation was getting out of hand. Claims situated miles away from Virginia City were readily sold on both sides of the mountains. Clerks, washerwomen, teamsters, laundrymen were dealing in mining stock. One young easterner who had just arrived in San Francisco was swept up in the excitement, bought two Washoe claims for $1,000 from the first promoter he encountered, sold out a few months later for $20,-000, and took steamer passage home. When telegrams giving the status of various claims were delayed en route to San Francisco, the telegraph operators were accused of holding the information for their own advantage. And when the editor of the San Francisco *Bulletin* visited Virginia City, one brokerage house staged a fake demonstration for his benefit—and that of his readers. While the newspaperman remained in the office, a perfect bedlam was manufactured by those supposed to be buying and selling stocks, the "buyers" almost begging for the chance to put down their money.

235

*A bearded miner at work in the Gould and Curry silver mine in Virginia City,*

*Nevada. Taken by Tim O'Sullivan, this was one of the first American flash photos.*

Undeceived and disgusted, the *Bulletin* editor returned to San Francisco and hurled thundering editorials against the Washoe fever. It was the beginning of the end of the first Comstock stampede. Stock prices tumbled in San Francisco; Washoe suddenly lost its magic name. Of an estimated 4,000 claims located in Washoe by 1860, only 300 had been opened, and only 20 were considered by experts to be sound investments. As one observer in Washoe told the San Franciscans, "fools at your end of the telegraph were deceived by knaves at our end . . ."

Early in May a savage Indian uprising in the Washoe country knocked the remaining steam out of the first rush. But such setbacks could not down the Lode, which was basically sound to the extent of an estimated one-third of a billion dollars. The tide to the Comstock rose again in the summer of 1860 and ran heavily until '63. Its riches helped to finance the Union side of the Civil War. Through the sixties and early seventies its wealth was the first fact of economics on the Pacific Coast. For the rest of the century its legend inspired the countless prospectors who scoured the Great Basin for "another Comstock."

Among them were many of the same wild army that had populated Washoe in its dawning hour. Peter O'Riley, one of the two discoverers, had sold out for $40,000, which he had then lost in mining speculation. For years he pursued silver with pick and shovel, driven by an obsession that finally conquered his mind. Bitter fortune also dogged Henry Comstock, who wandered through Idaho and Montana in search of another treasure, and finally committed suicide.

Violence overtook others of that original band. While on one of his sprees, "Old Virginny" was killed when he fell from his horse—possibly the same half-blind nag for which he had traded his share of the Lode. Julia Bulette, the tarnished queen of Washoe, was murdered for her jewels; the Comstock showed its heart by giving her its greatest funeral and her slayer its most elegant hanging. As for the cutthroat Sam Brown, he met his fate by bullying the wrong man: an inoffensive innkeeper pursued him through Washoe and brought him down with a double blast of a shotgun. And the frontier coroner's jury gave a verdict that has become classic: "It served him right."

But to others, Washoe dealt fantastic cards. George Hearst won a vast fortune that became the foundation for the career of his son, William Randolph Hearst. John Mackay, the honest miner from the Yuba diggings, bent all his energies to the study of mining. He rose from mucker to superintendent, then to mine owner. In the early 1870's Mackay and three partners gained control of the Big Bonanza, a glittering new underground treasure that gave Virginia City its second tumultuous boom, threw the Pacific Coast into a new frenzy of stock speculation, and made its owners the lords of the Comstock.

Still others were unable to play the hands they were dealt. Judge James Walsh sold out his interests too soon and missed his chance for great fortune. Eilley Orrum had married her star boarder, Sandy Bowers, and the two held on to their mining shares long enough to become the only original owners to reap millions. Part of it they poured into Washoe Hall, a sumptuous Victorian mansion in Washoe Valley. They spent more of it on a grandiose tour of Europe, scandalizing the Continent with their extravagance. But there came a time when they scraped the bottom of their mine. After Sandy died, Eilley became the lone proprietress of Washoe Hall, sitting amidst its decayed splendor, living on the admission fees of curiosity-seekers.

Today Virginia City itself has become a public museum for a vanished race. Gone now are the hearties—unshaven and unwashed—who filled her streets with pandemonium, and her coffers with coin. They have moved on; first to new silver strikes from Idaho to Arizona, then to windswept graves. They were crude, ribald, greedy—all of that. But no other breed could have tamed the fierce wasteland east of the Sierra and west of Salt Lake. As they staggered, snowblind and frostbitten, out of the Sierra a century ago, an early Comstocker welcomed them with a salute that became a prophecy: "Let no man speak disparagingly of these men. Let [no one] sneer at the ragged miners. They are the pioneers in a great era . . ."

*Trains from east and west about to meet at Promontory, Utah, on May 10, 1869*

# THE IRON SPINE

By HENRY STURGIS

t Promontory, Utah Territory, on the raw afternoon of May 10, 1869, Leland Stanford, the beefy, pompous president of the Central Pacific Railroad, hefted a silver-plated sledge hammer while David Hewes, a dedicated railroad booster from San Francisco, stood by the golden spike he had donated to complete the laying of the nation's first transcontinental rail line. At a nearby table sat a telegrapher, his hand on the key. Across the country lines had been cleared; when Stanford's sledge struck the golden spike, cities on the shores of both oceans would know that America was finally and forever bound by a single spine of iron. A parade four miles long stood ready in Chicago, and at Omaha on the Missouri River, whence five years before the Union Pacific tracks had started west to meet the Central, one hundred cannon were primed for a thunderous salute. Before Stanford squared himself away to swing, a crew of Chinese tracklayers from the Central stepped forward with the last rail of the 1,775 miles of line between San Francisco and Omaha. Just then a bystander, alive to the import of the scene, shouted to a cameraman, "Shoot!" The Chinese dropped the rail with a loud clang and scrambled for cover. It took several moments to round up the gun-shy Orientals and convince them that this shooting would not be like those they knew all too well from brutal months of pounding the line through a lawless wilderness. The rail was duly set in place.

Stanford drew back his hammer. A hush came over the assemblage — politicians, railroad dignitaries, track foremen, gandy dancers, Irish and Chinese track hands, hunters, mountain men, gamblers, gunfighters, ex-convicts, and *nymphes du grade* — massed in the heavy mud where the rails joined. The prevailing sounds were the hissings from the Central's handsome locomotive Jupiter and the U.P.'s gleaming Number 119, standing one hundred feet apart at the junction point.

The telegrapher clicked the penultimate message: "All ready now. The last spike will soon be driven. The signal will be three dots for the commencement of the blows." Leland Stanford swung, the silver hammer head flashing in the sun.

He missed.

The hammer thonked dismally against the tie, leaving the golden spike undriven; nonetheless the telegrapher signalled, "Dot, dot, dot." Across the United States cannon fired, bells rang, parades went forward, prayers were said, men cheered, and ladies wept. Jupiter and 119, aswarm from headlamp to cab with shouting, bottle-waving men, nosed gingerly across the last rail until their cowcatchers almost touched. Bottles popped and champagne splashed. So far as everyone but Stanford and a group of discreet onlookers was concerned, the United States was now truly — physically — one nation indivisible. One of those looking on was Thomas C. Durant, vice president of the Union Pacific. No sooner had Stanford committed his historic gaffe than Durant took the hammer and himself whacked the tie next to the golden spike, as if to suggest that Stanford had missed on purpose. (The spike was eventually driven home.) If it *was* the superb bit of tact that it seemed, it was the first evidence of cooperation between the two roads. Ever since the rail companies were chartered, they had been almost as busy wrangling or picking each other's pockets (and those of Uncle Sam) as laying track. As the railroad historian Stewart Holbrook has written, "Americans do not build a railroad from Omaha to the Pacific in five years, making grade and laying track under almost impossible conditions, meanwhile fighting savage tribes and prehensile politicians, without at least a trace of corruption."

There had been a number of proposals earlier in the century

*Officials of the Central Pacific Railroad, which laid track from west to east*

for a transcontinental railroad, but most congressmen had found them foolish. Nevertheless, the idea gradually became more respectable. In 1845 Senator John M. Niles of Connecticut put before Congress a proposal, drawn up by his friend Asa Whitney, to set aside for a railroad 75,000,000 acres in a strip sixty miles wide from the Mississippi to the Columbia River valley. The project would finance itself from land sales, industrial development, and mining and lumbering along the route. Besides tying the northern free states to the New West, the route would be the fastest means of transshipment for ocean trade between Europe and the Far East—trade that now labored around Cape Horn or the Cape of Good Hope.

European-Asiatic trade considerations aside, glowing reports were reaching Washington from explorers in the lush Mexican province of Upper California. There was mounting agitation for the United States to annex this splendid land and make it into a free-soil state, and that agitation gave pro-railroad men yet another reason to urge the laying of a transcontinental line. But Congress failed to act favorably on the Whitney proposal. Such

*At the crossroads of two eras: a wagon caravan halts for the train taking Leland*

schemes sat poorly in the minds of southerners like Sam Houston, of the new proslavery state of Texas, and the well-connected railroad promoter James Gadsden of South Carolina, who plumped for a southerly route to the Pacific. California was indeed a rich prize, made far richer by the discovery of gold in 1848. The only way to get there was still the Overland Mail's seventeen-day stage ride from St. Joseph, Missouri, or the even longer sea voyage from New York to San Francisco with a Central American land-crossing en route. Men could sail around the Horn or go by ox-drawn wagon across the desert, but both ways took six months and neither could guarantee a safe arrival. Despite the need for a transcontinental line, attempts in the late eighteen forties and early fifties foundered on the question of route location — North or South?

In 1853 Jefferson Davis, Secretary of War, pushed Gadsden into the position of minister to Mexico. Gadsden thence was able to bamboozle his government into buying a strip of parched borderland from the Rio Grande to California as part of the right-of-way for a projected Deep South railway to the Pacific.

*Stanford, Central Pacific president, and guests to the Promontory ceremonies.*

Congress concurrently approved Davis' proposal to dispatch five survey teams to investigate possible transcontinental rail routes, North and South. When the field reports came back to Washington late in 1854, Davis leafed through them and found, unsurprisingly, that of the five the Gadsden route would be the shortest, cheapest, and easiest to build.

While such notions were being batted around in the great councils, a number of remarkably able young railroad men were at work in the Middle and Far West. Among them were Theodore Judah, Collis Huntington, Thomas Durant, and Grenville Dodge. In the fifteen years before the union at Promontory, each of them would play a crucial role in the realization of a transcontinental line. Ironically, the one whom fate would scorn was the real inspiration for the project. Ted Judah had just finished work as a location engineer for the Niagara Gorge & Erie rail line when promoters asked him to build a short line from Sacramento to Folsom, California. The job called for only twenty-one miles of local road, but Judah had something much bigger in mind — a railroad across America. "He had always read, talked, and studied the problem," his wife, Anna, recalled years later. She remembered his saying more than once, "It will be built, and I'm going to have something to do with it."

By August of 1855 the Sacramento-Folsom line was operative, and Judah quickly moved to a series of new surveying jobs. He got to know a few of the right Californians, probed deeper and deeper into the Sierra Nevada to locate the magic route to the East — and tried to convince those who would listen that California's destiny was bound up in his dream road.

He was so passionate and persistent that a number of people called him "Crazy Judah," writing him off as a harmless if tiresome lunatic. They were wrong. He helped to inspire the Pacific Railroad Convention that met at San Francisco in September, 1859. A month afterward he set off for Washington, D.C. (via the trans-Isthmus route) as the convention's lobbyist for a transcontinental road.

Judah did not get his great railroad charter from a Congress now preoccupied with slavery and possible secession, but he did set some sort of record low in expense-accountmanship. At the end of the six-month venture he handed in his summary account: "For printing bill and circulars — $40."

Back in California by the summer of 1860, Judah hurried to

the mountains to resume his surveys, which carried him into the fall and early winter. Riding out of the mining camp of Dutch Flat one day, Judah came upon Emigrant and Donner passes, a pair of defiles about two miles apart through which an old wagon route crossed the Sierras from the Truckee River gorge and the Nevada flats beyond. This was it—the way through the mountains for the Pacific railway. The going would be rugged, he must have realized, for tunnel hogs and blasting crews. But with careful engineering a practicable route could be laid out.

Judah charged back to Dutch Flat, went to his headquarters at the drugstore of Dr. Daniel Strong, and, on a piece of paper that was laid atop a counter, drew up "The Articles of Association of the Central Pacific Railroad of California." He sold a few shares of stock to Strong, and left the doctor to solicit area residents (Strong peddled $46,500 worth of stock). Judah went chumming for bigger fish.

These he found early in 1861. After a number of fruitless talks with various San Francisco financiers, Judah called a meeting for a dozen prospective underwriters above a hardware store on K Street, Sacramento. Most noteworthy among them were Leland Stanford, a wealthy wholesale grocer and gubernatorial aspirant; Charles Crocker, a bull-shouldered adventurer who had made a quick pile in dry goods and now was looking for new, more exciting action; and the partners who owned the hardware store downstairs, Mark Hopkins and Collis Huntington. Hopkins was a quiet, sensible accountant, the inside man who kept the figures straight. Huntington, whom one observer later described as "a hard & cheery man, with no more soul than a shark," was a manipulator, a money raiser.

Ted Judah was quite shrewd that night. He rightly guessed that these local merchants would not go for any pie-in-the-sky scheme about a railroad to the Missouri. So for once he suppressed his dream and sold them on the fat, short-term profits to be had by monopolizing the traffic to Nevada's booming silver mines. Impressed, the merchants invested. Next morning a triumphant Judah told his wife at their Sacramento rooming house, "If you want to see the first work done on the Pacific Railroad, look out of your bedroom window; I am going to work there this afternoon, and I am going to have these men pay for it." Anna's somewhat sour rejoinder was, "It's about time somebody else helped."

The Central Pacific Railroad of California was officially incorporated on June 27, 1861. Its officers were Stanford, president; Huntington, vice president; Hopkins, treasurer; and Crocker, a director and chief of construction. By mid-September, Judah had completed his surveys for the line, and in early October the board resolved "that Mr. T. D. Judah, the Chief Engineer of this Company, proceed to Washington . . . for the purpose of procuring appropriations of land and U.S. Bonds from the Government, to aid in the construction of this road."

Lobbyist Judah found that the Civil War, now well in progress, was a distinct asset: there were no southern legislators around to wrangle over the route or to block the bill; besides, such a line would help hold California and Nevada Territory—and their gold and silver—in the Union. Thus, at last, on July 1, 1862, President Lincoln signed the Pacific Railroad Act; its provisions were generous enough for the most wild-eyed promoter.

The act specified that two companies would build the Pacific line. The Central would lay track to the California-Nevada border, and a new concern called the Union Pacific Railroad Company was to build west from Omaha. Federal aid would include a right-of-way strip and ten alternate land sections per mile of route, on both sides of the line, for the entire distance. Furthermore, the government would lend each company—in the form of low-interest thirty-year bonds—$16,000 per mile of track in flat country, $32,000 in intermediate terrain, and $48,000 in the mountains.

A happy Ted Judah wired Sacramento: "We have drawn the elephant. Now let us see if we can harness him up."

What Judah did not know was that, having planned the road and helped to guide the bill through Congress, he was no longer considered an asset by his colleagues in California. Crocker, Hopkins, Stanford, and particularly Huntington had decided that Judah was much too earnest—nay, passionate—an engineer to see that the real purpose of a transcontinental line was to make piles of money. He was bound to disapprove of their business methods—and sure enough, he did.

Stanford had been elected governor of California in 1861. By the freewheeling ethics of that era it was considered perfectly respectable for the governor to go right on being president of the Central Pacific as well. In his dual role, through some backroom arm twisting and by scattering money among voters on local bond issues, he managed to take in well over a million dollars in public money to help get the railroad moving. Judah was horrified.

Next, Huntington perceived that it was poor business to lay track at a base subsidy of $16,000 per mile if with a little imagination, the payment could be trebled. He got a team of geologists to swear that the Sierras began at the limit of alluvial soil just outside Sacramento, rather than twenty-two miles east at the foothills. President Lincoln, distracted by the war, agreed, and the money rolled in at $48,000 to the mile. Judah was scandalized.

Finally, the "Big Four" created a company called the Associates, later renamed the Credit & Finance Company. This dummy concern was to build the railroad—at exorbitant rates. The cronies were, in effect, hiring themselves with an eye to overcharging themselves and pocketing the overage. (The device worked magnificently: it was later estimated that the directors took the government and other investors for about $36,-000,000). The Associates were too much for Judah. He spoke his mind, and found himself excluded from a number of private conferences. After one such meeting the directors offered to buy him out for $100,000; alternatively, he was given the option of buying out the others if he could raise the money. Exhausted from six years of uninterrupted work and depressed with the turn of events, Judah once more boarded a steamer for the East, this time to look for backers who would buy the road for him. But he contracted yellow fever in Central America; carried ashore in New York, he was delirious for a week, and then, on November 2, 1863, he died. He was thirty-seven. Back in Sacramento the directors called a quick meeting to pass a resolution of sympathy for the widow. Then they got on with their business.

Before the act of 1862 was passed there had been no Union Pacific Company. Two and a half years later there still was not much of one. True, Durant had pasted together a company of which he was vice president, general manager, principal stockholder, and prime mover. In the best Central Pacific style, Durant had devised a holding company called the Crédit Mobilier, whose function was identical to that of the Central's Credit & Finance front.

By the spring of 1864, however, Durant had managed to lay not a single rail out of Omaha; but he did have some promising

*Thomas Durant (seated, third from left) and other directors of the Union Pacific*

schemes afoot. For instance, Durant gave the construction contract for the first 100 miles to a crony named Herbert Hoxie. Hoxie then assigned the contract to the Crédit Mobilier at $50,000 per mile. (The U.P.'s chief engineer, Peter A. Dey, had made an honest per-mile estimate of $30,000.) Hoxie received $10,000 worth of U.P. bonds for being the stooge, and the men of the Crédit Mobilier pocketed roughly $20,000 a mile on this particular deal.

Just as the Associates' manipulations had been the last straw for Ted Judah, so the Hoxie contract was the end for Dey. "I do not approve of the contract for building the first hundred miles from Omaha west," he noted in a terse resignation, "and I do not care to have my name so connected with the railroad that I shall appear to endorse the contract." Then to his friend Grenville Dodge he wrote, "I am giving up the best position this country has ever offered any man."

Durant now began to look for a chief engineer who could lay plenty of track in a hurry, handle huge gangs of hard-handed men in the field, fight Indians if necessary—and not worry about company finances. He didn't have to look far. In return for a salary of $10,000 plus a packet of Crédit Mobilier stock (in his wife's name), Grenville Dodge had the job. He also had a few tough words for Durant. "I will become chief engineer only on condition that I be given absolute control in the field," he said. "You are about to build a railroad through a country that has neither law nor order, and whoever heads the work . . . must be backed up. There must be no divided interests."

Though mildly set back, Durant was certain Dodge was the right man. He had surveyed all through Iowa and Nebraska and knew the land to the west. In 1859 Lincoln himself, visiting Nebraska, may have consulted Dodge about a possible route for the western road.

When the Civil War broke out, Dodge entered the Union army as a colonel, and eventually was promoted to major general on the basis of his fighting abilities and his work in rebuilding war-torn railroads. Reassigned to Missouri, he was ordered to pacify some of the more troublesome local Indians. With several troops of horse, he pacified so energetically that the Army nearly lost track of him. A wire attempting to locate Dodge was answered by a telegraph official: "Nobody knows where he is but everybody knows where he has been."

Earlier, in 1864, some quick-footed lobbying by Durant and Huntington had produced an amended Pacific Railroad Act. The land grants were doubled, and the government loans were switched from a first-mortgage to a second-mortgage basis. The railroads could now issue their own first-mortgage bonds. The gates were open for private investors. The government assumed all risks. It was the gravy train par excellence.

The stage was set for the actual driving of rails across the western half of the continent. Dodge wrote: "There was never any very great question, from an engineering point of view, where the line . . . going west from the Missouri River should be placed. The Lord had so constructed the country that any engineer who failed to take advantage of that great open road out of the Platte Valley, and then on to Salt Lake, would not have been fit to belong to the profession." There were, however, two major hazards: distance and Indians.

Dodge conquered distance by hiring a tough rail-laying boss named Jack Casement and his brother Dan. The Casements put together an ingenious train that functioned as an assembly line, and — along with the shanty town that attached itself to the train — was called Hell on Wheels by the men who worked it.

The leading unit of the Casement train was a rail-laden flatcar. Up ahead of it, grading crews levelled the roadbed and dropped the ties onto it. Beside the flatcar, ten "iron men," five for each 500-to-700-pound rail, pulled the iron from the car at the foreman's command, "Away she goes!" Then, at the word "Down," the rail boomed onto the ties with such precision that the track liners barely had to move it before the spikers and clampers fastened it into place. The flatcar also carried iron rods, steel bars, cable, rope, switchstands, and the like, as well as a complete blacksmith's shop at the rear.

The number of cars in the train could vary. A reporter from the Salt Lake City *Deseret News* described a twenty-two-unit version: the flatcar; a feed store and saddler's shop; a carpenter's shop and wash-house; two sleeping cars; two eating cars; a combined kitchen, counting room and telegrapher's car; a general store; seven more sleeping cars; two private cars (a kitchen and a parlor); another sleeper; a supply car; and two water cars.

*Some of the Central Pacific's Chinese laborers and their work train in the High*

So efficient was the Casement train and the supply system backing it up that from the outset, in the spring of 1866, the Union Pacific set a record by laying one mile of track a day. The pace was gradually stepped up to two and three and more in the final, frantic race with the Central.

As the construction crews moved west, they found to their considerable joy that they were being accompanied by a movable feast of gamblers, peddlers, and prostitutes, all eager to help them spend their money. These early camp followers posed no serious threat to the road's progress, but by the time the rails had reached Julesburg, Colorado Territory, the pleasure-mongers had been joined by a vicious auxiliary of pimps, bouncers, muggers, thieves, and gun-slingers. "Watchfires gleam over the sea-like expanse of ground outside the city," wrote one correspondent, "while inside soldiers, herdsmen, teamsters, women, railroad men are dancing, singing, or gambling. I verily believe that there are men here who would murder a fellow creature for

*Sierras. Their stoic efficiency during the terrible winters surprised everyone.*

five dollars. Nay, there are men who have already done it, and who stalk abroad in daylight unwhipped of justice."

"These women," he reported of the Julesburg bawds, "are expensive articles, and come in for a large share of the money wasted. In broad daylight they may be seen gliding through the streets carrying fancy derringers slung to their waist."

Gambling, wenching, and drinking were one thing, but shooting and knifing would not do: good track hands were too hard to find. Dodge ordered a cleanup, and Jack Casement, passing out rifles to a picked group of his toughest ironmen, walked slowly through town one summer night. Soon afterward General Dodge inquired, "Are the gamblers quiet and behaving?"

"You bet they are, General," said Casement. "They're out there in the graveyard."

Cleanups had to be repeated at Cheyenne and Laramie, and once more at Corinne, Utah.

Farther west, Union Pacific workers ran into Indian trouble. Several small advance parties of grading crews were bushwhacked. In another raid an engine was derailed and the crew trapped, tomahawked, and tossed into the flaming wreckage. Occasionally a lone meat hunter or a careless stroller was scalped. But the Indians didn't always win. One bold but not particularly bright party of braves tried to capture an iron horse alive. Taking a forty-foot leather rope that their medicine man had infused with magic, two braves lay on either side of the track, the rope slack as an engine approached. When the locomotive was a few yards away the Indians leaped up and strained against the medicine rope. The two closest to the tracks were swept under the wheels, and the others limped home with their bruises.

Occasionally Dodge, who had a dramatic flair, issued such ringing pronouncements as, "We've got to clean the damn Indians out or give up building the Union Pacific," but the fact was that the Indian trouble was more terrifying in the telling than in the fighting. The majority of Casement's more than one thousand men were mustered-out Confederate soldiers—among the best bushfighters the country had ever known. They were supplemented by a force of ham-handed Irish ironmen, freed slaves, and a fair number of just plain tough characters from the slums of eastern cities. On the few occasions when the Indians tried to hit the main work force they were beaten off easily, with little or no damage to the railroad.

While the work of road building continued, the work of money-making more than kept pace. The Hoxie contract remained in effect for the first 247 westward miles of track. It was superseded for the next 667 by the so-called Ames contract. Oakes Ames was a member of the Crédit Mobilier, brother of the president of the Union Pacific—and a United States representative from Massachusetts. Ames was to assign the contract to a group of men (brother Oliver among them) representing the Crédit Mobilier.

Actually, the first 228 miles of trackage under the Ames contract had already been laid, at a per-mile *cost* of $27,500. Nonetheless, the contract specified per-mile *payments*—by the Union Pacific to the Crédit Mobilier—of $43,500. The Crédit Mobilier, then, had realized a profit of $3,648,000 on the Ames contract even while the ink on it was drying.

The fact that Oakes Ames was a member of Congress was a great help, since it allowed him to distribute juicy chunks of Crédit Mobilier securities "where they will do the most good"— among his legislative peers. The securities went to such friends of the Union Pacific as Speaker of the House (and Vice President-to-be under Grant) Schuyler Colfax, to Representative (and future presidential nominee) James G. Blaine, and to Representative (and future President) James A. Garfield. A score of others were implicated.

The kited profits from the Ames contract and succeeding arrangements have been estimated at anywhere from fourteen to fifty million dollars. Durant should have been content to let more than enough alone. But he began tampering with Dodge's road building, trying to make the route longer to get even more subsidy money. Dodge would have none of it, and one day shouted down Durant in front of the men. "You are now going to learn," Dodge bellowed, "that the men working for the Union Pacific will take orders from me and not from you. If you interfere there will be trouble—trouble from the government, from the Army, and from the men themselves."

Scraping up a pile of evidence on what he considered incompetence and nonfeasance, Durant gambled on an official showdown. The referee was none other than General U. S. Grant, Republican nominee for President.

On July 26, 1868, at Fort Sanders in Wyoming Territory, Grant heard the two men out. Durant charged that Dodge had selected a poor route, had wasted money, and had failed to get the line to Salt Lake. Grant said, "What about it, Dodge?"

"Just this," said Dodge. "If Durant or anybody connected with the Union Pacific, or anybody connected with the government changes my lines I'll quit the road."

Grant pondered, then spoke again, slowly. "The government expects the railroad company to meet its obligations. And the government expects General Dodge to remain with the road as its chief engineer until it is completed."

That was plain enough. Durant leaped up, stuck out his hand to his chief engineer, and said heartily, "I withdraw my objections. We all want Dodge to stay with the road."

Out in California the Central Pacific had had an entirely different set of problems. Once Judah was out of the way there was little but harmony within the line's management. The Indians were no trouble at all—Crocker kept them happy by handing the chiefs passes to ride the day coaches and by letting the braves hitchhike on freight cars. The terrain, however, was another matter. The rugged defiles of the Sierras had killed off hundreds of pioneers; they claimed hundreds of railroad laborers before the Central got through.

The man chosen to lead the assault on the Sierras was Charley Crocker, who noted modestly that he "grew up as a sort of leader." (Later he would boast, "I built the Central Pacific.") Of all the people who had a hand in its building, Crocker certainly

*In July, 1868, at Fort Sanders, Wyoming, Republican presidential nominee U. S.*

was the most colorful. Roaring up and down the grade cease-
lessly, bragging, bullying, paying the men from a bag of gold coins
slung from his saddle, Crocker drove the track layers toward the
summit passes. Yet, amid all this energy would come sudden
lapses into complete torpor. Flat on his back, with a Chinese
manservant fanning him with a branch, he would not speak, get
up, or even do paper work. Then, just as abruptly, he would be
back in the saddle, full of bombast and shouting profane orders.

But the Central was having labor troubles. In the spring and
summer of 1865 roughly ninety per cent of the white workers
who had signed on in San Francisco deserted after a week or so
at railhead — they had been looking for a free ride toward the
gold and silver mines of the Sierras. Crocker considered replac-
ing them with Mexican peons but finally brought in a trial batch
of fifty Chinese from San Francisco. The other Central directors
protested the scheme, and the remaining American laborers
hooted at the tiny, pig-tailed coolies, most of them under five
feet in height and averaging 110 pounds, padding along in their
floppy blue cotton trousers.

The Chinese ignored the jibes, silently pecking at the grade
with their shovels and wheeling away earth in modest barrow-
loads. At the end of the first day, to the embarrassment of the
regular hands, the Chinese grade was smoother and the work-
line farther advanced than any of the others. Better yet, instead
of getting drunk, fighting, and generally disrupting the camp in

*Grant (standing under bird cage) settled the quarrel between Dodge and Durant.*

the evening, the Chinese carefully bathed with buckets of hot water, boiled their tea and rice, and then retired to pray, read, or smoke opium.

Crocker ordered up another group of Chinese, then another; by the winter of 1866-67 there were more than 2,000 Orientals in the Central work force. As the going got tougher so did the Chinese. These men were, as Crocker had maintained from the outset, descended from the people who built the Great Wall; the matter of building a rail line over the Sierras, at the cost of a few hundred lives, was barely to be noticed in the great scheme of things.

When the line hit a sheer wall of rock thirteen miles from the summit, the Chinese wove baskets of reeds, lowered themselves down the sides of the precipice to plant nitroglycerin charges, and then hauled quickly up the rock face while the nitro blew.

Crocker decided against using a steam drill on the summit tunnel because his one steam-power machine was already being used to hoist blasted rock. So the coolies stoically burrowed down through twenty-foot snowdrifts to chip away with hand chisels. They worked week after week in the frozen gloom of the shafts; sometimes progress was no more than eight inches a day through the solid granite.

In the fall of 1866 Crocker had come to feel that the Central's slow progress was giving the U.P. a big advantage in the race for mileage (and government subsidies), so he decided to bypass the unfinished summit tunnel and try to lay track down the eastern slope of the Sierras before spring. Teams of five hundred Chinese hitched themselves to enormous log sleds and hauled three locomotives, forty cars, and enough iron for forty miles of track through the blizzards of the High Sierra. Avalanches swept through the work camps, carrying whole bunkhouses full of men to death in canyon bottoms; the Chinese offered quiet prayers, and waited for spring to retrieve their dead. The phrase "Not a Chinaman's chance" was coined that terrible winter. It was just as applicable the next.

At last, by May 4, 1868, the Central's rails reached the Truckee River at the Nevada border. The Sierra ordeal was over. There remained the safe though still arduous business of racing eastward to beat the U.P. out of as many $32,000 miles as possible. Since the government had never bothered to specify a meeting point, Crocker and the Casement boys spurred ahead.

*Cutting ties at the start of the Echo Canyon bore in northeastern Utah. The tunnel was 1,100 feet long, the longest along the Union Pacific's section of track.*

When they came to rivers or ravines, both Central and U.P. gangs threw up sometimes flimsy trestles, promising to finish the job later. At the few remaining tunnel sites, they carved out hasty bypasses and rushed on. Through the final winter of 1868-69, they flung down track on snow and even across river ice. At one point Dodge laid rail on a frozen stream bank so narrow and precarious that the track, together with an entire train, slid off into the water.

When the tracks finally approached each other on the great curve around the northern end of Great Salt Lake, the grading crews—working as much as 150 miles ahead of the ironmen—began to carve parallel roadbeds within sight of each other. The directors of both lines gleefully collected their separate fees of $32,000 per mile for duplicate work that proceeded for nearly two hundred miles.

In early April of 1869 President Grant informed Dodge that he had had enough of the nonsense and would do his best to withhold future bonds if the U.P. and the Central could not

*The Union Pacific's wooden frame bridge at Dale Creek, Wyoming, cost $200,000.*

agree on a junction point. Dodge, Durant, and Huntington conferred. The Central agreed to stop at Promontory if the Union Pacific would sell its trackage thence east to Ogden. That was mutually acceptable, and Congress approved the agreement by joint resolution.

Even with the meeting place set and the money virtually counted, the rivals seemed unable to stop battling. U.P. crews had, at one point, set a one-day's trackage record of eight and a half miles. Crocker, who could not stand to be beaten, is said to have boasted that the Central could lay ten. Durant allegedly bet $10,000 against it. On April 29 a handpicked gang of Crocker's men did indeed lay 3,520 rails, with 55,000 spikes and 14,080 bolts, from sunup to sundown (including a brief lunch break) for ten miles and two hundred feet.

But the two U.P. officials had more to worry about than wagering.

The day before the record was set Durant was kidnapped from his special train by workers striking for back pay. Dodge had to scramble to obtain nearly a million dollars from back East to placate the angry track hands.

On May 7 it began to rain, and for the next two and a half days it poured. Officers from each company squished through the mud to champagne parties in the various rail cars that had pulled in for the spike-driving ceremony. The track hands, meanwhile, were getting drunk in Promontory's ramshackle saloons.

And then, on the tenth, the rails met, and Stanford swung his futile swing. In San Francisco young Bret Harte, editor of the *Overland Monthly*, jotted down a poem for use in his next editorial:

> *What was it the engines said,*
> *Pilots touching, head to head,*
> *Facing on a single track,*
> *Half a world behind each back?*

What they may have said was that this was one hell of a way to build a railroad. For in addition to all the haste, waste, and thievery, two of the reasons for rushing ahead with the road had evaporated — and a third was yet to come into being. In 1869 the Suez Canal opened, scrapping the European-Oriental trade route scheme. The Civil War had ended long since, and with it the serious North-South rivalry for political domination of the

West. Third, although a railroad had indeed crossed the great American desert, there was precious little freight and passenger traffic. "Building railroads from nowhere to nowhere at public expense is not a legitimate enterprise," rumbled Cornelius Vanderbilt.

Not a great many years after the line was completed, the Union Pacific was sometimes hauling one lone passenger a day; and ultimately it ended up in receivership. By 1872 the stench from Crédit Mobilier had finally become too much even for Congress; an investigation led to a vote of censure for Oakes Ames, and left spatterings of mud that could never be expunged from the coat-tails of the others involved.

But despite everything — the financial flop, the congressional scandal, the misplaced hopes for an Oriental trade route, the travail of the building work, the blizzards, raids, gunfights, and interminable wrangling — two decades after the line was completed, a continent had been transformed. The Indians, pushed

*Parallel to the railroad tracks, a town of tents and wooden shacks sprang up at*

back and hemmed in now by rail-borne troops carrying repeating rifles and Gatling guns, began to sink into the despair of their impoverished reservations. The buffalo, too, were doomed by the railroad. Forever after the high plains and mountains would belong to the white man.

By 1880 three more lines had crossed to the Pacific, and parts of the prairie bloomed into food-growing regions as lush as any in the world. Desert shanty towns touched by track were transformed into shining cities. Boston and Philadelphia now dined on Colorado beef, and fresh-caught Pacific salmon became a delicacy in Minneapolis. Chicago grew to be the world's busiest railhead, and America was becoming the most powerful industrial nation the world had ever seen. As one Gilded Age President put it for an audience at Hudson College in New York: "The railway is the greatest centralizing force of modern times." And President James Garfield was something of an authority on the value of railroads.

*Promontory, Utah, where the Union Pacific and the Central Pacific railroads met.*

*The most dramatic moment in the Battle of Beecher Island, from a 1901 painting*

# "DON'T
# LET THEM
# RIDE OVER US"

By GEORGE M. HEINZMAN

For five days, beginning September 17, 1868, a party of fifty frontier scouts under the command of Major George A. Forsyth held off an estimated four hundred to one thousand Cheyenne, Sioux, and Arapaho warriors on a small sand island in the nearly dry Arikaree fork of the Republican River in eastern Colorado. The island was later named Beecher Island, in honor of Lieutenant Frederick H. Beecher, a nephew of Henry Ward Beecher, who died there in one of the most dramatic battles ever fought between Indians and white men.

Less than a year before, in October, 1867, more than two thousand Comanches, Kiowas, Cheyennes, and Arapahoes had gathered on Medicine Lodge Creek in southern Kansas and had held a conference with a United States government peace commission.

By terms of the Medicine Lodge treaty, those tribes were denied their ancestral lands and were assigned to reservations south of the Kansas state line, though they were permitted to roam north of it to hunt. Congress did not ratify the treaty until July, 1868, however, delaying food, clothing, and other supplies that had been promised to the Indians.

During August of 1868 Cheyennes and Arapahoes as well as Sioux from the north began raiding along the Saline and Solomon rivers in Kansas and attacked the Smoky Hill road in Kansas and Colorado, killing over 100 settlers. They captured at least a dozen women and children, and burned more than a score of ranches.

The slashing August raids called for fast retaliation, but General Philip H. Sheridan, commanding the Department of the Missouri, was short of troops. In the emergency he decided to organize a scouting party of fifty civilian volunteers to track down and engage the roving marauders and, if possible, head them back to Indian Territory. When Major Forsyth, who was on General Sheridan's staff, asked for an active command, "Little Phil" put him in charge of recruiting and leading the scouts.

Forsyth, only thirty years old, had participated in sixteen pitched battles and sixty minor engagements of the Civil War. He had been an aide-de-camp to General Sheridan, who had told Secretary of War Stanton that Forsyth was one of the bravest men in the war.

Forsyth recruited his men at Fort Harker and Fort Hays, Kansas, arming them with Colt revolvers and seven-shot Spencer repeating rifles. With Lieutenant Beecher, another regular, as his second-in-command, he headed west from Fort Hays on August 29. Many of his fifty scouts were plainsmen wise in the ways of the Indians—traders, trappers, buffalo hunters, government scouts—but some were merely young drifters. About half had served in the Civil War, coming from both the Union and Confederate armies. They were at Fort Wallace in western Kansas when Indians attacked a wagon train nearby, killing two teamsters and running off some stock. Forsyth and his men (who called their commander "Colonel," his Civil War brevet rank) at once set out after the raiders. Fortunately, several of the scouts later wrote accounts of this expedition, and we can trace in their own words the course of the battle that followed.

SCOUT JOHN HURST: As soon as the news of the killing reached Fort Wallace we started in pursuit with six days' rations. We found their trail . . . but soon lost it on account of the Indians scattering, as they generally do, when they do not want to be followed. We kept travelling north, as that was the direction the trail went as far as we found it. . . . the morning of the fourth day we found a small trail running up the [Republican] river which we followed until evening. . . . Next morning we started on the trail, which kept enlarging, and soon we discovered the trail of the lodge poles; then we knew that they had their families with them. The lodge poles are strapped on each side of the ponies, one end dragging on the ground, and their movables are fastened to the poles behind the ponies.

SCOUT LOUIS MCLOUGHLIN: It was evidently a large body of Indians; some estimated that there must be four of five hundred lodges, and that would mean nearly a thousand warriors. . . .

*Major George A. Forsyth, commander of the fifty defenders of Beecher Island*

Some wanted to get out in the night and try to reach Fort Wallace, as there did not seem to be much show of [our] little band ever getting away from the immense body of Indians, but the Colonel, believing that the Indians were concentrating to make a great raid on the settlements, decided to throw his little band between them and the settlements. . . . and hold them or cripple them so that they would give up the raid.

HURST: . . . we went into camp early on the north side of what we thought was the south branch of the Republican River, but which proved to be Arickaree Creek. It was a beautiful place opposite a small island.

SCOUT SIGMAN SCHLESINGER: . . . on September 16, 1868, Colonel Forsyth decided to camp on a spot that [had] good grazing, much earlier [in the afternoon] than usual. [This] proved to be an act of providence. Had we travelled about a half mile further we would have fallen into an ambush, ingeniously prepared . . . so that had we passed that way not a mother's son would have escaped alive, but we were ignorant of the fact at that time.

SCOUT ELI ZIGLER: . . . we unsaddled our horses and picketed them out to graze, and built our fires and went to rustling our suppers. . . . about dusk . . . we saw a signal light go up south of us . . . and then we saw more go up in different directions, so we were pretty certain we would have more for breakfast than we

*This early photograph shows a band of Plains Indians staging an attack. Major*

had for supper. . . . the Colonel put on more guards that night and ordered us to be ready at any moment. . . . and as my horse and Mr. Culver's were picketed out close to the river, we took our blankets and went out close to our horses and spread them down.

. . . they came a little earlier than we had expected them and woke us up. I heard the first whoop they gave, but I was so sleepy I thought it was a flock of geese; just then the guards fired. I gave a jump and said to Culver, "They are here!"

As we were dressed and our revolvers and cartridge boxes buckled on and our carbines lying by our sides we were ready for action. . . . It was not hardly daylight yet, but we . . . could see the flash of their guns. Culver and I made for our horses as they rode by; they were whooping and yelling and shouting and shaking their blankets to make a stampede.

HURST: Colonel Forsyth gave orders to saddle up, which we did, and were standing by our horses . . . when some of the men got permission to drive off some Indians that were hiding behind rocks on the side hill north of us. When they got onto the high ground they shouted to us to look up the creek, and by this time the Indians were in full view, and such a picture! All were mounted on their war horses, in war costume, with feathers and plumes flying, shouting war whoops, their horses running at full speed and seeming to have partaken of the spirit of the fray. . . . We . . . knew that we would be no match for that army of red

*Forsyth and his volunteer frontier scouts set out to retaliate for such raids.*

men, in the open, and as we were close by the small island . . .
Forsyth gave orders . . . to move onto the island.

McLoughlin: The island was about three feet above the level of
the sandy bed of the creek and was about 40 feet wide and 150
feet long. The upper end was covered with high blue stem grass
and small cottonwood trees, none larger than six inches in diam-
eter. The dry channel of the creek was about 70 feet wide on
each side of the island.

Hurst: We made a grand rush for the island, without order,
and tied our horses to the trees. Some ran across to the south
side and crouched down in the long grass . . . and were hardly
located when the Indians were charging through us. Comrade
Armstrong was close by my right, and another comrade on my
left, each one by a tree. John Stillwell and his party were on the
east end of the island, and Jack Donovan and his party were on
the west end, and some were in the central part, all pretty well
hid, and all [were] shooting when the Indians came in close
range. . . . Our bullets coming from all directions seemed to be-
wilder them.

A warrior coming from the north almost ran over me, and
would have but for his horse shying to one side, which saved me.
It rather surprised me, as my attention was directed toward the
south. . . . as he rode straight away from me I had a good chance
to shoot. . . . I think I must have hit him. . . .

Armstrong and the other comrade were both wounded . . . I
was afraid the Indians would get between me and the other men.
. . . Soon [I] saw an Indian creeping through the grass toward
our horses. . . . Well, I did not want to be scalped out there on
the island alone, so fired at the Indian . . . and without waiting to
see the effect of my shot jumped up and ran to where some of
the comrades were located. Some had dug holes and made banks
of sand around them, and some were using the dead horses for
protection, and so I dropped down beside an unoccupied dead
horse and went to digging. . . . While I was busy digging,
Comrades McCall and Culver came in . . . and went to work
digging. . . .

Comrades inside the circle shouted, "If you fellows on the
outside don't get up and shoot, the Indians will be charging us."

McCall and Culver got up to look for Indians to shoot, and
some sharpshooter fired at their exposed heads. The bullet

grazed McCall's neck, stunning him, and hit Culver in the head, killing him.

ZIGLER: I saw George Clark and Farley and a couple of others running across the river; they got behind a bank on the north side, so I thought that would be a good place to go. As I started, the Indians made a charge down through that way so I had to stop. I stopped where there was a little bunch of brush and a few horses tied; some of the horses were hit by the flying bullets and commenced charging and jumping, so I had to get away from there. . . . Just then the Colonel saw me . . . he said, "You can come with me, I want you around on this side."

We went a few steps toward the east; the Indians were making another heavy charge. . . . we got down on our knees. . . . As we shot a time or two I heard something strike and the Colonel said, "I'm shot," and put his hand on his leg. . . . He turned over a time or two and said, "I am shot again." . . . the first chance we got, we carried him farther in, near the center of the bunch.

*Later in the day, Forsyth sustained a third wound when a bullet grazed his head. Though he was unaware of it at the time, that bullet fractured his skull. On the fourth day of the fight, the ball in his right thigh became so painful that he removed it himself with a razor.*

ZIGLER: About the time I had dug a hole that I could partly lie in, I heard [Henry] Tucker say, "I'm shot through the arm and I would like to have someone tie this handkerchief around it to stop the blood."

John Haley was nearer to him . . . but before he got it tied, a bullet struck him. I told [Tucker] to come over where I was. . . . We lay facing each other. He wanted me to draw the handkerchief pretty tight . . . and just before I got done tying the knot . . . I felt an arrow strike me on the upper part of my right leg. Looking down, I saw the arrow had passed through Tucker's left leg above the knee. . . . I examined the arrow and found that just part of the steel had come through. Tucker asked me to pull it back, so I pulled once; it was very painful to him . . . and I could not move it. I then took hold of the point of the arrowhead that was sticking through his leg, and with the other hand hit the feather end of the arrow and drove it through. After tying the arrow wound, I left him . . . thinking I might yet get across the river, but just as I came to where Jack Donovan was lying behind a little bunch of grass, with a little sand thrown up around, he said, "You stop here. One of us can dig while the other shoots and we will soon have a hole big enough for both of us."

HURST: . . . Comrade Burke then came in and dug a hole near by us and kept digging until he came to water. He filled his canteen and passed it over to the next, and so on . . . until all in reach had been supplied. . . . Burke then told us his experience. He had crawled along [toward an Indian] until he reached a hummock, and raising himself, almost bumped noses with the Indian and it so surprised him that he . . . punched his gun at [the Indian] and shouted, "Booh!" and ran for us. He said he thought the Indian ran the other way, as he did not hear him shoot. . . .

. . . two warriors had been shot by Louis Farley as he lay on the north bank with a broken leg. They were in full view of him as they crept along a ridge of sand made by the water where it divided to go around the island. Both were shot through the head. . . . This had an intimidating effect on the rest and so stopped that mode of warfare.

*Frank Harrington and George Clark were on the north bank with Farley from early morning until after dark, and though they were all wounded, they did not cease firing. Several times the Indians rode over them. Harrington was wounded by an arrow in the forehead over the left eye. Clark, who lay next to him, tried to remove it but could not. Shortly afterwards a bullet hit a little above the arrow, cutting through the skin, but not fracturing the skull; it came so near that it knocked the arrow loose.*

McLOUGHLIN: The Indians expected to get the scouts in a very short time and kept charging in a circle. With short intervals they charged on every side at the same time. They expected the scouts would fire all their shots and when they stopped to load would ride onto them and slaughter them. The Indians nearly all rode on the opposite side of their horse and shot under their necks.

The scouts were all good shots and the slaughter of the Indians and their horses was terrible. . . . Two or three times if the Indians had kept on a minute or two longer they would have got us, as sometimes we would hardly have a shot left when they broke. Finally . . . about half of them crept up all around [us] as close as they could get shelter and commenced to sharpshooting, and the rest kept charging.

. . . we dug holes in the sand. In the meantime, they shot our horses down. . . . At this time Wilson and Culver were dead, Lieutenant Beecher and Surgeon Mooers were mortally wounded, the Colonel was shot through the thigh and the ankle. About seventeen of the men were wounded, some severely. Louis Farley was mortally wounded, and he died nine days later.

*Spurred on by confidence that great magic protected him against harm, the Cheyenne warrior Roman Nose had often acted with extraordinary fearlessness during battle. He believed, though, that his special "medicine" could be destroyed if his food was touched by iron after being cooked. Shortly before the battle, the warrior had visited the lodge of a Sioux chief where he was served food that his host's wife had lifted with an iron fork. Roman Nose had eaten before he discovered what had happened, and the battle at Beecher Island had begun before he could go through a purification ritual. Believing that without the protection of his magic he faced certain death, Roman Nose entered the battle only after much urging by his men. Scout McLoughlin described what happened in the first charge Roman Nose led:*

About noon a large body under Roman Nose formed out of gunshot in the stream and charged us. There must have been 700 or 800 of them. Roman Nose himself led the charge. Just as they got to the upper end of the island he was mortally wounded, and we poured such a terrible fire into them that they broke and scattered. That was the last charge they made that amounted to anything.

*McLoughlin's estimate of numbers involved in the charge is probably high. Others have estimated the Indian force at four to six hundred.*

SCOUT SIG SCHLESINGER: As the fighting progressed, it began to tell on us. Every once in a while the cry went up that this one, or that one, was hit. . . . I have often been asked whether I have killed any Indians, to which my answer must truthfully be that I don't know. . . . I did not consider it safe to watch the results of a shot. . . . [I took] general observation by suddenly jumping up and dropping back into my hole, which enabled me to take a shot . . . without undue exposure and yet be in touch with the general situation. Several times [I saw] two horsemen drag a body away between them. I saw bodies of Indians both on foot and horseback coming toward us. These I considered good targets. . . .

In the south channel of the dry creek was a tree trunk. . . . From this stump came many shots, to the annoyance of Lou McLoughlin and myself. McLoughlin was wounded. . . . I employed my tactics of suddenly going up in the air and firing at the stump. After several shots, the sniping . . . ceased.

An Indian, evidently a chief [was] standing on a high elevation a little south by west of our position, talking loudly and giving commands. He was in sight of all of us. Grover, who was in the next pit east of ours, and next to Colonel Forsyth, interpreted to us the chief's orders, stating that he wanted his young bucks to persist in charging, as we had only a handful of cartridges. Grover yelled back at the chief in his language to "send on the bucks, that we each have a hat full which we will give them."

*The Cheyenne battle leader Roman Nose was mortally wounded at Beecher Island.*

ZIGLER: About dark . . . one of the party came from across the river and said the rest were alive but badly wounded; we went over and found them. Farley's leg was badly broken and we carried him over.

We first cared for the wounded the best we could and then . . . built small fires in the rifle pits and then went to the [dead] horses and cut off small pieces and roasted them. . . . After supper we held a council. . . . We thought our best show was to try to send a dispatch to Fort Wallace. It looked almost impossible to get out, but Jack Stillwell came forward and volunteered to go if they would let him pick a man to go with him. . . . [He] chose Pierre Trudeau . . . and as Pierre was older and a good Indian fighter, the Colonel agreed. . . . The Colonel then wrote a dispatch to Fort Wallace. Jack was the best imitator of an Indian I ever saw, so they fixed themselves up as Indians as best they could and took off their boots and tied on some rags and blankets on their feet so that if Indians saw their tracks next day they would think it some of their own party and not follow them. . . . We . . . roasted them some horse meat, enough to last three or four days. . . . At a late hour they . . . crawled out. We listened, expecting to hear them run into some Indians and fire, but we heard nothing. The next thing in order was to fix our rifle pits. We had been keeping in our holes as much as possible; we commenced digging to one another so as to connect them all together and by working hard all night we got all connected together and enlarged our hospital, as we called it.

[They came early]—just before the sun rose. It seemed to me that there were just as many . . . as the first day. . . . Our orders were about the same, "Hold your fire till they get close, but don't let them ride over us."

It seemed to me that the Indians were more determined than ever to get us out, as they charged in from every direction, and it seemed to take more than one volley to stop them. . . . When we summed up the [second] day's work, we had one man killed and one wounded, so we got off easy from a hard day's fighting and I think we broke their backbone that day. We heard nothing from Stillwell and Trudeau and fearing they had not succeeded in getting through [two more] attempted to go out the second night, and after having been gone three hours returned saying they could not get through the Indians' line. The [third] morning about daylight a smaller party of Indians charged down on us.

There were not as many as the other two mornings. We laid low and let them come close; then we raised up and gave them a couple of volleys and started them back. . . . They continued their fight all day but not as strong, I did not think, as it had been the other two days.

. . . we still did not believe that Stillwell and Trudeau had got through, [so that night] Jack Donovan and A. J. Pliley said they would try it again. The Colonel . . . wrote another dispatch. They fixed themselves up to imitate the Indians, [and] . . . we cut them off some of that poor, rotten horse meat.

ZIGLER: [Fourth day] Our horses lay just where they were shot down the first day, and were getting pretty badly spoiled and the smell was not very pleasant, but our appetites were good so we made out a fair breakfast. . . . We got our supper from the same source, only now it was a little more tender. [Fifth day] Our breakfast . . . still came from the same place, and was getting very tender by this time.

HURST: The Indians left us after the fifth day. . . . We had nothing then but our horses that had been dead six days, and when we would cut into the meat we found it had green streaks through it and was fast decaying. . . . [We sprinkled] it with [gun] powder while it was cooking, which partially took away the bad odor, but we could only eat it when we were starving.

. . . our systems cried out for [salt]. One of the men found a small piece of pork rind in his haversack and chewed it until he thought he had all the good out of it and spit it out; when another comrade took it up and chewed it for a while and spit it out, and then I took it and chewed it up and thought it tasted delicious on account of the salt.

*The action of the Indians in breaking off the siege is readily understood in light of the fact that the Plains Indian loved the fast hit-and-run fight, the raid, and had little stomach for a long siege, particularly after suffering a few casualties. But Forsyth had no way of knowing how many of his attackers might still be lingering in the vicinity, waiting to finish off his command. His horses were dead, he had no food, and if he moved out he would have to do so on foot, slowed down by the burden of his wounded. It seemed more sensible to stay where he was, hoping that at least one of his messengers had gotten through and that relief was on the way.*

UNKNOWN SCOUT: On the evening of the sixth day our leader called us to him. How gray and drawn his face looked in the shadowy gray light, but his eyes were clear, and his voice was steady.

"Boys, we've got to the end of our rope now." [He pointed to the low hills.] "Over there the Indian wolves are waiting for us . . . but we needn't all be sacrificed. . . . To stay here means you all know what. Now, the men who can go, must leave us to what's coming. I feel sure now that you can get through together somehow, for the tribes are scattering. It is only the remnant left over there to burn us out at last. There is no reason why you should stay here and die. Make your dash for escape tonight. . . ."

When the response came, it was: "It's no use asking us, Colonel. We have fought together, and, by heaven, we'll die together."

ZIGLER: [Sixth day] [The] sour horse meat was so rotten and alive with maggots we thought we would try to find some game . . . so we rustled out a little and found nothing but prickly pears. We lingered along on our old butcher shop until the eighth night. [Ninth day] I went to the old slaughter house and after looking over several, I found them all of the same material and price, so I cut off a slice and laid it on the coals and roasted it and ate it. [Fletcher Villot and I] took our guns and started north across the river [to hunt]. . . . [Fletch] looked way over to the south on the far hills, and asked, "What is that?"

I said, "That's some rock." We sat there talking a few moments; my eye caught an object on the far hills. "There is something moving out there," I said.

We jumped to our feet and walked up the hill a little farther, where we could plainly see that they were coming over the hill toward us. . . . We fired a [warning] shot . . . and hurried back to camp to make ready in case it was Indians.

"I think it is the relief," the Colonel said. "But get the men all in, and we will be ready for anything." I thought there were two of the boys out of sight around the hill to the south of us, so I went across that way.

HURST: . . . the ninth day I went out to the [prairie] dog town [we had found the day before], but [again] no dog came out. . . . I began to think I would starve to death, and was having the blues pretty bad when I started back for camp. I had not gotten

*The Indians of the Plains were among the world's most skillful horsemen, and*

*their resistance to white settlement long made them a danger to reckon with.*

far when . . . some of my comrades . . . motioned to me to come to them, and the thought that Indians were coming took possession of me and I started to run as fast as I could, but soon got tired and thought they would surely get me before I could make camp, so I thought I might as well die fighting, and turned around and sank down on the ground and saw three horsemen coming directly toward me. . . . the closer they came the more they looked like white men.

ZIGLER: In a short while I saw a man at full gallop. When he got a little closer . . . it was my old friend, Jack Peate. He asked, "How are the rest of the boys?" and I said, "Have you got anything to eat?"

[Peate] reached into his saddle pockets and brought me out a hardtack and a little piece of bacon. . . . Then he put spurs to his horse and rode on to the island. When I got there the boys were laughing and cheering and the tears were running down their cheeks and Peate said that Donovan was coming . . . and Colonel Carpenter and his command. . . .

*Forsyth's hopes had proved well-founded. Stillwell and Trudeau had gotten through to Fort Wallace, and the commanding officer there sent word to Cheyenne Wells, about 100 miles from Forsyth's position, where a company of the 10th U.S. Cavalry under Lieutenant Colonel Louis H. Carpenter was on patrol. Jack Peate was one of Forsyth's scouts who through a mixup in orders had been left behind when the main body moved out. Now he was temporarily attached to Carpenter's command, which headed immediately to Forsyth's relief. On the way, quite by accident, the troopers ran into Donovan, who, with Pliley, had also reached Fort Wallace and was returning to the Arikaree with a group of scouts.*

SCOUT JACK PEATE: Crowned king nor conquering general ne'er received so royal and hearty a welcome as I did when I rode into that island among those staunch-hearted men, who lifted me from my horse, embraced me, and strong men though they were, wept, as cheer upon cheer arose. . . . All had that wolfish, haggard look on their countenances which indicates hunger. . . . None of the wounds had been properly dressed, as the doctor had been killed in the battle. A terrible stench from the dead horses, which lay where they had fallen, filled the air. . . .

Louis Farley was the most desperately wounded, and died that night after his shattered leg had been amputated. . . . Blood poisoning had already commenced in [Colonel] Forsyth's wounds and had medical attention been delayed twenty-four hours, he could not have lived.

TROOPER REUBEN WALLER: Jack Stillwell brought us word of the fix that Beecher was in . . . and in 26 hours [actually about 48 hours — G.M.H.], Colonel Carpenter and myself, as his hostler, rode into the rifle pits. And what a sight we saw . . . wounded and dead men in the midst of 50 dead horses, that had lain in the hot sun for [nine] days. And these men had eaten the putrid flesh of those dead horses for eight days. . . . we began to feed the men from our haversacks. If the doctor had not arrived in time we would have killed them all by feeding them to death. . . . Sure, we never gave a thought that it would hurt them. . . .

The Battle of Beecher Island, one of the finest stands against long odds by a small force, was not a key fight in the Indian wars. The scouts sustained losses of five killed and eighteen wounded. George Bird Grinnell, in *The Fighting Cheyennes*, wrote that in later years the Indians could identify only nine warriors killed. Other estimates have placed their losses as high as four or five hundred. Forsyth officially reported that he counted thirty-two dead Indians, and was later told by a Brulé Sioux, who participated in the battle, that there were seventy-five killed. The truth probably lies between these latter two figures.

After Beecher Island General Sheridan abandoned his idea of using civilians to bring peace to the plains. But he was still confronted with the problem of marauding Indians, and decided that the only way to pin down the elusive foe was to hit him in his winter camps, where he would lose his advantage of mobility. Accordingly, the General organized a campaign against the large bands wintering in Indian Territory — now Oklahoma. George Custer's 7th Cavalry struck the first blow in a surprise attack on Black Kettle's camp of Cheyennes on the Washita River at dawn, November 29, 1868. His orders from Sheridan had been to hang any warriors not killed in battle, to take prisoner all women and children, to destroy all lodges and supplies, and to kill all ponies. Custer carried out these instructions with a relish. The engagement at Washita River was followed by other punitive measures, and by the following spring most of the Indians of the central plains had been brought under control. But as George Custer discovered seven years later, the control was only temporary.

*In 1874, the first year of the great grasshopper plague, Iowa farmers tried to drive off the swarming insects by burning straw covered with damp grass.*

# PHARAOH
# HAD IT EASY

## By SENATOR WARREN G. MAGNUSON

"*T*hey are awful!" wrote General Alfred Sully in a dispatch to headquarters. "They have actually eaten holes in my wagon covers and in the tarpaulins that cover my stores!"

The General's outrage was evoked during a march across the Dakota Badlands in 1864. "A soldier on his way here," the report went on, "lay down to sleep on the prairie in the middle of the day—the troop had been marching all night. His comrades noticed him covered with grasshoppers and awakened him. His throat and wrists were bleeding . . ."

Fortunately, General Sully's encounter with the insects was a brief one. It was merely an unpleasant foretaste of the plague of Rocky Mountain locusts—or grasshoppers, as they were more often called—which was to blight the Great Plains area from Manitoba to Texas and from the Rockies to the Mississippi. These modestly proportioned but insatiable creatures suddenly materialized in overwhelming numbers during the spring of 1874, ravaged the countryside for four successive summers and then, without so much as a wave of their antennae, mysteriously vanished. Originally identified as *Caloptenus spretus*, and now known as *Melanoplus spretus*—one of four gluttonous and migratory species known to the North American continent—this grass-hopper was occasionally seen in small numbers during the re-mainder of the century, but not a single live specimen has been reported since 1904.

Had it not been for the sudden easing of the plague, the course of civilization in the Great Plains might very well have been changed, for at its peak billions upon billions of grasshop-pers were rendering agriculture of any sort impossible. There is little dispute that in outright intensity this plague of the mid-seventies stands unrivalled in the history of the North American continent. The Mormon crickets may have been equally as dam-aging over a restricted area, and no doubt the boll weevil has, in its time, created comparable economic loss. But for dramatic impact, neither of these is in a class with the Rocky Mountain locust.

Though archaeologists have discovered Indian relics embel-lished with representations of grasshoppers, and New England-ers were complaining of locust plagues as early as 1743, probably the first recorded instance of trouble with the notoriously de-structive Rocky Mountain locust was reported by a Captain Jona-than Carver. In 1766, while exploring the region west of the Great Lakes, Captain Carver took the word of the Indian inhab-itants that "the Locust is a septenniel insect, as they are only seen, a small number of stragglers excepted, every seven years, when they infest these parts and the interior colonies in large swarms, and do a great deal of mischief."

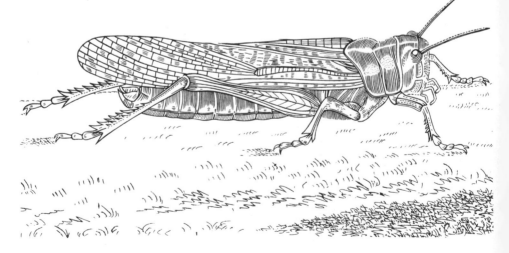

*Eighteenth-century lithographs (above and opposite) of the migrating grasshopper*

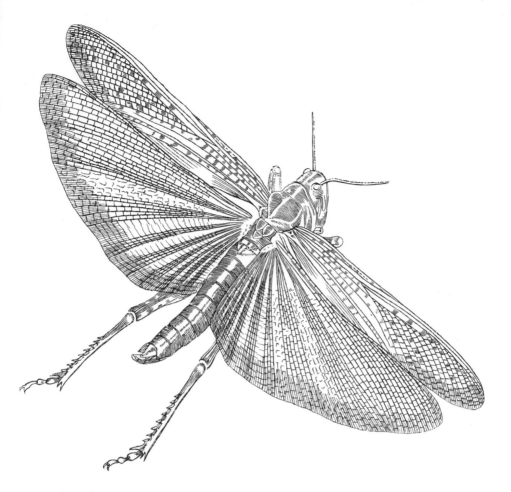

The famous Canadian fur trader, Alexander Henry the Younger, who settled near the present site of Pembina, North Dakota, observed in a journal entry dated June 25, 1808, that "Swarms of grasshoppers have destroyed the greater part of . . . my kitchen garden, onions, cabbages, melons, cucumbers, carrots, parsnips and beets. They had also attacked the potatos and corn, but these were strong enough at the root to sprout again." "The very trees," he added more menacingly, "are stripped of their leaves."

A decade later the settlers of the Red River valley received an even more convincing preview of the plague to come. A number of farmers were driven from their land, which the grasshoppers left "as barren as though swept by flame." Having devoured the crops and defoliated the trees, the insects began on the bark.

With starvation in prospect, the leaders of the colony at Pembina spent six thousand dollars to send a relief party overland to Prairie du Chien, Wisconsin, on the Mississippi, to purchase food. More than three months later the mission returned, paddling three Mackinaws full of wheat, oats, and peas. The first locust-relief expedition had followed a devious water route of hundreds of miles, and manhandled their heavily laden boats over lengthy portages with rough-hewn wooden rollers.

The following year the locusts, who had abandoned their seven-year cycle (if indeed they ever maintained one), came back to plague the Pembina settlement. As the years passed, reports of locust incursions grew in frequency and scope, doubtless because there were more humans present to voice complaint, as well as more cultivated fields to attract the interest of the six-legged raiders. It appears, however, that these outbreaks, which occurred up through the early seventies, were merely local in character; just how many may be blamed on the Rocky Mountain locust remains a question. Certainly the locusts were migratory. As one settler commented, "They came one year and left us the next when the young had acquired wings, and so they came and went all the time."

As the snows melted in the spring of 1874 the grasshoppers suddenly seemed to appear everywhere on the Plains. So rudimentary were communications at the time that the widespread nature of the assault was not immediately realized. "Such a host of insects I never saw," reported a Kansas homesteader. "The ground is completely covered and the branches of the trees are bending down with their weight. In my orchard of nearly twenty acres the trees are covered by myriads. The grove on the north is one huge, moving mass."

"Thirty acres of wheat which looked beautiful and green in the morning is eaten up," he continued. "Six hundred and forty acres, two miles south of me, that was looking fine at the beginning of the week, looks this morning as though fire had passed over it."

Later that season, as the insects developed wings and began their aerial migrations, the St. Louis *Republican* printed this report: "A glance upward toward the sun revealed them filling the air as far as vision could extend, as thick as snowflakes in a storm, and they drifted along with the breeze, and fluttered down at your feet occasionally or lit on your nose, with as much unconcern as if they had been part of the elements."

The swarms described in this newspaper dispatch were a dark omen of what the next few years would bring. The plague of 1875 proved even more severe, and it, in turn, was surpassed by the grasshopper invasions of 1876 and 1877.

Probably the main deterrent to unlimited multiplication, year by year, was the food supply. The grasshoppers had their taste preferences, and even a minor invasion could be economically disastrous, for the insects invariably went straight for exposed cornsilks, the heads of young wheat, and the juicy stems of cotton bolls, thus destroying what they did not consume.

But there was little they would not eat when their favorite foods were exhausted or unavailable. Onion bulbs, comparatively impervious to insect pests, became a target when the locusts had finished off the other produce in sight. Their ravages would leave the onion patches pocked with holes where the bulbs had been, while the air hung heavy with acrid fumes.

With grain and vegetables disposed of, the locust hordes took the weeds—everything from "Jamestown weed" to wild hemp (now known as marijuana)—and the trees. As a final parting ges-

*Grasshoppers, also called locusts, preparing to strip a flourishing grainfield*

ture they nibbled whatever clothing and harness they could reach, and even chewed on the handles of spades and pitchforks. For dessert, they ate each other.

They did not eat silently. While a keen ear might have been needed to detect the gourmandizing of a single individual, the noise produced by several million tiny mandibles was audible for a considerable distance. This did little to improve the disposition of the property owners who unwillingly played host to the insect visitors.

Next to their propensity for omnivorousness, the Rocky Mountain locusts specialized in reproduction. Still in dispute is the exact number of offspring turned out by each female in a season. The figure seemed to vary with climatic conditions. Whereas in some cases Mrs. *Spretus* laid three to four batches of eggs, there were times when she would make a single deposit and call it a summer.

The female grasshopper would seek a dry, firm, sandy soil for her nest, which she gouged out of the ground to the depth of one inch with a pair of strong "valves" at the tip of her abdomen. This drilling process, even in hard earth, would take but a few hours. Then, with her entire abdomen below ground level, she would begin extruding her twenty to thirty cigar-shaped eggs in a careful arrangement that permitted those young at the bottom of the hole to make their escape if their brothers and sisters nearer the surface chose to over-incubate. Next the female would seal the eggs with a waterproof but easily broken cellulose film, shove a little dirt into the neck of the hole to conceal it, and wander off, perhaps in search of another mate.

The following spring the infant would struggle up into the sunlight encased in a pellicle, which was soon split open and discarded. At first the youngster would be relatively inert, resting from the exertion of hatching and letting the warmth of the sun permeate its muscles. Presently, assuming more of the outward appearance of a mature grasshopper, it would commence to move about more actively in search of food. After quickly denuding the vicinity of its birthplace, the entire colony of nymph locusts would begin to march.

The direction of movement appears to have been chosen entirely at random. During the plague, many eyewitnesses reported seeing one army of grasshoppers surging down one side of a road while a second passed going the other way. Once on the move, however, they were not easily deflected. From time to time one locust army would encounter another coming head on, or from the flank. Without pause, they would simply scramble around and over one another, each individual steadfastly maintaining his original course without regard to the cross-traffic.

Railroad tracks, to the grasshoppers, were no deterrent whatever, and this was to prove a source of major annoyance to train crews. Since locomotives would instantly lose traction on the rails made oily by the insects' crushed bodies, trains were forced to carry quantities of sand against this contingency.

The same unswerving attitude prevailed when the locusts came upon natural obstacles. In 1875 several million crossed Pottawatomie Creek near Lane, Kansas, at a point where the stream was more than seventy feet wide. Another observer watched the crossing of the Big Blue and Little Blue rivers near Independence, Missouri, which were in several places a good one hundred feet across! "They would march down to the water's edge and commence jumping in, one upon another, till they would pontoon the stream, so as to effect a crossing. Two of these mighty armies also met, one moving east and the other west, on the river bluff . . . and coming to a perpendicular ledge of rock 25 or 30 feet high, passed over in a sheet apparently 6 or 7 inches thick, and causing a roaring noise similar to a cataract of water."

The rate of advance of the half-grown locusts was three yards per minute at best. The pace was one-fourth hopping and three-fourths walking. Any single individual, forced to hop a dozen times consecutively, would halt from fatigue. Theoretically then, a locust army might cover thirty miles during its walking and hopping phase, but in practice this range was sharply reduced. The grasshoppers were choosy about marching in the rain. They seldom got started before ten in the morning and usually halted for the night by four in the afternoon.

In the final chapter in the life of the Rocky Mountain locust, its wings sprouted and it took to the air to migrate almost unbelievable distances and spawn. To this day the naturalists are trying to resolve the available evidence into a meaningful pattern of movement. They are handicapped by the fact that in flight the locusts were disposed to meander a good deal, guided largely by the direction of the wind. The same swarm that blackened the sky for hours over a particular locality going east one day might conceivably repeat the performance a day or two later traveling west. With a favoring breeze and no succulent young grain to provide a distraction, the locusts sometimes flew two hundred miles in a day. To travel at the rate of fifty miles an hour with a forty-mile tail wind was, of course, no startling accomplishment.

No farmer could witness the destruction of his crops with equanimity, and from the outset of the plague plainsmen tried to devise ways to combat the locusts. Probably no living species has brazenly defied so many different attempts at extermination.

The first instinct of a property owner, upon noticing his wheat being eaten down to the nub, was to run out into the field, shouting and waving his arms. This procedure only mildly alarmed the locusts, who would surge into the air in small clouds and immediately settle back to earth and resume their interrupted meal.

*Clouds of grasshoppers stop a westbound train in Nebraska. Train crews had*

From this point, human ingenuity conjured up a multitude of devices and techniques both simple and complex to squash, bury, trap, burn, asphyxiate, trample, crush, drown, or poison the common enemy.

One of the simplest methods was the destruction of unhatched grasshopper eggs. Through some rough calculation it was widely advertised that a bushel of eggs removed from circulation equalled the saving of one hundred acres of corn. On this basis, states like Minnesota and Missouri offered bounties of up to five dollars—a fair weekly wage—for a bushel of locust eggs.

The bounty laws made strict provision for measuring the catch and insured that no egg was brought in twice for the reward. A bounty of one dollar per bushel was offered for young grasshoppers, the price being progressively reduced as the season wore

*to sprinkle sand on rails made slippery by the oily bodies of the crushed insects.*

on. It was the reasonable contention of the authorities that by June the average locust had eaten his fill. Locusts captured in May were redeemed at a mere quarter a bushel.

No public budget was ever seriously thrown out of balance by the payment of locust bounties. Though as many as twenty thousand eggs might be laid within the space of a square foot of ground, there was widespread misconception about the best place to find them. While the eager bounty hunters were meticulously sifting shovelfuls of earth scooped from the cultivated fields where the grasshoppers had been seen feasting, the majority of the embryos might be peacefully developing in the hard-packed adjacent pastureland.

Once the quarry was visible, pure manpower was brought into the fray: for example, a long wire wrapped in burning oil-soaked rags and stretched taut between two farmhands would be carried close to the ground over the fields where the infant grasshoppers were beginning to convene; from Europe was borrowed the design of a flat-bladed, shovel-like implement to flatten the locusts with lusty blows. This latter method facilitated collection of the bounty, but even at the top rate there was no giveaway involved: some seven thousand corpses were needed to fill a bushel basket.

Would-be efficiency experts turned their livestock into the infested areas in the expectation that the hoofs of the cattle and swine would appreciably decimate the locusts. The hope proved vain. As for domestic fowl, they soon gorged themselves into a stupor without making substantial headway against the tide; further, they became "crop-bound" by the more indigestible parts of the insects. And too, the flesh of turkeys that had been on extended grasshopper-control duty became tainted and unfit to eat.

A United States government entomologist, Charles V. Riley, who was very much on the scene during the critical years of infestation, industrially gathered all available data on the grasshoppers' behavior and issued bulletins as to effective countermeasures.

"When the insects are famishing, it is useless to try and protect plants by any application whatever," he wrote resignedly, "though spraying them with a mixture of kerosene and warm water is the best protection we have tried." Riley instructed the fruit farmers to whitewash the trunks of their trees; the lime flaked off as the creatures tried to claw their way into the foliage, depriving them of a foothold. The whitewash applications had to be repeated frequently, and Riley tacitly acknowledged the partial ineffectiveness of this strategy by recommending that the farmer shake his young trees vigorously from time to time.

Experiments proved that locusts on the march might be blocked and destroyed in great numbers by digging in their path ditches two feet wide and two feet deep. The majority stumbled blindly into these traps and could mangle each other fatally in their mad struggles to get out again. It was further found that they could be channelled into death pits by arrangements of converging strips of netting or muslin. These devices were not geared, however, to exterminate locust armies advancing on a one-mile front, which often happened.

All this while, to be sure, inventive-minded individuals were deep in designs for machinery to combat the scourge. In general, the contraptions that emerged from the workshops and smithies were known as "hopper-catchers" or "hopperdozers"; some actually worked.

Usually horse-propelled, the hopperdozers attained widths of up to forty feet. The principles of operation varied. The Flory Locust Machine, for example, sought to crush the locusts between two rollers. Several horse-drawn scorching-machines were produced. The King Suction Machine was built on the vacuum-cleaner concept, with eight-inch tubes, flattened at the mouth, running close to the ground and drawing the pests into a chamber where a large fan rotated at twelve hundred revolutions per minute, providing the necessary air flow and effectively pulverizing the grasshoppers.

The glaring weakness of these designs was the assumption by their creators that most locust-ridden farmland was as smooth and level as a village green. On rough, sloping ground the machines were as helpless as a full-rigged ship in a creek bed.

Many farmers put their trust in machines that plunged the grasshoppers into a bath of water and coal oil. Equipped with a projecting unit called a "disturber," which impelled the quarry to leap into the air, these machines were supposed to catch the insects against a wire screen and deflect them into the pan filled with the oil-and-water mixture. Advocates of this method were aware that many of the insects scrambled out of the pan, but were comforted by the belief (it turned out to be unfounded) that a brief exposure to the fluid would be fatal.

The development of such fearsome contrivances, and others like them probably does not explain the virtual absence of *Melanoplus spretus* when the spring of 1878 arrived. Many factors may have caused its disappearance: the weather the year before had not been favorable for breeding; parasites that preyed on the grasshoppers and their eggs had multiplied; and it was noted repeatedly that the locusts of the summer of 1877 had been sluggish and, as the farmers phrased it, "used up."

In August, 1876, the Georgetown, Colorado, *Miner* carried a dispatch illustrating the susceptibility of the locusts to atmospheric turbulence and sudden temperature change: "As the ravenous millions were driven up against the high ranges about Mount Evans, they were chilled and commenced falling into the little stream that flows near Sisty's place, until for days, the rivulet was transformed from a sparkling stream of limpid water into a floating mass of dead grasshoppers, the water becoming so corrupt and offensive that neither man nor beast could tolerate it. The trout pond in Mr. Sisty's meadow became so putrid that he was compelled to cut away the dam and let the accumulated filth flow off."

Uncounted millions of Rocky Mountain locusts died in the snows of upper Yellowstone Park. They may be seen today, by those intrepid enough to survive the trip by jeep, horseback, and foot to the Grasshopper Glacier. In layer upon layer, the insects lie in this 11,000-foot-high deep-freeze. It is impossible to pinpoint the exact years in which they died there, but scientific tests have established that these grasshopper deposits very possibly coincided with the great plague, the victims chilled in flight like those that fell on Mr. Sisty's farm.

True, the disappearance of the grasshoppers during the seventies may have been in some part due to the efforts of the settlers who had become organized, equipped, and inspired by their political leaders to fight back. Ex-Governor Robert W. Furnas of Nebraska set the tone in words meant for prospective immigrants: "While in the West we have room for millions more people, and are glad to have them come, and with us occupy and utilize the broad fertile acres God has bequeathed to the Far West, those who have not 'sand and grit' enough to clean out a crop of young locusts are not the men wanted!" Days of prayer were freely proclaimed as the farmers girded themselves for the massive insect assaults.

Public leadership was not confined to the rostrum. With the formation of relief societies to aid the destitute, various state legislatures authorized bounty payments and emergency allotments of new seed and even ordered the conscription of manpower to join in the antigrasshopper crusades. In Kansas all able-bodied males from twelve to sixty-five were subject to the call of the road overseer; in Minnesota the levy applied to all men from twenty-one to sixty, "except paupers, idiots and lunatics."

Entomologists refuse to agree that *spretus* is extinct. Modern experts feel certain that a time may come, when conditions are ripe, when new swarms will range again over the fields they once denuded.

Should this occur, however, the grasshoppers will face weapons considerably more potent than the Suction Machine. In the face of lesser outbreaks that have materialized from time to time in the United States, and together with foreign-aid programs in Asia and Africa, insecticides have been developed that should make another plague out of the question. No longer experimenting with cumbersome bait, like bran impregnated with Paris green, the locust-fighters are now prepared to spread highly concentrated synthetic contact poisons from low-flying aircraft, which will not only kill any locusts present but destroy through residual effect those that may follow.

*Melanoplus spretus,* if he still exists in some remote sanctuary, will be well advised to stay out from under foot.

*Clarence King (far right) and James*
*Gardner (far left) with a survey team*

# THE GREAT DIAMOND FRAUD

By HARRY H. CROSBY

*I*n previous winters when Clarence King and James Gardner finished their work in the Nevada desert and boarded a river boat for San Francisco, they were the center of the attention of the other passengers. Clarence King was the director of a geological survey of the land along the new transcontinental railroad, and Gardner was his first assistant. They were trying to discover what minerals could be found out in the desert waste, what crops could be grown, and how much water was available.

But in October, 1872, when rains and high winds stopped the survey's work again and King and Gardner once again headed for winter quarters, none of the other passengers paid any attention to them at all. The passengers were talking about something that thrilled every Californian. Somewhere out in the American Desert, two prospectors had stumbled across a whole mountain of diamonds.

If the story was true, the prospectors had come across something King and Gardner and all their assistants and their scientific knowledge and equipment had missed in five years of exploration and study. King had written that there were no precious gems in the American Desert.

King and Gardner listened with astonishment to the report that the project had been taken over by William C. Ralston, the town's leading investment banker. Twenty-five of the city's most reputable men had each put up $80,000 to form what they called "The San Francisco and New York Mining and Commercial Company." Baron Ferdinand Rothschild of London, Charles Tiffany and Horace Greeley of New York were members of the company. Such men did not ordinarily subscribe to fairy tales.

For young men, Clarence King and James T. Gardner had come a long way. Both of them had put themselves through scientific school with little financial help from their parents. They had traveled across the continent with a wagon train. They had several years' experience working with the great Professor Whitney and his California Geological Survey. At the age of 24, King had talked his way into the command of the most ambitious federal geological exploration survey ever undertaken.

They both realized, however, that the diamond strike could ruin them. The United States Congress would not be likely to support an expensive survey that supplied misinformation.

King and Gardner decided they would go immediately to the Pacific Union Club when they arrived in San Francisco. The Union was the garish, noisy rendezvous not only of the richest men in northern California but also of the men who would know the truth about mining developments.

When their cab reached Montgomery Street and stopped in front of the Pacific Union building, the two men walked upstairs to the clubrooms. Within a few minutes, they saw a friend who could give them more than rumor. The story was a long one.

Early in February, two disreputable-looking miners had been seen in various saloons talking furtively to each other. Eventually the pair entered Ralston's bank with a heavy bag which they asked the cashier to deposit in a vault. Before he locked up the sack, the cashier found that it contained several hundred uncut diamonds, and many raw rubies, sapphires and emeralds. In ten minutes, William Ralston had been told that someone had discovered a fabulous gem mine.

After several weeks of profitless investigation by many curious people, a former Army general, George D. Roberts, discovered that one of the miners, a southerner by the name of Arnold, was a former employee. General Roberts, of course, resolved to renew his acquaintance.

The General found Arnold almost grateful to meet an old friend whom he thought he could trust. His partner turned out to be a quiet fellow named Slack who nodded his head to agree with Arnold but never disputed the other's leadership.

It took but gentle prodding to get the talkative Arnold to tell the story; although Arnold and the shrugging Slack seemed afraid to share their secret, they appeared even more frightened at the thought of not sharing it. The two miners told the General how they had happened upon a mountain filled with gems of every description. The find was so profuse that diamonds, sapphires, emeralds and garnets could be scratched out by boot heels. Although they had brought back a large sack of the stones, they were certain they had hardly touched the vast store. With this, the miners closed their mouths. Arnold and Slack hinted that the mine might be in Arizona, but beyond that they would tell no more.

When this vague information spread about the city, many parties set out for an exploration of Arizona. Finally, when the month of February was almost gone, Roberts called on Ralston, the master persuader of them all, to talk sense to the prospectors.

Whereas Roberts had been talking about taking rocks out of a hole in the ground, Ralston began to plan a whole gem industry with Arnold and Slack as key figures. Ralston promised the simple fellows lavish offices with solid walnut desks, rich homes with servants and great power. Under this strategy, the miners began to appreciate that there were many advantages to having experienced partners.

Once the miners became interested, Ralston convinced them that they should take two mining experts to the gem fields. Arnold and Slack agreed, demanding only the stipulation that the men should be blindfolded when they reached the vicinity of the field.

In a few weeks two dazzled mining experts returned. They had little idea where they had been, but they were wild with tales of diamonds jutting out of the ground and gleaming in crevices. They brought with them another bag of jewels and deposited it in Ralston's Bank of California with the earlier sack, which had been assayed at $125,000.

Ralston was already dreaming of a California empire. He began to plot the removal of the whole diamond industry to San Francisco. He would import miners from South Africa and lapi-

*Clarence King fathered the U.S. Geological Survey and wrote on mountaineering.*

daries from Holland. He would control the gem market in London.

He never lost his caution. He demanded that Arnold and Slack permit him to submit the gems to Tiffany of New York, the most reputable American authority on precious stones. If Tiffany confirmed the value of the treasure, Ralston and his associates were to choose a mining expert of international repute for a final investigation of the mine.

To all of this, Arnold and Slack agreed.

Ralston lost no time in establishing the directorate of his corporation. He sent a long cablegram to his old friend Asbury Harpending and persuaded him to return from England and become general manager of the enterprise. He asked General Roberts to be a director. David Colton, an engineer whose father had owned the hall where California declared its independence from Mexico, was elected president; Ralston became the corporation's secretary and treasurer.

This small group of men, working with showy secrecy, sketched in the outlines of a corporation with a capital stock of $10,000,000. To represent the New York affairs of the enterprise, they engaged Samuel Barlow, one of New York's most eminently successful lawyers.

To expedite passage through Congress of a law permitting them to claim a great area of mining land, Ralston added Senator Ben Butler to their legal staff. An influential member of the United States Senate, Butler had a strong voice in establishing mining policy.

Barlow and Butler arranged the meeting with Tiffany. It was full of drama and they provided an appreciative audience. Besides the company officials, the group included George B. McClellan, Lincoln's deposed commander in chief and presidential opponent of 1864. Although Horace Greeley had resigned as editor of the New York *Tribune*, his friendship with his successor, Whitelaw Reid, would insure some valuable publicity, and he was in the audience. The impresarios also invited the president of Duncan, Sherman and Company, one of New York's largest investment firms.

When the group assembled, Barlow dumped the contents of a huge cloth bag onto a tablecloth before Tiffany. In a few words, Barlow told the audience that a fabulous store of gems had been found in the West. Mr. Tiffany was to see if they were valuable.

Tiffany played the part of the expert with gusto, holding up each stone to the light carefully, peering at it with his jeweler's glass.

"Gentlemen," he finally pronounced, "these are beyond question precious stones of enormous value. But before I give you the exact appraisement, I must submit them to my lapidary and will report to you further in two days."

For the next 48 hours, they all waited. At the announced time the group reassembled, this time to witness an even more dramatic presentation. Tiffany paused for a moment until he gained full attention. Then he stated firmly that, when cut, the gems would be worth $150,000. Since the westerners had brought only one-tenth of the treasure, the whole collection presumably would be valued at $1,500,000.

Ralston had only one more step to take before he could feel that his gem industry had a sound foundation. All that remained was a full investigation of the mine itself by a mining expert. When Ralston looked for the right man, he hit immediately on Henry Janin, a consulting engineer. Janin was one of the most dependable mining authorities in the United States. Although he had examined over 600 mines, he had never caused a client to lose a dollar. He agreed to make an appraisal, for a fee of $2,500 cash; all his expenses were to be paid, and he was to have the right to take up 1,000 shares of the stock at a nominal price.

Janin's trip to the gem field was staged as dramatically as every other episode. Arnold and Slack led the party, all of whom were blindfolded when they left the train.

Now that they had the whole story, King and Gardner were perplexed. Diamonds, they knew, were found either in placer conditions in the alluvial deposits of rivers and creeks, or in lode conditions in rocks of heavily variegated states of metamorphosis. Rubies and sapphires required completely different conditions. King and Gardner were sure that the proper conditions had not existed in the American West. But surely Janin knew this too. Could their own information be wrong? They had to know more.

Although no one in the company would divulge anything officially, the president, David Colton, had already opened impressive offices and hired twenty clerks. He had refused fifteen offers of over $200,000 each for claims at the mining fields. He answered every request only with a glowing prophecy of the corporation's future.

King and Gardner learned that the fever was not confined to San Franciscans. In New York, investors were besieging Barlow and Butler with demands for stock. When someone who signed his letter "An Old Miner" wrote the New York *Sun* that he had seen a stone worth half a million dollars taken from the gem field, which he said was in southwestern Arizona, he started a wildcat movement to that state.

In England, Baron Rothschild was watching developments. After the testimony of Tiffany and Janin, the Baron ordered his agents to get control of the gem enterprise. Ralston laughed at this move but he had Rothschild's agent, A. Gansel, elected to the board of directors.

Meanwhile, Arnold and Slack decided they had had enough of the fast company. After showing several corporation officials how to locate the diamond field, they sold out. They took for their interest $300,000 each and a percentage of the future profits.

King and Gardner still were sure that the mine was fraudulent, and they decided that they must talk to Henry Janin. Since they did not expect Janin to want to talk to them, they learned where he customarily ate dinner and waited for two days until he appeared. When he entered the restaurant, King invited Janin to eat with them.

To their astonishment, Janin opened the conversation by asking if they had heard about the Arizona diamond discovery. He was proud that his name was associated with it.

He related that the journey on horseback had followed an erratic course. Even with their blindfolds, he could tell that at times Arnold and Slack seemed lost. Perplexed, they argued about the position of the sun; Arnold left the party to climb a high peak in search of landmarks. Long after the San Franciscans were ready to give up the search, the guides removed their blindfolds and announced that they had reached their goal. The spot was at a high elevation, about 7,000 feet above sea level, and near a conical mountain.

Immediately all fatigue and irritation disappeared. The party began to scratch and dig where Arnold and Slack pointed. Within ten minutes a San Franciscan found a diamond. Then they all began to have fantastic success. Diamonds were everywhere; occasionally the hunters found a ruby, a garnet, a sapphire, or an emerald. Janin swore that twenty rough laborers could wash out a million dollars' worth of diamonds per month indefinitely.

When Janin was spent, King and Gardner began a cross-examination. "Of course, you know exactly where the place is?" King asked.

"No. No, I don't. I was taken a long distance on a train, about 36 hours. Then we left the railroad at some small station where there was no attendant. We were brought out of the station blindfolded and put on horses which our guides secured in some way. For two days we rode, and at last they took our blinds off when we got to this mountain. If I hadn't gone through it all myself, I should hardly believe it."

"Why?" Gardner asked.

"It's a curious place, a desert with a conical but flat-topped mountain rising right out of it, and on the mountain you find everything from garnets to diamonds!"

King then commented, "It's a pity you had such bad weather to ride in."

"Why, we had splendid weather," Janin said. "In fact, we had the sun in our faces for the entire two days during the trip; it was quite too hot."

When the mining expert left, King explained to Gardner why he had asked Janin about the weather. Janin was fooled about the mine's location, or he had not been entirely frank with them. It was impossible to get to Arizona by a 36-hour train trip followed by a two-day ride on horseback. Thirty-six hours on the Central Pacific would have taken the party east of Promontory Point in Utah and on into Wyoming. This checked with some information they had about rainfall. Almost all the mountainous areas in Nevada and Utah had been covered with rains and storms at the time of the trip, yet Janin had said that his trip was dry. Only southwestern Wyoming and northern Utah had escaped the deluge. The party must have been traveling generally southward since Janin made such a point about facing the sun for the entire day. Unless they had wound and twisted a great deal, two days' trip to the south would have taken them into Utah.

King and Gardner studied their maps. They had a faint recollection of the mountain Janin had described, but neither could place it exactly. In a few minutes, they found such a mountain on the edge of the Uinta Range east of Salt Lake City, which they had surveyed only a year before.

Thirty-six hours later, King arrived at Rawlings Springs, near what is now Green River, Wyoming. Here he hired an elderly German prospector who had some horses to carry the barometers, transits, sextants, food and books King found necessary for

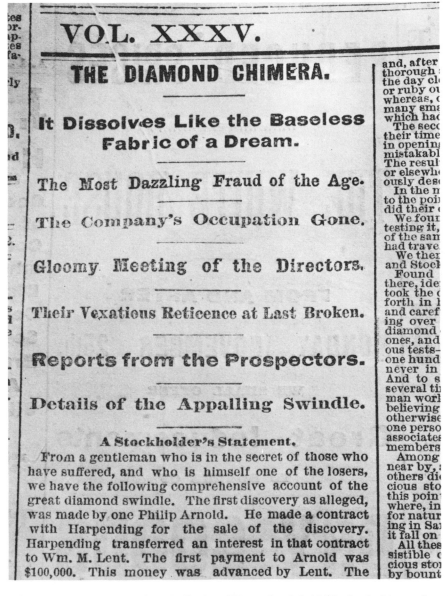

# VOL. XXXV.

## THE DIAMOND CHIMERA.

### It Dissolves Like the Baseless Fabric of a Dream.

### The Most Dazzling Fraud of the Age.

### The Company's Occupation Gone.

### Gloomy Meeting of the Directors.

### Their Vexatious Reticence at Last Broken.

### Reports from the Prospectors.

### Details of the Appalling Swindle.

#### A Stockholder's Statement.

From a gentleman who is in the secret of those who have suffered, and who is himself one of the losers, we have the following comprehensive account of the great diamond swindle. The first discovery as alleged, was made by one Philip Arnold. He made a contract with Harpending for the sale of the discovery. Harpending transferred an interest in that contract to Wm. M. Lent. The first payment to Arnold was $100,000. This money was advanced by Lent. The

*The San Francisco* Evening Bulletin *of November 26, 1872, shocked its readers with its account of Clarence King's discovery of the great diamond swindle.*

all his trips. King and the German cut across Red Canyon and the valley of the Green River and up into the gulches and ravines of the Uinta foothills, about 140 miles east of Salt Lake City. Finally they climbed onto the mountain of their destination, Table Rock, a plateau of 6,840 feet elevation. They arrived on November 2.

At first they found nothing. Quickly satisfied that their search was profitless, King quit scratching around in the rocks and began to cook supper; the old prospector, however, still continued digging. Just as the meal was ready, the German called from a spot several hundred feet from their camp site. He had discovered what Janin and the San Francisco reports had promised: raw diamonds, emeralds, rubies and sapphires.

The geologist and the prospector pitched camp and went to bed, but neither of them slept much. At sunrise, the prospector was again scurrying around picking up the valuable stones. Suddenly he held up a stone and shouted, "Look, Mr. King. This diamond field not only produces diamonds but cuts them also!"

King ran to the prospector and grasped the half-cut diamond. Clearly it bore the smooth surface left by a lapidary's tool. He knew for certain now that the field was a fraud. The ground had been "salted" with rough stones. He began to discover evidence he had previously overlooked. Occasionally he found a straight hole at the bottom of which rested a gem as though it had been pushed down by a miner's bar. He found ant hills jammed with gems. Any crevice of rock or shale might contain a diamond, but the rock was likely to have scratches on it from a steel tool.

On November 10, King and his aide returned to the Union Pacific station and flagged a train. At the next stop, the geologist sent a brief telegram to Colton stating that the company was duped.

In San Francisco, the board of directors hurriedly identified King and established his reputation. When they learned that whatever he said about mining and geology would be authoritative, the company president, two directors and Henry Janin traveled the mountainous way to Rawlings Springs. Two days later, they sent Ralston the telegram he had been dreading. As Ralston read the telegram to his associates, they knew their dreams were dead.

By the time King returned to San Francisco, Ralston had started a nationwide search for the men who had tricked him.

He never located Slack, but found Arnold ensconced in Hardin County, Kentucky. When the Californians brought suit, the southern state refused to extradite Arnold. The courts in Kentucky were solidly in support of the successful son who had made a foray into Yankeedom and returned with a third of a million dollars. After months of wrangling, Arnold surrendered $150,000 for immunity from further litigation. The only other satisfaction the Californians got was that Arnold, who used the balance of his gains to start a bank in Elizabethtown, Kentucky, was promptly shot to death by a competitor.

The recovery of only one-fourth of what he had paid to Arnold and Slack left Ralston a heavy loser, especially since he made it a point of honor that no one else should lose a penny. Because he sold no stock and paid back to each one of the charter members the $80,000 originally invested, he was freed by public opinion of any taint.

Gradually the Californians began to understand how they had been gulled. Amsterdam gem merchants remembered that two "crazy Americans," one talkative and the other taciturn, had been "throwing their money away" on inferior, uncut gems for almost a year before the great strike. The stones they had bought were rejects, worth less than $25,000.

The embarrassed Tiffany could offer slight excuse. His lapidaries were the best in America, but none of them had ever before seen uncut gems. Only the most experienced cutters, all of whom were members of the gem monopoly at Amsterdam, were aware how much of a raw stone is lost when its heart is fashioned into a jewel. Janin, who had sold his 1,000 shares for $40,000 before King's discovery, had an even lamer excuse. The enthusiasm of Ralston and the reputation of Tiffany had confused him. He was convinced about the authenticity of the mine before he got off the train at Rawlings Springs.

The most acceptable explanation of how so many shrewd and reputable men were so thoroughly fooled probably lay in two facts. In the first place, Arnold and Slack must have been skilled actors. Their "air of simple rugged honesty" made them master swindlers. When they learned that Tiffany had agreed to appraise the gems they were convincingly exultant, and they were equally delighted with the selection of Henry Janin. At all conferences they affected being both nervous and relieved that they had found some honest men with whom to share their secret.

307

*Clarence King's successful sleuthing made him a nationwide hero overnight.*

The second fact was that in the 1870's everyone had abundant confidence in the "Manifest Destiny" of California and the West. After the completion of the transcontinental railroad, settlers began a drive for the productive lands on the coast. Their success stories added to the legends of fortunes made earlier in gold, silver and trade. At that time, anything good was expected of the West.

As for King, the fame he acquired from the exposure was almost blinding. The New York *Times*, the Philadelphia *Inquirer*, the Chicago *News*, and the *Rocky Mountain News* gave the exposé more space on their front pages than they did the arrest of Jay Gould and the first reports that Horace Greeley had gone insane, stories which broke at the same time. The London *Times* publicized King's act extravagantly, including in its story the first account of how Arnold and Slack had secured the rough diamonds of Amsterdam.

Immediately, of course, rumors began to exaggerate his triumph. There is an unsubstantiated claim that officials of the corporation offered King a tremendous bribe to delay his announcement until they had sold enough stock to get their "investment" back. To this, King is supposed to have returned a declaration that is today preserved in the histories of science: "There is not enough money in the Bank of California to induce me to delay this announcement a single hour."

Ironically, if the bribe was offered and King did say that there was not enough money in the Bank of California to tempt him, his reply had a dreadful pertinency. An investigation made soon after King's exposé revealed that Ralston's bank was insolvent. The next morning Ralston's body was found in the Bay, and his whole empire crashed.

The magnitude of the swindle and King's independent method of frustrating it caught the fancy of America. He was praised in the newspapers and eulogized from the pulpits. One of the leading churchmen in New York, Reverend Horatio Stebbins, declaimed, "One scientific man, whose untarnished fame alone is worth all the diamonds in the world, has found occasion to prove to the world the value of science and his own moral worth; and that result alone compensates for all the shame of this great fraud. . . . To have learned that we have one such man is enough to make us look upon the whole stupendous wrong and its results as a cause of thankfulness."

*Nathan Meeker, the Utopian, and his wife*

# THE
# BLOODY END OF
# MEEKER'S
# UTOPIA

## By MARSHALL SPRAGUE

On September 29, 1879, a small band of Ute Indians went wild on the Western Slope of Colorado and murdered their Indian agent and all his employees at the remote Ute Agency on White River. A few hours earlier, another small Ute band ambushed a relief force of soldiers at Milk Creek 25 miles away. All told, the White River Utes, who had never hurt anybody before, killed 30 white men and wounded 44 more.

The murdered agent, Nathan Meeker, did not resemble the average second-rater sent out by the Indian Office as a political favor. Meeker was a newspaper editor and a writer of wide repute, and his violent death in the romantic Rocky Mountain wilderness shocked and thrilled the whole nation. In addition, the White River massacre gave Coloradans the pretext they had sought for a decade to take from the Utes their vast hunting paradise of 12,000,000 acres.

The hideous climax of Meeker's career derived from starry-eyed idealism, which he had cultivated all his life. He was born in 1817 on a breezy Ohio homestead overlooking Lake Erie. At seventeen he ran away from home to become a poet, starved a while as a young intellectual on MacDougal Street in New York and returned prosaically to Ohio to run a general store. He married a sea captain's gray-eyed daughter, Arvilla Delight Smith, who bore him three daughters and two sons. She was a plain, pious girl, always a little embarrassed about her fecundity and apprehensive about her husband who theorized brilliantly but disliked manual labor and talked of Jesus Christ as though He were a fairly sound but not entirely respectable neighbor down the street.

Meeker was often broke and twice bankrupt during the first twenty nomadic years of their marriage. In Ohio, and later in Illinois, Arvilla and the children often tended his store while he dabbled in Fourier socialism, Phalangist economics, planned parenthood, Brook Farm Transcendentalism, a Buddhist sort of Christianity, and the practice of nibbling carrots for better vision at night.

His yearning to improve the world expressed itself at last in his first novel, *The Adventures of Captain Armstrong,* the hero of which was tall, handsome, cool-headed, plausible, and indestructibly hopeful like himself. The captain was shipwrecked on a Polynesian atoll and in jig time created among the naked savages a co-operative Utopia of modern industries and crafts. Meeker was a great admirer of Horace Greeley, the famous editor of the New York *Tribune.* He mailed his novel to Greeley, who found a publisher for it. Later, Greeley made Meeker his war correspondent to cover for the *Tribune* Grant's Mississippi campaign. Then he brought him to New York to be his agricultural editor.

Meeker was a persuasive columnist and he became a national oracle on farm problems. But in 1869 his Utopian dreams crystallized in a plan for a co-operative farm colony near Denver in semi-arid Colorado Territory. Horace Greeley approved the plan and gave him free space in the *Tribune* to promote it. Members of this Union Colony (Meeker called his new town "Greeley") had to be temperate, industrious, moral, and tolerant in their religious outlook.

The founder visited the Cache la Poudre region northeast of Denver and chose a flat, wind-swept tract which was to become the most successful co-operative venture in the Rockies. The tract, like the rest of the Great Plains, had no rainfall to speak of. Meeker's colonists watered their new farms by an elaborate system of ditches which distributed the snow water flowing down from the mountains seventy miles away. Their irrigation methods were copied widely. Their success made it possible to grow crops and livestock in quantity on small acreages. Colorado villages began expanding into cities, the mining districts swarmed with new people, and homesteaders poured into Colorado Territory, enabling it to win statehood in 1876.

Meanwhile the fates conspired to destroy Meeker. He was not a good executor of his own theories (his first irrigation ditch at Greeley cost Union Colony $25,000 and watered less than 200 acres, including the basements of several business establish-

*Eastern tabloids allowed themselves considerable license in reporting the White River massacre. That Josephine Meeker fired on the attackers is pure fantasy.*

ments). He frittered away his small capital on his Utopia and on his newspaper, the Greeley *Tribune*. He went deeply in debt to Horace Greeley, himself, before the great editor died in 1872. By degrees, his colonists watered down his idealistic aims and eased him out of power. As his frustrations accumulated, he grew brusque and opinionated. He denounced traveling theatricals and dancing and picking wildflowers. He blackballed from membership in the Greeley Farmers' Club all those who opposed his views.

In 1877 the executors of Horace Greeley's estate demanded the money which he owed to it. Desperately Meeker sought and

313

failed to get a postmastership. He applied for but was not accepted for duty at the Paris Exposition. Then he heard that an Indian agent was needed at the White River Ute Agency in northwest Colorado. He had no special interest in Indians as yet, but the job paid $1,500 a year. To get it, he sought the aid of old newspaper friends back East and some influential Coloradans like Senator Teller. Because of their recommendations, Carl Schurz, secretary of the interior under President Hayes, assigned him to the White River Ute Agency.

The assignment transformed the harried Utopian. He was only 61, but the bitter disappointments at Greeley had given him a defeated look. He had grown thin and stooped, as though bent by the burden of his own despair. As hope returned, his imagination resumed its extravagant soaring. His blue eyes sparkled. His stoop vanished. His shoulders swung confidently when he walked, like the swinging, confident shoulders of his fictional superman, Captain Armstrong.

As he applied his idealism to the problems of the Utes, he began telling himself that maybe he wasn't through yet. Maybe he could achieve Captain Armstrong's Utopia after all. And perhaps, after he had taught the wonders of modern society to these simple White River savages, a grateful President Hayes might ask him to perform the same miracle for the Sioux and Apaches and all the other suffering red men!

Leaving the Greeley *Tribune* in the hands of a friend, Meeker set out for his new post early in May, 1878. Arvilla and his youngest daughter Josie were to follow him there in mid-summer. The other two girls agreed to run the family home as a boarding house. The new Indian agent was hardly aware of the explosive situation into which he stepped during his five-day trek to White River. The seeds of bitter conflict over possession of Colorado's Western Slope had been a long time sprouting. The Colorado Utes, anciently of Aztec breeding, had endured centuries of misery as pariahs until the seventeenth century, when they became among the first, if not the very first, Indians to adopt the horse from Spanish colonists on the Rio Grande. This magical creature so inspired them as to completely change their tribal personality. They developed into superb horsemen and found themselves able to hold the Colorado highlands for their exclusive use. Thereafter their reverence was boundless for the divine beast which had raised them from the depths of human degradation to great happiness, prosperity, and dignity.

Eventually some 3,500 of these Utes divided into six loosely allied Colorado bands, led by an extraordinary man named Chief Ouray. He was 45 in 1878 and had a mind as spacious as his mountains. He had risen to power in 1863 and had set his political policy then. The Utes, he decreed, must live in peace with white men. They must modify their wasteful hunting economy, sell off bits of land as required by events, and learn to prosper on the reduced acreage as white men prospered.

Ouray's masterpiece was the Treaty of 1868 by which the U.S. Senate gave his six bands most of Colorado's Western Slope forever (4,500 acres for each Ute man, woman, and child). In 1873 he had to release the 4,000,000-acre San Juan silver region but the Utes had a 12,000,000-acre reservation left. They were still the richest Indian landed gentry in the nation. And they were the pets of the whites, befriending settlers and doing a big buckskin business with traders.

But Ouray played a losing game. By 1878 the tenfold increase in the state's white population had created a huge demand for more land. Politically, the demand was expressed in an outcry for the removal of the Colorado Utes and the liquidation of their vast Western Slope estate. Senator Teller and the land grabbers around him dreamed of herding them off to army-guarded desert camps. But the Teller crowd had to move with caution because of the good reputation of Ouray's people. Their strategy was to try to destroy this reputation by accusing the Utes falsely of all kinds of outrage, arson, theft, and murder.

The Utes were deeply disturbed by the charges, the resentment being highest among the two White River bands under the aging Chief Douglas and Chief Jack. This Jack was a young, forceful leader and he reacted to the white campaign of slander by urging an end of Ouray's peace policy. He wanted the Utes to fight for their homeland, though Ouray warned him that he was playing into Senator Teller's hands. Ouray added that if the Utes went on the warpath, they would abrogate their treaty rights and lose all they possessed.

Chief Jack was not convinced. The government, he said, had always mistaken Ouray's peace policy for weakness and was preparing to dispossess the Utes anyway. He stressed that Interior Secretary Schurz had just dismissed the White River agent who had protected their rights for years. Schurz had replaced this

*Ute leaders and their white friends in 1874. Chief Ouray is in front row, second*

*from right; Jack and Johnson are in the back row, second and third from right.*

good agent with a Teller appointee named Nathan Meeker. In Jack's opinion, such an appointee could have but two aims; to steal Ute land and destroy the Ute way of life.

On May 10, 1878, the new agent arrived blithesomely at the cluster of tumble-down log buildings in White River valley at the utter end of the 185-mile road south from Rawlins, Wyoming. The bleak agency setting did not resemble Captain Armstrong's charming atoll in the South Seas, but Meeker did not care. He was abloom with love for and faith in his Utes and had high hopes of easing their presumed misery. He was not worried about the hostility which greeted him at first. He placated many Indians soon by his success in obtaining better rations and distributing annuities on time. They were pleased too with his agency staff—eight good-natured young men hand-picked by Meeker from the best families in Greeley.

The agent outlined his Utopian dream to the principal chiefs, Douglas and Jack, and to the head medicine man, Johnson, a distinguished horseman who was also Ouray's brother-in-law. Meeker explained how he would teach them modern farming and irrigation so that they could all be rich, live in houses, ride in carriages, use privies, sleep in beds, wear underwear, and send their children to the agency school. He described plans for associated industries to raise their living standard still higher—saw mills, orchards, wool plants, coal mines, and a railroad to Rawlins.

He observed that Douglas and Johnson were mildly intrigued by his dream. But Jack had an irritating way of asking loaded questions. He asked whether or not white men would allow Utes to compete in business with them. He wanted to know if the high living standard of the whites was worth all the work and worry they had put into it. He asked if white men enjoyed working as much as the Utes enjoyed their lordly leisure of hunting and fishing and riding their ponies about their Colorado estate.

That fall agent Meeker discovered a perfect site for his model Ute farm at Powell Park a dozen miles down White River. He was sure of its value because the Utes pastured thousands of ponies on it in winter. To Meeker's surprise, Douglas objected heatedly to moving the agency there.

Meeker thought it over and concluded that this pony business did indeed present an obstacle to his whole bright plan for Ute salvation. The Utes, he perceived, were obsessed with these confounded ponies. They could never achieve the happiness which he held out to them as long as they had so many ponies to care for. It was a ticklish matter. And yet he was sure that Captain Armstrong had more than enough persuasive power to make the Indians see that the ponies were millstones around their necks.

And, sure enough, in the ensuing winter months, Douglas and Johnson let him have his way. The agency buildings were moved downstream to the richest part of Powell Park. Neat streets were laid out, ditches were dug, and forty acres of pony pasture were plowed, fenced, and planted to wheat. The young employees from Greeley built a nice house for Johnson and put cook stoves in the tepees of four families. Meeker's gentle daughter Josie induced three children to attend her agency school.

But serious trouble from outside the reservation came in the spring of 1879, and Meeker watched with mounting anguish as his dream faded. Colorado's new governor, Frederick W. Pitkin, had been elected on a Utes-Must-Go platform which he was trying hard to implement. The Denver papers were full of incendiary anti-Ute propaganda. Senator Teller forced Chief Ouray's Uncompahgre band to sell 10,000 acres of prime farm land for $10,000—and failed to produce the promised money. It was a terribly dry spring. By mid-June the state's forests burned in hundreds of places, and the Teller crowd charged that the Utes had deliberately set all the fires.

At White River Agency the Indians took out their anger at all this unfairness toward them by ceasing to co-operate with Meeker further. And, as his dream collapsed, the agent's optimism faltered. His all-embracing love for his charges turned rapidly to hate. He spent much time alone nursing grudges against Douglas, against Johnson, against the ponies, even against his agency staff and his daughter Josie, who sided often with the Indians.

A particular irritation to him was the attitude of Arvilla Meeker's Ute housemaid, Jane. To say that this tall, pretty, bilingual girl of 22 disturbed Meeker is to understate probabilities. He had done everything he could to please her, including weeding her garden for six weeks in 1878 while she was off hunting. When she had returned, she had rewarded him with a sort of smile and nine beets out of a total crop of thirty bushels. In that tense spring of 1879, Meeker decided to coddle Jane no longer. He summoned her to his office one morning and began the conversation in a gentle kindly vein:

MEEKER: Now Jane, you will be planting your garden soon. I just want to warn you that last summer's style of gardening is played out.

JANE: Played out? How so?

MEEKER: Well, I'll tell you. After the things are planted, it will not do for you to run off and leave me to plow, hoe and pull weeds. You or some of your family must stay here all three moons and work your crops, for no one will touch them, and in that case you will have nothing. Or they will be given to some other Indian to work and he will have all.

JANE: You say we must stay three moons? What for? Hoeing the things once is enough.

MEEKER: You must hoe them three or four times, and must keep watch of them and you need not undertake to tell me how the work is to be done.

JANE: But we never done so before and we had heaps.

MEEKER (warming up): But I tell you the thing is played out. If you get anything you must work for it.

JANE: Why can't white men do the work as before? They understand it. We don't.

MEEKER: It won't do. Now I worked your garden last year. I carried hundreds of pails of water to it. You had a nice garden and got lots of money. But this year we have a big ditch and plenty of water. You must attend to things yourself.

JANE (sweetly): But, Mr. Meeker, ain't you paid for working?

MEEKER: No. Not to work for you.

JANE: Well, what are you paid money for if not to work for us?

MEEKER (momentarily stumped): Yes, I see how it is. . . . I'll put it this way. I am paid to show you how to work.

JANE: But the Utes have a heap of money. What is the money for if it is not to have work done for us?

MEEKER (coming to a boil): I'll tell you, Jane. This money is to hire me and the rest of us to teach you to help yourselves so that you can be like white folks and get rich as they are rich — by work. You are not to be waited upon and supported in idleness all your lives. You have got to take hold and support yourselves or you will have trouble.

JANE (black eyes wide): Ain't all these cattle ours, and all this land?

MEEKER: The cattle, yes. The land, no.

JANE: Well, whose land is it, and whose is the money?

MEEKER (almost yelling): The land belongs to the government and is for your use, if you use it. If you won't use it and won't work, and if you expect me to weed your garden for you, white men away off will come in and by and by you will have nothing. This thing can't go on forever. As to money, it is to be used to make you helpful. It is time you turn to and take care of your-selves and have houses and stoves and chairs and beds and crock-ery and heaps of things. Do you understand?

JANE (very quiet): Yes. But I can't tell you, Mr. Meeker, how bad you make me feel.

She left the office and Meeker watched her straight proud form as she walked across the office porch, past his hitching rack and down the street which ended at Douglas' lodge on White River. She walked stiffly and rapidly, keeping her handsome head straight ahead.

We may guess that the agent was aware that he had said too much. He had asserted not only that the Utes didn't own White River valley, but that they couldn't even stay there if they didn't follow his orders. To make matters worse, Meeker sat down now and wrote out the entire conversation verbatim for publication in the next issue of the Greeley *Tribune*.

Tension at the agency became so unbearable by early September that Meeker feared for the safety of Arvilla and Josie Meeker. But he would not call for troops from Fort Steele in Wyoming 200 miles away. The agent knew that to ask for soldiers would be to accept final defeat.

On the morning of September 8 he mailed a list of complaints to the Indian Office. Also, he called in the medicine man Johnson and accused him of stealing water for his ponies from Josie's school water barrel. Ponies! Always the ponies! Meeker was be-coming psychopathic about them. Johnson denied stealing any water and left Meeker's office muttering. After lunch he returned and stood before the agent talking fast and loud. Meeker leaned easily back in his office chair, his pale blue eyes cold and a set smile on his weary face. He did not catch all that Johnson said, but it seemed to concern the plowing up of pony pasture and his suspicion that the agent was sending lies about the Utes to Washington.

Suddenly Meeker decided that he had heard enough. He raised an imperious hand and said, very deliberately, "The trouble is this, Johnson. You have too many ponies. You had better shoot some of them."

Johnson stared at the agent for a long moment, utterly dumfounded. Then his brown eyes blazed with the fire of a reasonable man who had just heard the consummation of blasphemy. He moved slowly toward Meeker, grasped his shoulders, lifted his long spare body from the chair and hustled him across the office and on to the porch. There, two employees ran up and grabbed Johnson as he flung Meeker hard against the hitching rack.

That was all. Johnson did not touch Meeker again. The agent tottered back to his chair, felt himself over and found that he was not badly hurt. Next day, he penned a telegraphic request to Washington for troops, stating that his life and those of his employees were in danger. As his courier rode north toward the Western Union office in Rawlins, Meeker must have known that

*The Utes "ambushed" the troops sent to help Meeker, an action that set off the*

his life's dream went with him.

In Washington the Indian Office passed Meeker's wire on to General Sherman who ordered a force of 153 soldiers and 25 civilians under Major Thomas T. Thornburgh to go to White River from Rawlins. Presumably the Major did not care for the task. As an army officer he detested the Indian Office and all its works. The Ute Agency was not even in his military department. He had no decent maps, no proper guides. He had had fighting experience only with Plains Indians. He knew nothing about these Utes, with whom he tended to sympathize.

The Major took his time. On Monday morning, September 29, his force reached the Ute Reservation line at Milk Creek, 25 miles north of White River. Thornburgh had exchanged messages earlier with Meeker and had agreed to ride alone over Yellowjacket Pass to the agency for talks with Douglas and Jack, leaving

*attack on the agency. It was six days before reinforcements lifted the siege.*

his soldiers outside the reservation. But he found that Milk Creek was almost dry because of the record drought. He had to have fresh water for his men and for his 400 animals. Therefore he ordered his force to move some miles into the reservation to a spot where water was available.

From the sage ridges above Milk Creek valley, Chief Jack and his band watched this unexpected movement with enraged astonishment. Suddenly the soldiers spied the Indians. Someone fired a gun. Then everyone was firing. Men began falling to earth. After some minutes Jack's courier leaped on his pony and galloped

*Flora Ellen Price was held hostage.*

southward to bring the awful news to Douglas' band at the agency. Before noon Major Thornburgh, eleven of his troopers, and many Utes lay dead. Forty-odd white men were wounded. Nearly 300 army horses and mules were out of action. Without the use of these animals, the army survivors were completely trapped. They forted up behind their wagons and dead horses and barely managed to hold Jack's warriors off until relief troops arrived from Rawlins six days later.

On that same fateful Monday morning, everything seemed peaceful at White River Agency. The tension of recent weeks was as bad as ever, but the boys from Greeley and Douglas' men and the white women did their best to ignore it. Several young Utes loitered about begging biscuits at the big agency kitchen which Josie Meeker ran for the nine employees. She was helped by Flora Ellen Price, the plump, blond, teenaged wife of Meeker's plowman. The agent, preoccupied and wan, spent all morning describing his difficulties in his September report. Soon after lunch he appeared at Josie's kitchen window to get from her the key to the government gun closet. He walked with a stoop again as in his unhappiest Greeley days. There was a grim smile on his strained face. And still he retained enough of his old spirit to ask Josie if

*Meeker's daughter Josie survived the massacre.*

she knew what day September 29 was. When she shook her head, he said jauntily: "On this day in 1066, William the Conqueror landed in England!"

At 1:30 P.M. Josie, Arvilla, and Flora Ellen were still in the kitchen, washing and wiping the dinner dishes in the Indian summer heat. A small Ute boy stopped to borrow matches, announcing proudly, "Now I go smoke." Flora Ellen stepped outside to fetch her two small children. She saw some Greeley boys spreading dirt on the roof of a new building. Beyond them, on the street down to White River, she saw Douglas and a dozen of his men. Then she saw an Indian on a sweat-flecked pony galloping up to

Douglas from the direction of Milk Creek.

The Indian said something to the old chief and immediately after that Flora Ellen saw doom come. It came without signal, like the spontaneous firing at Milk Creek. Some of Douglas' men simply raised their Winchesters and began shooting at their white friends, the unarmed Greeley boys. Flora Ellen watched one boy fall from the new roof. She watched another as he begged the Utes not to shoot him. She saw her husband collapse holding his stomach. She snatched her crying children, joined the other women, and went with them and Frank Dresser, a Greeley boy, to the adobe milk house while the Indians fired some of the log buildings.

The three women, two children, and Dresser sat in the milk house for four hours, too stunned, too helpless, too hopeless to entirely comprehend the horror which was upon them. Arvilla Meeker picked at her faded calico dress, wept and stopped weeping, and prayed for her husband's safety. Josie was mixed sorrow and gentle compassion for the Utes, whom she had learned to understand. Flora Ellen was pure terror, dying the deaths of all the Indian-ravished heroines she had met in fiction.

At last they left the milk house in the cooling twilight and ran back to Meeker's unburned house. In the agent's office, peaceful as a church, Josie stood a moment, a tall, slender, white-faced girl of 22, her lips parted in anguished query. She was staring at Pepys' Diary lying open on her father's desk where he had left it, apparently, just before stepping outside to investigate the firing. Through the window she saw Utes looting the agency storehouse. She said to the others, "Let's try to escape north while they are busy."

They went through the gate into Meeker's wheat field. Frank Dresser ran like a deer and disappeared in the sage, but later was wounded and died before he could reach help. The Utes saw the three women and the children and came for them. Arvilla fell when a bullet grazed her thigh and lay still on the ground. A young Ute named Thompson reached her and helped her to rise. "I am sorry," he said. "I am heap much sorry. Can you walk?"

Arvilla whispered, "Yes, sir."

The young Ute offered her his arm politely and led her toward White River. Near the agent's house, he asked if she had money inside.

"Very little."

"Please go and get money."

She limped into the quiet house calling "Papa! Papa!" and somehow found twenty-six dollars in bills and four dollars in silver. Then Thompson helped her to walk to Douglas near his tepee and she gave him the money. Near him was Josie on a pile of blankets holding little May Price on her lap. Further away were Flora Ellen and her son.

Arvilla limped from Ute captor to captor. Where, she asked, was the agent? The Utes shrugged. As night came on she watched the great full moon yellowing in the east. She began to shiver and she spoke to Douglas about the thin dresses she and the girls were wearing. Douglas told Thompson to take her back with a horse and lantern to get some things.

Meeker's house was burning at one end. Entering, Arvilla called, "Nathan!" but low and sorrowfully now, almost to herself. Then she loaded Thompson with warm clothes, towels, blankets, and a medicine box. She donned her hat and shawl, put a handkerchief and a needle packet in her pocket, and limped out hugging her big volume of *Pilgrim's Progress*.

A hundred yards south of the house she came suddenly on a man's dead body, startlingly white in the moonlight, and clad only in a shirt. It was Meeker. He had been shot in the side of his handsome head and a little blood trickled still from his mouth. But he lay entirely composed, straight as he had stood in life, his arms tranquil beside him as though he were about to tell Arvilla what had happened to William the Conqueror on September 29, 1066.

She cried softly and knelt to kiss him. But she did not actually kiss him. Young Thompson was beside her and she realized that he would not understand the gesture. Then she stood up and left the body, hoping that Nathan Meeker's Utopia would be easier for him to come by in the land where he was now.

The massacre of Meeker and his eight young men by Douglas' band, the "ambush" of Thornburgh's soldiers by Jack's band, and the holding of the three white women as hostages for 23 days by both bands caused as much consternation as the Custer massacre in 1876.

Millions of people were especially upset when the women testified after their rescue that Josie's person had been outraged repeatedly during their captivity, that Flora Ellen had been forced twice to submit, and that even old Douglas had insisted on "having connection" with Mrs. Meeker once.

# THE UTE MASSACRE!

## Brave Miss Meeker's Captivity!

### HER OWN ACCOUNT OF IT.

ALSO,

## The Narratives of Her Mother and Mrs. Price.

TO WHICH IS ADDED

FURTHER THRILLING AND INTENSELY INTERESTING DETAILS, NOT HITHERTO PUBLISHED, OF THE BRAVERY AND FRIGHTFUL SUFFERINGS ENDURED BY MRS. MEEKER, MRS. PRICE AND HER TWO CHILDREN, AND

# BY MISS JOSEPHINE MEEKER.

———

PUBLISHED BY

THE OLD FRANKLIN PUBLISHING HOUSE,

PHILADELPHIA, PA.

*The furor aroused by the White River massacre cost the Utes their rich lands.*

The punishment of the alleged guilty was all the landgrabbers could have asked. The two White River bands were branded as criminals en masse by a political commission without any judicial powers whatever. Though only twenty White River Utes had staged the massacre, all 700 were penalized in that money owed to them by the government was paid instead to relatives of victims. Chief Ouray's Uncompahgre Utes, who had had nothing to do with the massacre or the "ambush," were held equally responsible. The 1868 treaty rights of all three bands were canceled. Their rights to be Americans as set forth in the Fourteenth Amendment were ignored. Title to their ancient Colorado homeland was extinguished and they were moved at gun point to barren lands in Utah. By these means the last and largest chunk of desirable Indian real estate was thrown open to white settlement.

And still, the year 1879 marked a happier turning point. It was the beginning of the end of indefensible white attitudes toward red men. Interior Secretary Carl Schurz was only one of many people who probed beneath the surface causes of the White River tragedy and then had the courage to say, and to keep on saying, that it would not have happened if the Utes had lived under the same laws as other Americans.

This novel notion took root and the roots spread far and wide. Before another decade passed, white men generally were agreeing that perhaps Indians were human beings too. Though the living Nathan Meeker failed to build his Utopia, in dying he made a contribution of far more value to his country than persuading an outdoor people to sleep in beds.

*Aware of his fame, Geronimo assumed a fierce pose for this 1887 studio portrait.*

# GERONIMO!

## By E. M. HALLIDAY

*J*ust before sunrise on May 15, 1885, Lieutenant Britton Davis, of the United States Third Cavalry, awoke in his tent at Turkey Creek, Arizona Territory. He stretched, pulled on his clothes and boots, and stepped into the clear cool of the morning.

In the forest glade where usually, at this hour, only the dark trunks of great pines were to be seen, he was instantly aware of the shadowy figures of perhaps forty Indians, huddled silently before his tent. Among them Davis recognized the chiefs and sub-chiefs of the most dangerous Apache band on the reservation: the Chiricahuas.

That in itself was not alarming, since Davis often met the chiefs for sunrise discussions. But on this morning things looked different. The chiefs seemed sullen. On top of a nearby knoll, keeping watch toward Fort Apache seventeen miles away — the nearest army garrison — Davis could see a pair of Indians; their silhouettes showed rifles. Another ominous circumstance was that Davis' Apache scouts — Indians who had been enlisted on the theory that the Chiricahuas could be best policed by their own people — were also gathered in the glade in groups of four or five, and they too were armed. Clearly they expected trouble.

Through Mickey Free, a half-Irish, half-Apache interpreter, Davis learned without surprise that the chiefs wanted to make formal complaints. He ushered them into his tent, and the Indians squatted in a semicircle. Loco, an elderly chief, began a long, slow speech, but a younger man, a subchief named Chihuahua, broke in impatiently. The trouble was easily explained, he said. The Apaches were angry because Davis, as the officer in charge of their camp, had jailed some of them for exercising two time-honored customs: drinking tiswin (a strong beer made from corn) and beating wives. They had surrendered and come to live peacefully on the reservation, Chihuahua said, but they had made no agreement to alter their domestic habits. He maintained that what they drank, and how they disciplined their wives, was no business of the U.S. Army.

Davis began an explanation of why General George Crook, his commanding officer, had felt it necessary to prohibit these folkways, but he was shortly interrupted by Nana, the oldest of the Chiricahua leaders.

"Tell the Stout Chief [Davis]," Nana said harshly to the interpreter, "that he can't advise me how to treat my women. He is only a boy. I killed *men* before he was born." And with as much dignity as his bent and wrinkled body could command, Nana stalked out.

Davis knew now that the situation was serious. Nana, despite his eighty-odd years, had only recently surrendered his warriors after a frightening series of bloody raids on Mexican and American ranches, and his status among the Chiricahuas was still far from emeritus. The other chiefs were muttering their approval, and Chihuahua was launching into a more defiant speech, the gist of which was that there was no Army guardhouse big enough to hold all five hundred of the Apaches assigned to the Turkey Creek part of the reservation. Almost more disturbing than Chihuahua's open defiance was the glowering look on the eagle face of Geronimo, whom Davis regarded as "thoroughly vicious, intractable, and treacherous"—the worst of the Apache leaders. If looks could kill, the Lieutenant was about to join the already extensive company of Geronimo's victims.

Deciding to play for time, Davis told the Indians he would telegraph General Crook, at Prescott, and ask him what to do about the complaints. He knew that the chiefs feared and respected Crook, who had put them on the reservation in the first place. The meeting broke up in a mood of tense and temporary compromise.

Having posted his most trusted Apache scouts as watchmen, Davis rode to Fort Apache and sent his telegram. Necessarily it had to go by way of the army post at San Carlos, sixty miles to the south, and Davis knew it would be at least a day before he heard from Crook—maybe more, since it was already the end of the week. After alerting the officers and men at the fort for possible action, the Lieutenant whiled away some uneasy hours on Satur-

*General Miles called Crook's Apache scouts a "turbulent, disreputable band."*

day in the limited weekend diversions of a far-western garrison. Periodically, scouts came in from Turkey Creek to report a state of restless suspense there: the Chiricahuas were waiting.

By Sunday morning there was still no reply from Crook, but Davis hopefully assumed some sort of military preparations must be under way at the General's end of the line. (He was to discover later that an officer at San Carlos, acting on the advice of a drunken colleague, had never forwarded the message at all.) Late Sunday afternoon there was a post baseball game at Fort Apache. Davis was umpiring, in what was undoubtedly a distracted state of mind, when Mickey Free and Chato, top sergeant of the Apache scouts, galloped in to report that an undetermined number of the Chiricahuas under Geronimo and Nana had broken from the reservation and were heading for their old haunts across the Mexican border.

Davis immediately told the telegraph operator to wire Crook again. Nothing happened: the line had been cut. While the bugles at Fort Apache blew boots and saddles, Davis hurried back to his camp at Turkey Creek to investigate. He was relieved to find his company of Apache scouts in formation in front of his tent, awaiting orders. He knew, however, that among them were many blood relatives of the renegades who had gone with Geronimo. The next few moments would tell whether or not he had a full-blown mutiny on his hands.

The Lieutenant ordered the scouts to ground arms while he went into his tent for extra ammunition to issue before they took up the pursuit. Dusk was coming on, and he would have to light a lamp in the tent—an easy mark for a sniper. He stationed Chato and another Apache sergeant at either side of the tent fly, facing the company.

"Shoot the first man who raises his gun from the ground," Davis ordered. He went into the tent and lit the lamp. At that moment three Apache scouts slipped from the formation and disappeared quickly into the darkening brush—but that was all. Very shortly the rest of the company was on the march, the best trailers in the outfit tracking the fugitives' hoofmarks slowly but surely under the Arizona stars. But Geronimo and Nana had mounted their people on good horses, and by now were off to a long head start.

Thus began what was in some ways the most extraordinary Indian campaign in the history of the West. Lieutenant Davis himself, looking back many years later, summed it up as succinctly as anyone ever has, and with a proper degree of wonder:

In this campaign thirty-five men and eight half-grown or older boys, encumbered with the care and sustenance of 101 women and children, with no base of supplies and no means of waging war or of obtaining food or transportation other than what they could take from their enemies, maintained themselves for eighteen months in a country two hundred by four hundred miles in extent, against five thousand troops, regulars and irregulars, five hundred Indian auxiliaries of these troops, and an unknown number of civilians.

That terse statement goes far to explain the fact that, of all American Indian leaders, Geronimo may well be the most famous. It is nevertheless a curious fact, for he was not a man of great stature—a "patriot chief," like Tecumseh, Crazy Horse, or Chief Joseph, leading whole tribes in a noble but hopeless stand against the rape of their homeland. Nothing in Geronimo's record suggests that he was capable of deep thought or feeling; nor was he a chief by reason of family precedent. He became the leader of a small band of Apache raiders much the way a gangster takes over a "mob": by hard force of personality and skill in conducting field operations.

But when it came to making a mark in history, there was much in Geronimo's favor. It was his fortune to be the *last* of a succession of Apache leaders who for well over a hundred years terrorized Mexico and the Southwest with harrowing raids from their mountain hide-outs. His depredations of 1885–86 were committed when Arizona and New Mexico were strenuously working to emerge from the raw frontier and become a reasonably civilized part of America. Miners, ranchers, and farmers clamored for protection; territorial newspapers constantly upbraided the Army for its failure to destroy this last Apache menace, and the territorial governors again and again petitioned Washington to take more drastic steps. By the autumn of 1885 the whole country was aware that large segments of the United States and Mexican armies were unable to catch one fugitive remnant of Apache desperadoes, and the pursuit began to take on the fascination of a particularly dangerous fox hunt.

The fox, moreover, had an intriguing name. It seems doubtful that Geronimo would have become a semilegendary figure if he had been widely known by his Apache name, which was Goyakla—"the Yawner." No one can imagine World War II para-

*Geronimo (left) rides with Naiche, his constant companion throughout the Apache*

*deportation to Florida and then Alabama, and the final settlement in Oklahoma.*

troopers shouting "Goyakla!" as a war cry when they plunged from airplanes; nor could they have aroused much adrenaline with such a name as Nana. But "Geronimo!" rolls off the tongue with satisfactory resonance and impact; for obscure linguistic reasons it carries intimations of excitement.*

There was, of course, a long and sensational historical background for the popular image of the Apache raider. Unlike other southwestern tribes—the Navahos, for instance, or the Pueblos—the Apaches had made only a truculent adjustment to the arrival of Western civilization. They seemed disdainfully uninterested in settling down to weave blankets, raise sheep, or farm. A relatively primitive tribe with nomadic habits, they lived in small, semi-independent bands, in the simplest kind of improvised shelters—brush "wikiups," covered with whatever was handy—which would have looked uninhabitable to the Plains Indians with their proud buffalo-hide tepees. In summer the Apaches climbed into the high mountain parks of the Rockies and the Sierra Madres; in winter they came down to the warmer lands, along the banks of the rivers. They ate almost anything. Venison, beef, or horseflesh was fine when they could get it easily; otherwise jack rabbits or even field rats were meat to them, supplemented by mescal, fruit of the cactus, sunflower seeds, acorns, berries, and nuts.

Physically, the Apaches had become a specialized type. Implacable natural selection, helped along by infanticide when a child seemed to be feeble, had produced over the course of a few centuries a formidably rugged breed. Not tall—the typical Apache warrior was perhaps five foot seven—they were lean and muscular, broad of shoulder, deep of chest, and with legs that seemed thewed with spring steel. Their women, though they aged fast, were lithe and tough: childbirth, for instance, was but an hour's interruption to whatever other labor a wife happened to be occupied with at the time. It was no news to hear that a band of these Indians, including women and children, had travelled forty miles a day on foot, across precipitous mountain canyons or the most arid stretches of desert. The Apache's resistance to heat and his water metabolism almost rivalled that of the camel: he could be "hilarious and jovial" (observed an army officer who knew the tribe well) "when the civilized man is about to die of thirst."

*In Spanish, the name was pronounced Heronimo; but the Americanized form became common in Geronimo's own lifetime.

But the most important fact about the Apaches was simply this: they were marauders by profession. As far back as the oldest of them could remember, plunder had been their regular way of life. Above a bare subsistence level they depended on their victims for nearly everything: horses, cattle, weapons, ammunition, domestic utensils, clothing, tobacco, liquor — and amusement.

Apaches hunted Mexicans almost as the Plains Indians hunted buffalo: they seemed to be natural prey, and there was a sporting aspect to a raid on a Mexican settlement that overlaid the practical matter of replenishing supplies. An Indian camp high in the Sierras would become wildly excited when plans for a big sortie were afoot.

Yet once a raid was actually in progress, a sinister efficiency took over. Masters of stealth, the Apaches would meticulously survey the scene so as to anticipate just what resistance they might encounter; then they would pounce out of the night upon their quarry, killing all males over ten or twelve, and capturing women and little children for use as slaves or hostages. It is significant that scalping was not a common Apache practice: loot, not trophies, was what they were after, and honor was to be measured as much by material gain as by valor. Their ferocity was, so to speak, of a professional variety.

The history of American-Apache relations, starting with America's acquisition of much of the Apache homeland after the Mexican War, was a bloody one, relieved only by scattered attempts at peaceful coexistence. Both Confederate and Union troops in the Southwest fought Apaches during the Civil War, and grew grimly accustomed to their maddening guerrilla tactics. The Confederate governor of Arizona, Colonel John R. Baylor, declared to Jefferson Davis that "extermination of the grown Indians and making slaves of the children is the only remedy." Davis, shocked by the harshness of the prescription, indignantly vetoed it. But General J. H. Carleton, Union commander in the Southwest, instituted a scarcely gentler policy by ordering that all Apache men "are to be slain wherever and whenever they can be found"; the women and children were to be taken prisoner. Meanwhile, in 1863, Mangas Coloradas, the greatest of Apache chiefs, was "captured" by Federal soldiers while discussing a possible peace treaty; then he was provoked into "trying to escape" and was shot to death.

339

*General Crook (above with Apache guides) often broke with Army conventions.*

*He shunned regulation uniforms, used mules, and trained Indians as scouts.*

But by the 1870's, the most sanguine and sanguinary hopes for wiping out Apache manhood were foundering. The ravished towns and haciendas of northern Mexico lay more helpless than ever under the strokes of the marauders, and across the border in Arizona and New Mexico settlers were endlessly haunted by the Apache spectre. An investigator appointed by President U. S. Grant reported in 1871 that the "extermination" policy "has resulted in a war which, in the last ten years, has cost us a thousand lives and over forty millions of dollars, and the country is no quieter nor the Indians any nearer extermination than they were at the time of the Gadsden purchase." It was decided to combine the stick with the carrot: as many Apaches as possible would be lured onto reservations, while the adamant hostiles would be hunted to earth by new and more vigorous methods.

It was to effect this approach that General William T. Sherman, the Army chief of staff, sent to Arizona an officer who, when his long career was over, would often be called the greatest Indian fighter the West ever knew. General George Crook, however, was more than a successful subduer of the red man: he was at the same time a sympathetic friend. He was free of the ethnic bias that made most Americans regard Indians as possibly higher animals but decidedly lower humans: "With all his faults," Crook once declared to a graduating class at West Point, ". . . the American Indian is not half as black as he has been painted. He is cruel in war, treacherous at times, and not over cleanly. But so were our forefathers." Along with such blunt views as these, Crook had a personal demeanor that was disconcerting to some but impressive to all. He disliked official uniform, usually dressing in comfortable hunting clothes; he had a great, forked beard which he sometimes braided for convenience; he was taciturn and often moody — and he attracted to his staff some of the most intelligent and devoted young officers in the frontier army.

As a result of a fine Civil War record plus some outstanding exploits against the Yakimas and Paiutes in the eighteen fifties and sixties, Crook already had a high reputation when he was assigned as commander of the Department of Arizona in July, 1871, at his brevet rank of brigadier general. With characteristic vigor and contempt for the orthodox, he launched a program of negotiation salted with chastisement that in four years had most of the Apaches on reserves in New Mexico and Arizona. His campaign innovations included heavy reliance on pack mules instead of horses —

because of their greater endurance and mountain-climbing ability—and selection and training of a corps of Indian scouts who soon gave new meaning to an old saying of the Southwest: "It takes an Apache to catch an Apache." The idea of Chiricahua ex-warriors being deliberately armed and equipped by the Army and sent out to pursue their own kin struck many frontier observers with dismay; but Crook had learned that a counterpart to Indian ferocity was Indian loyalty—if his employers proved to be worthy of his trust.

Unfortunately, Crook had more to contend with than Apaches. His surprisingly successful efforts to teach the new reservation Indians the rudiments of farming were sabotaged by white greed for money and land. The business of supplying rations to the government for use by peaceful Indians was already one of the dirtiest in the annals of American enterprise. To cheat an Indian was commonly regarded as a perfectly good way to make a living, and Crook's young officers fought an endless struggle against watered stock, false weights, and adulterated supplies. Nor could many white settlers tolerate the sight of Indians becoming self-sufficient on good, fertile land: it meant less business for contractors, and less land for whites. Through political manipulations, and against the protests of Crook and his staff, the Apaches were moved from the better reservations and concentrated at places like San Carlos, Arizona—an arid, treeless waste to which Lieutenant Britton Davis referred, not humorously, as "Hell's Forty Acres." It was small wonder that Apache warriors, remembering the free life of the cool and lovely mountains, drowned their bitterness in tiswin drunks or stupefied themselves with rotgut whiskey bootlegged in by avaricious white traders.

Crook's policies were nevertheless so generally successful that in 1875 the War Department moved him to the northern plains, where he was soon deeply involved, along with such officers as George Armstrong Custer, against the hostile Sioux. By the time Custer and Crazy Horse had gone to their doom and things had quieted down in that region, the Southwest was again afire with Apache terror. Cochise, one of the tribe's great patriarchs, had died as a reservation Indian. But other chiefs who still revered the valiant memory of Mangas Coloradas had now taken over the leadership of the Chiricahuas and their cousins the Mimbreños: Nana, Loco, Victorio, Naiche (son of Cochise), Chato—and Geronimo. Operating sometimes together and

*Apache scouts employed by the United States Army. One is applying war paint.*

sometimes only with small, individual bands, these tireless outlaws rejected the miserable certainties of the reservation for the desperate freedoms of the old Apache way. Weaving back and forth across the Mexican border, they repeatedly ambushed both Mexican and American troops sent in pursuit of them; they slaughtered scores of civilians as well as soldiers, and stole hundreds of horses and whole herds of cattle. The success of their baffling maneuvers drew Indian recruits from the American reservations every time they swooped into New Mexico or Arizona, and the whole situation began to go—from the white point of view—precipitately downhill.

To try to halt the debacle, General Crook was ordered back to Arizona in the late summer of 1882. He began a series of patient interrogations and conferences with Apache leaders to discover their grievances, and he set about the unpleasant task of ridding the reservations of unscrupulous and grafting agents, squatters, and traders. In October he issued general orders to his troops that emphasized an approach to Indian affairs almost eclipsed since his departure from the Southwest in 1875. "One of the fundamental principles of the military character," he said, "is justice to all—Indians as well as white men. . . . In all their dealings with the Indians, officers must be careful not only to observe the strictest fidelity, but to make no promises not in their power to carry out." It was a noble ideal, and the final crisis of Crook's career would come in a strenuous effort to make it a reality.

Crook's enlightened attitude, coupled with the growing efficiency of his corps of mule-pack troopers and enlisted Apache scouts, soon began to bear fruit. Slowly but steadily the restlessness of the reservation Apaches subsided, and Crook was left free to operate against the holdouts, most of whom were Chiricahuas. The word from Mexico was that Victorio had been killed in action; but Chato, old Nana, and Geronimo were still enjoying themselves, stripping isolated Mexican settlements of everything worth taking and swiftly disappearing into the fastness of the Sierra Madres, where they drove off pursuing Mexicans with ridiculous ease.

Chato—who later became Lieutenant Britton Davis' most devoted scout—unwittingly made a serious mistake in the spring of 1883. Like many of the Apaches still at large, his fighters had managed to equip themselves with Winchester repeating rifles—

345

*Geronimo and his defiant band (photographed here before their surrender to Gen-*

booty from assaulted pack trains and ranches. The Winchester was a fine weapon, with a more lethal capacity than the ordinary rifles of the Mexican and American armies. But ammunition for it was hard to get. Usually it meant a sally across the border into American territory, where opposition from the far-ranging troopers was sure to be tough and persistent.

Chato took the risk, and in true Apache style engaged in a certain amount of rapine along the way. Near Silver City, New Mexico, on the morning of March 24, 1883, his band of twenty-six encountered Judge H. C. McComas, driving his wife and six-year-old son toward Lordsburg in a frontier wagon. They were a prominent family, but to Chato they were just ordinary white settlers, and fair game. His band descended on the McComas wagon like wolves, shot the judge seven times, clubbed the resisting Mrs. McComas to death, and rode off with Charlie McComas as a captive. A stagecoach reached the scene soon afterward, and by the next day a new wave of public exhortation was demanding an end to the Apache menace in the Southwest.

Chato and his party by this time had acquired their ammunition and slipped back into Mexico, having killed a couple of dozen other settlers in the process—but one of their number, a young man whom the American soldiers called Peaches because

*eral Crook in 1886) managed to evade both Mexican and American troops.*

of his unusually light complexion, stayed behind. Britton Davis found him visiting some of his relatives near San Carlos, and arrested him without difficulty. More important, Peaches asserted that many of the Apache outlaws were growing tired of war, and he agreed to guide General Crook into the heart of the Sierra Madres—to their secret and almost inaccessible retreat. It was an opportunity not to be missed.

Crook's carefully planned campaign into Mexico got under way on May 1, 1883. It was in several respects a novel expedition. For one thing, the American and Mexican governments had explicitly agreed that there was to be no difficulty about crossing the border as long as the object was the destruction or capture of the hostile bands. For another, the make-up of Crook's force was a kind of double-or-nothing bet on the reliability of Indian auxiliaries: 193 of his fighting men were Apache scouts, well armed and selected for their superb physical fitness, while there were only 42 enlisted white soldiers and nine officers. Equipment was cut down to bare necessities. Except for the personal kit that no Apache warrior would travel without—a knife, an awl for sewing moccasins, and a pair of tweezers for plucking face hair—each man carried only his rifle, forty rounds of ammunition, one blanket and a canteen of water. Rations and

347

camp equipment were packed on the backs of hand-picked mules, which were then organized into five trains and tended by Mexican packers.

According to Crook's adjutant, Captain John G. Bourke, most of the outfit was in high spirits as they descended into northern Mexico toward the Sierra Madres, despite the rather depressing character of the countryside:

On each hand were the ruins of depopulated and abandoned hamlets, destroyed by the Apaches. . . . The sun glared down pitilessly, wearing out the poor mules . . . slipping over loose stones or climbing rugged hills . . . breaking their way through jungles of thorny vegetation. . . . Through all this the Apache scouts trudged without a complaint, and with many a laugh and jest. Each time camp was reached they showed themselves masters of the situation. They would gather the saponaceous roots of the yucca and Spanish bayonet, to make use of them in cleaning their long, black hair, or cut sections of the bamboo-like cane and make pipes for smoking, or four-holed flutes, which emitted a weird, Chinese sort of music. . . .

Passing through the little towns of Bávispe and Basaraca, where they were feted with enthusiasm but little else by poverty-stricken Mexicans, they began to hear lurid tales of recent Chiricahua operations. The name of Geronimo was frequently mentioned, and Bourke concluded that the Mexicans regarded him as a kind of devil incarnate, "sent to punish them for their sins."

By May 9, the expedition was well into the Sierra Madres. The going was extremely rough, up mountain trails so steep and narrow that five supposedly sure-footed mules plunged over precipices to their death. Peaches led the command up and down the corrugated ridges and across deeply gashed canyons into country none of the white men had ever seen, and eventually they emerged from a gorge into a small natural amphitheatre some 8,000 feet up — a favorite camp site, the guide said, of Geronimo's band. This eyrie was empty now; but a few days later Captain Emmett Crawford, pushing on with an advance party of Apache scouts, surprised a Chiricahua encampment, killed several of the hostiles, and captured four children and a young woman.

This proved to be the beginning of the end of the campaign. As the young woman told General Crook, her people were "astounded and dismayed" when they realized that the Americans, with Apaches as guides and allies, had penetrated to the innermost reaches of the Sierra Madres, where they had always felt safe from pursuit. Geronimo and Chato, she said, were away on a raid; but she was sure that when word of this new development reached them, they would find most of their warriors in a mood to surrender.

She was right. She herself was sent out as an emissary with the bad tidings that the Chiricahuas' stronghold was no longer impregnable, and within twenty-four hours smoke signals from a nearby peak indicated that some of the hostiles were coming in to surrender.

At first only old men, women, and children appeared, but on May 18 a small band of warriors came cautiously into the American camp. Leading them was Chihuahua; and on May 20 Geronimo, Chato, and thirty-six other first-class fighters arrived, back from their raid and full of consternation at what they found awaiting them.

During the next few days, as more renegades continued to give themselves up, Crook began a close acquaintance with Geronimo that was to continue off and on for seven years with little admiration on either side. Unlike many of the Apache leaders, in whom an easy candor and ingenuousness offset courage and ferocity, Geronimo struck the General as deceitful, arrogant, and vindictive — "a human tiger," Crook said later. The Apache headman was a windy talker, and he now gave a long discourse on how badly misunderstood he and his people had been, and how anxious they were to live on the American reservation and work peacefully — if only they could be guaranteed good treatment. Crook, as usual, said little, but made it clear that fair treatment could be reasonably expected if they returned with him, while the alternative, which he was perfectly willing to undertake, was relentless warfare against any Chiricahuas who did not care to come in.

After much further talk, mostly from the Apache, it was agreed that Geronimo, Chato, and some of their followers would be allowed a respite of "two moons" in which to gather up the elements of the Chiricahua bands still scattered in the Sierra Madres. They then would make their way to the United States, where General Crook would have preceded them with the Indians already in hand, and all would go onto reservations.

The remarkable thing was that Geronimo kept his part of the agreement, though admittedly several months later than he had promised. Crook brought over 300 Apaches back from Mexico in June, 1883 — an amazing achievement — but nearly 200 remained in the Sierra Madres. In October, with territorial newspapers snarling at Crook's "folly" for not having destroyed them all when he had the chance, Lieutenant Britton Davis was sent to the border to see if he could discover what was going on in Old Mexico. After a wait of about a month, he was rewarded by the arrival of several bands including those of Naiche and Chato. Geronimo, these Indians assured Davis, was on the way — but it was spring of 1884 before the famous outlaw rode into Davis' camp, leading approximately eighty Chiricahuas.

It was Davis' first encounter with the man who a year later was to give him so much trouble at Turkey Creek, and it occurred in a manner that the Lieutenant found highly expressive of Geronimo's character. As the Indians approached his camp, Davis sent Apache scouts to meet them and explain that the American soldiers were there purely as an escort. The human tiger did not appreciate this courtesy. "Riding up to me and checking his pony only when its shoulder had bumped the shoulder of my mule," Davis wrote, "his first words were an angry demand to know why there was need of an escort. . . . He had made peace with the Americans, why then was there danger of their attacking him?"

Davis explained that certain members of Arizona's civilian population, often fortified by whiskey, were ranging the border area looking for Apaches to shoot or hang, and that the Army's role was to conduct the Indians safely to San Carlos. This might not be easy, especially since Geronimo, a do-it-yourself prodigal, had brought with him a herd of 350 fatted cattle — stolen from Mexican ranches to trade to his tribesmen when he reached the American reservation. It meant slower travelling, and more chance of interference.

Sure enough, when the whole party was camping one night near a ranch house, there appeared on the scene two men in civilian clothes — who identified themselves, however, as a U.S. marshal and a collector of customs. The marshal handed Davis a subpoena and announced that they were there to take Geronimo's band under arrest to Tucson, to stand trial for smuggling and murder. If Davis failed to help them, they would organize a posse in a nearby town, and the Lieutenant could take the consequences.

Davis was amicable, but underneath he had no intention of giving up his charges before they got to San Carlos. That evening he entertained the marshal and the collector with such generosity that both of them went to bed in the ranch house numb with whiskey. Then Davis told Geronimo that at sunrise the marshal was planning to take all of his cattle away from him, and that a sneak departure toward San Carlos was advisable. Ge-

W·A·ROGERS.

*Led by an Apache, General Crook penetrated to recesses of the Sierra Madres never before seen by white men. Here the octogenarian Chief Nana surrenders.*

ronimo, at first irascibly unwilling, was moved to action by a gibe from Davis that the feat might be too much for even Chiricahuas to pull off. Ho! said the chief. When the marshal and the collector came sleepily out of the ranch house the next morning, they found only Britton Davis, sitting patiently beside his mule, waiting to explain that Geronimo and the Apache scouts had unexpectedly decided to leave in the middle of the night. He was not quite sure, he said, where they had gone. The marshal told Davis he could go to hell, and the Lieutenant then rode off to catch up with Geronimo and the scouts.

No part of the Geronimo saga has been more romanticized for commerical consumption than the background of the outbreak of 1885, after the Chiricahuas had been on the reservation for over a year. A recent movie, for instance, supplied the Apache leader with a set of motives worthy of Sitting Bull: there were brutal army officers, scenes of public humiliation, and outrageous land grabs. The fact is that in officers like Crook, Bourke, Crawford, and Davis, the Apaches were extraordinarily lucky. Moreover, the Chiricahuas, at least, got good land: they were taken up above San Carlos to Turkey Creek, where there was plenty of water, a pleasant pine forest, and abundant game. True it was that the life of the farmer, to which Britton Davis reluctantly introduced them—for he was himself a sportsman by nature—was contrary to their long-established habits, and few of them took to it with any grace. Davis tells how, in the spring of 1885 shortly before Geronimo's last escape from the reservation, he was invited to view the chief's "farm." "When I arrived at the section of river bottom that had been allotted to him and his band he was sitting on a rail in the shade of a tree with one of his wives fanning him. The other two were hoeing a quarter-acre patch of partially cleared ground, in which a few sickly looking sprouts of corn were struggling for life."

But what moved a minority—about one-fourth—to the final break from the reservation was not so much what they were obliged to do in their new environment as what they were forbidden to do. As related at the start of this account, the prohibition against tiswin and wife-beating was particularly galling; and for some, including Geronimo and Nana, total abstinence from brigandage was more than they could bear. Davis felt that Geronimo never ceased to brood over the fact that "his" herd of cattle had been taken from him when he came in from Mexico. It was confiscation of rightful booty, from the Apache standpoint, and it engendered in Geronimo a wrath almost equal to that of Achilles, who, it will be remembered, retired to sulk in his tent for a similar reason at the beginning of the Trojan War.

Geronimo, together with Nana, Naiche, and something above a hundred of their compatriots, rode off from Turkey Creek on May 17, 1885, with Lieutenant Davis and his Apache scouts in pursuit. Their ultimate surrender took place on September 4, 1886. An odd thing about the long campaign which led to that surrender is that despite the tremendous national interest it aroused, most of its details are less than stirring. The truly exciting days of Apache-American warfare were already in the past: the odds were now much too heavy against the Indians, and their survival depended almost entirely on their skill at evasion. In this, however, Geronimo proved himself to be one of the virtuosos of all time. "It is senseless to fight when you cannot hope to win," the old warrior observed to an interviewer twenty years later, when he had become a celebrated captive. He knew, in 1885–86, that "winning" was out of the question—but he soon demonstrated that a fugitive freedom could be prolonged over an astonishing length of time.

The meager number of the renegades, while it made pitched battle unprofitable, greatly facilitated fast movement and effective concealment. They rode their horses at a killing pace, and then got fresh mounts by stealing them from the nearest ranch; the exhausted animals, after a quick butchering job, served as food. By ranging over eighty thousand square miles of exceedingly difficult terrain that he knew probably better than any man living, Geronimo continually frustrated pursuit by many separate detachments of American and Mexican troops. Sometimes, by the most dogged and strenuous effort, some of Crook's scouts would catch up with the hostiles; but the typical result was the capture of a few ponies and camp supplies and possibly a couple of women and children. The rest of the quarry vanished into the mountains, as Lieutenant Davis put it with much exasperation, "like quail when the hawk dives."

Whenever they camped, Geronimo designated a rendezvous point forty or fifty miles away: if an attack came, the Apaches broke up quickly into groups of two or three, or even took individual flight, and by as many different routes converged upon the chosen spot a day or two later.

353

The military obstacles were very hard for anyone not actually in the field to understand. Lieutenant General Philip Sheridan, now the commanding general of the Army, and a West Point contemporary of General Crook's, felt both his understanding and his patience dwindling as the months went by and as journalistic agitation for the capture of Geronimo steadily ballooned. Even President Cleveland, responding to political pressure, was irritably anxious to see the Apache gadfly disposed of — preferably, he said, by hanging, which would certainly have been most satisfactory to the enraged citizens of Arizona and New Mexico. If that was impossible, nearly everyone in government circles agreed, the thing to do was send all the Chiricahuas to some safe place in the East the minute they could be rounded up.

In January, 1886, things suddenly took a new turn. A detachment under Captain Crawford caught up with Geronimo's band, and with great good luck captured all of their horses and camp equipment. Eight months of running had tired the renegades, and they decided to negotiate. But on the day the talks were to occur, some Mexican soldiers from nearby Sonora towns suddenly attacked Crawford's camp, by mistake, and before the confusion was cleared up, Crawford had a fatal bullet in his brain. The parley was postponed until March, at which time Crook himself journeyed into the Mexican mountains near San Bernardino and met in conference with Geronimo, Naiche, and Chihuahua. To Crook's disgust, Geronimo was more windy-worded than ever, overblown with concern about his reputation and full of blame for everyone but himself for what had happened since May, 1885. Nevertheless, he agreed to surrender on condition that he and his band should not be held prisoner in the East for more than two years, and that their families should be allowed to go with them.

It looked like the end; but after Crook had returned to Arizona, leaving a small party of Americans and a group of Apache scouts to conduct the surrendered band, Geronimo and Naiche and some of their warriors got thoroughly drunk on hundred-proof liquor, allegedly sold to them by an American named Tribolet. That made everything look different, and in the middle of the night about half the band took off into Mexico again. Sheridan, who learned of this by telegram on March 31, was furious. He could not comprehend how Crook could have let the hostiles slip out of his grasp, but he was sure that reliance on Apache scouts as escorts was the heart of the trouble—and he implied as much in his answer to Crook. This was close to an insult: it challenged the one method by which, Crook was convinced, Apache renegades could be brought to bay. What Sheridan failed to realize, Crook explained in another telegram, was that Geronimo's band, far from being a flock of helpless refugees, was still "armed to the teeth, having the most improved guns and all the ammunition they could carry," and that only on the basis of mutual trust could they be taken into custody at all.

But it was too late to patch up the difference between the two old West Pointers. Another stiff exchange of telegrams ended with Crook asking to be relieved of his command. Sheridan quickly complied.

Now the last chapter in the "Geronimo campaign" was about to unfold. The man who replaced Crook was an old acquaintance, and (though Crook seems to have been largely unaware of it at the time) an old rival. General Nelson A. Miles had, to his chagrin, followed in Crook's footsteps from the time they both were bright young Union generals in the Civil War, through the Sioux campaigns of the 1870's, and the equally trying struggles for recognition and promotion amidst the narrow opportunities of the frontier army. Always Crook kept one jump ahead, and as Miles' letters to his wife reveal, he had gradually developed an almost paranoiac jealousy of his somewhat older fellow officer. At last his great chance had come: Crook had been discredited, and it was up to Miles to succeed where Crook had not—with the whole country watching to see what would happen.

By May, 1886, Miles was in full command in Arizona. In the eyes of Crook's loyal staff officers, most of whom were of course replaced, he was indeed a Johnny-come-lately, arriving on the scene when an absurdly small number of the hostile Apaches remained at large (to be exact, there were twenty-one men and thirteen women still with Geronimo). Nevertheless, it was a very big thing for Miles, and he made exhaustive preparations for the denouement. He reorganized his combat and supply forces, discharging nearly all of the Apache scouts—which must have pleased Sheridan—and distributing his troops so that there was hardly a ranch or water hole in Arizona or New Mexico that did not have a small detachment within easy call. One innovation, picked up from the British Army, did turn out to be highly effective: the heliograph. In the sunny climate of the Southwest, this scientifically designed mirror worked very well, and within weeks Miles had a system by which he could flash messages three or four hundred miles in a couple of hours, across country that no telegraph lines would decorate for many years to come. On the other hand, he quickly discovered something that Crook could have told him: when the Chiricahuas took to the Sierra Madres, the best United States cavalry was useless, and only foot soldiers, guided by Apaches, stood any chance of routing out the hostiles.

By Miles' own estimate, his men chased Geronimo more than two thousand miles in three months, and with highly impalpable results until the very end. Meanwhile Geronimo, to everyone's consternation, had the insolence to strike back across the border into Arizona, expertly running a gantlet of half a dozen detachments of soldiers, and so closely pursued that his band, as Miles expressed it officially, "committed but fourteen murders" before they plunged into Mexico again.

What Miles' troopers did succeed in doing—not surprisingly, since there were approximately five thousand of them—was to induce heavy fatigue in Geronimo's little group. The chief himself was in his late fifties and perhaps decided that it was time to retire from the more athletic activities of his career. Nonetheless, when he finally gave up once and for all, on September 4, 1886, it was a negotiated surrender, and not a capture. Borrowing from the tactical book of General Crook, possibly with some embarrassment, Miles sent a pair of formerly hostile Apaches to seek out Geronimo's camp and suggest a parley. This was achieved late in August, but only because Lieutenant Charles Gatewood, one of Crook's best officers and one who knew Geronimo well, agreed to be the intermediary. Miles supplied him with an escort of troopers, but Gatewood knew what he was doing, and made his way to the meeting place, near Fronteras, Mexico, all alone. His offer to Geronimo's band was simple: "Surrender, and you will be sent with your families to Florida, there to await the decision of the President as to your final disposition. Accept these terms or fight it out to the bitter end."

Gatewood added something else: that many of their relatives had *already* been sent East—to Fort Marion, Florida, which the War Department judged to be sufficiently removed from Arizona to prevent further trouble. That news visibly affected the hostiles. They talked it over, and agreed to surrender to General

Miles. After an eleven-day march, not as captives but still under arms and merely accompanied by American troops, they arrived at Skeleton Canyon, Arizona, where Miles joined them in a state of nervous excitement. His triumphal hour was near, but he was acutely aware that things could go wrong just at the last moment, as they had for Crook. He had never laid eyes on Geronimo before, and it may be supposed that he faced the famous renegade with intense—and tense—interest.

Geronimo, for his part, seemed to be relaxed, and even managed a humorous thrust at the moment of introduction. "Gen-

*General Nelson A. Miles, who finally succeeded in bringing in the wily Geronimo*

eral Miles is your friend," said the interpreter. The Indian gave Miles a defoliating look. "I never saw him," he said. "I have been in need of friends. Why has he not been with me?"

Miles had some of his men demonstrate the heliograph to Geronimo, sending a message to Fort Bowie and receiving a reply within minutes. If anything had been lacking to clinch the

*While curious and rather suspicious soldiers look on, Naiche (left) and Geronimo*

surrender, that did it, and on September 7, 1886, Miles was able to write to his wife, without undue modesty: "If you had been here you would have seen me riding in over the mountains with Geronimo and Natchez as you saw me ride over the hills and down to the Yellowstone with Chief Joseph. It is a brilliant ending of a difficult problem."

*pose for a photographer in September, 1886, just after their final surrender.*

There were many who thought the ending was not so brilliant, and George Crook was one of them. At Omaha, where he was now in command of the Department of the Platte, he heard that Geronimo and his braves had been sent by train to Fort Pickens, Florida, while their families went to Fort Marion, two hundred miles away. This was an outright violation of the terms of the surrender; and on top of that, 400 Chiricahuas at Fort Apache, who had remained loyal all through Geronimo's last rampage, were summarily rounded up and sent off to Fort Marion also. Not exempted were many Apache scouts who had served Crook with absolute fidelity, and to the end of his days the General never lost his smouldering indignation at this treatment.

Crook did more than just smoulder. He spent much of his time between 1886 and 1890 endeavoring to win better justice for his former enemies and allies, who were not exactly thriving in the steaming climate of Florida. Malaria and other "white men's diseases" took a lugubrious toll: even at the well-run Carlisle Indian School in Pennsylvania, where many of the children were sent to be civilized, thirty of them had died by 1890. Early that year, Crook made a visit to Mount Vernon Barracks, near Mobile, Alabama, where the surviving Chiricahuas had been transferred for reasons apparently having more to do with the convenience of the government than their welfare. The news swiftly got around that "Chief Gray Wolf" had come to see them,

*About 1905 Geronimo — in top hat — took some friends for a spin in his Buick.*

and soon they were crowding about him—Chato, Chihuahua, Naiche, and the rest—eagerly shaking his hand and laughing with pleasure. Geronimo hung about the edge of the crowd, but Crook had never forgiven him for failing to keep his pledge in the spring of 1886, and would not speak to him. At the schoolhouse, where some of the children recited for the General, the old chief made one last ploy, threatening unruly pupils with a stick, and looking to Crook for approval; but he got not a word.

On the first day of spring, 1890, George Crook died of a heart attack. But he had managed, against much public opposition in which Nelson Miles played a leading hand, to lay the groundwork for the Apaches' transfer to Fort Sill, Oklahoma, where the climate and terrain would be somewhat more like that of their beloved Southwest. It was another four years before the plan went through. Then the western trek took place, and by the turn of the century the remaining Chiricahuas, including the now-aging Geronimo, were more or less contentedly installed at Fort Sill. By that time the old renegade had become aware that he was something of a national celebrity, and he liked it. Though still nominally a prisoner of war, he was allowed to travel to various fairs and exhibitions, where he filled his pockets with change by crudely signing his autograph and looking fierce for snapshot portraits at a quarter or half dollar a snap. As much as possible of this legitimate loot he spent on liquor—and one day in February, 1909, riding back to the army post from a spree, he fell off his horse into some weeds, lay there all night, and contracted a mortal case of pneumonia.

Yet it may be that even in death Geronimo was true to his reputation. An interested group of people at Fort Sill raised a simple but dignified monument over his supposed grave, and there it still stands on Cache Creek, part of the Fort Sill reservation. But one day in 1943 a soldier reporter for the Fort Sill *Army News* happened to interview an elderly Apache who had been commemorating old times with a bottle of whiskey. Out came an intriguing story. Geronimo was not where they said he was, the old Apache claimed. No: One night, not long after his burial, a small band of his former warriors went to the grave and spirited his remains away to a secret place, clear of the white man's reservation. When this story was published, fervid denials came from several sources. But the elderly Apache just smiled and nodded. Geronimo, he insisted, got away in the end.

*A lynching party rides off, its grim work done, in a drawing by C. M. Russell.*

# THE JOHNSON COUNTY WAR

By HELENA HUNTINGTON SMITH

***O**n a blizzardy April morning in 1892, fifty armed men surrounded a cabin on Powder River in which two accused cattle rustlers had been spending the night. The first rustler was shot as he came down the path for the morning bucket of water; he was dragged over the doorstep by his companion, to die inside. The second man held out until afternoon, when the besiegers fired the house. Driven out by the flames, he went down with twenty-eight bullets in him. He was left on the bloodstained snow with a card pinned to his shirt, reading: "Cattle thieves, beware!"

So far the affair follows the standard pattern of frontier heroics, a pattern popularized by Owen Wister and justified to some extent by the facts of history if you don't look too closely: strong men on a far frontier, in the absence of law, make their own law for the protection of society, which generally approves.

Thus runs the cliché, but in Wyoming this time it went awry. In the first place the attackers were not crude frontiersmen taking the law into their own hands. They were men of means and education, predominantly eastern, who really should have known better; civilized men, at home in drawing rooms and familiar with Paris. Two were Harvard classmates of the year '78, the one a Boston blue blood, the other a member of a Wall Street banking family. Hubert E. Teschemacher and Fred De-Billier had come west after graduation to hunt elk, as so many gilded youths from both sides of the Atlantic were doing; had fallen in love with the country; and had remained as partners in a half-million-dollar ranching enterprise.

Our fifty vigilantes were truly a strange company to ride through the land slaughtering people. The instigators dominated the cattle business and the affairs of the former territory, which had recently been elevated to statehood, and more than half of them had served in the legislature. Their leader, Major Frank Wolcott, was a fierce little pouter pigeon of a man, a Kentuckian lately of the Union Army, whose brother was United States senator from Colorado. Accompanying the party as surgeon was a socially prominent Philadelphian, Dr. Charles Bingham Penrose, who had come to Wyoming for his health. It was not improved by his experiences.

These gentlemen had no thought of the danger to themselves as they set out, without benefit of the law, to liquidate their enemies. Convinced of their own righteousness, they expected nine-tenths of the people of Wyoming to be on their side, and they even looked for a popular uprising to assist them. Instead, thirty-six hours after their sanguinary victory on Powder River, they were surrounded in their turn by an enraged horde of citizens, and just missed being lynched themselves. They were saved only by the intervention of the President of the United States, who ordered federal troops to their aid. But it wasn't quite the usual scene of the cavalry riding to the rescue at the end of the movie, for while the cattlemen were snatched from imminent death, they were also arrested for the murder of the two men and marched off in custody of the troops—the latter all making clear that personally they regretted the rescue.

So ended the Johnson County War—tragic, bizarre, unbelievable. It was a sequel to the great beef bonanza, which began around 1880. The cattle boom combined the most familiar features of the South Sea Bubble and the 1929 bull market—such as forty per cent dividends that would never cease—with some special features of its own—such as a rash of adventuring English Lords and Honorables, free grass, and the blessings of "natural increase" provided by the prolific Texas cow. A man could grow rich without his lifting a finger.

Instead of the old-style cow outfit with its headquarters in a dugout and a boss who ate beef, bacon, and beans, there were cattle companies with offices in Wall Street, London, or Edinburgh; champagne parties; thoroughbred racing on the plains; and younger sons who were shipped out west to mismanage great ranches at fancy salaries. In a raw new city sprawled along the Union Pacific tracks, the Cheyenne Club boasted the best steward of any club in the United States, and its members were drawn from a roster of aristocracy on both sides of the Atlantic. Burke's Peerage and the Social Register mingled, though not intimately, with common cowhands from Texas, but only the latter knew anything about cattle.

To be sure, some of what they knew was a trifle shady: they knew how to handle a long rope and a running iron; how to brand a maverick right out from under the noses of the lords. But the mavericks, unbranded animals of uncertain ownership, were rather casually regarded anyhow; "finders keepers" was the unwritten rule which had governed their disposition in the early days, and they had been a source of controversy and bloodshed throughout the history of the West. While they were now claimed by the big cattle companies, the Texas cowboys were not impressed.

The boom crashed into ruin in the awful winter of 1886–87. Snow fell and drifted and thawed and froze and fell again, clothing the ground with an iron sheath of white on which a stagecoach could travel and through which no bovine hoof could paw for grass; and since the plains were heavily overstocked and the previous summer had been hot and dry, there was no grass anyway. Moaning cattle wandered into the outskirts of towns, trying to eat frozen garbage and the tar paper off the eaves of the shacks; and when the hot sun of early summer uncovered the fetid carcasses piled in the creek bottoms, the bark of trees and brush was gnawed as high as a cow could reach. Herd losses averaged fifty per cent, with ninety per cent for unacclimated southern herds, and some moral revulsion set in, even the Cheyenne *Daily Sun* remarking that a man who turned animals out on a barren plain without food or shelter would suffer loss of respect of the community in which he lived.

Meanwhile there were gloomy faces at the Cheyenne Club. "Cheer up, boys," quipped the bartender across the street, setting out a row of glasses, "the books won't freeze."

In the heyday of the beef bonanza, herds had been bought and sold by "book count," based on a back-of-an-envelope calculation of "natural increase," with no pother about a tally on the range. As the day of reckoning dawned, it turned out that many big companies had fewer than half the number of cattle claimed on their books. Now the terrible winter cut this half down to small fractions: faraway directors, grown glacial as the weather, hinted that blizzards were the fault of their underlings in Cheyenne; while the few surviving cows, instead of giving birth to sextuplets as was their clear duty, produced a correspondingly diminished calf crop to fatten on the gorgeous grass that sprang up after the snows.

In their bitterness, the cattlemen believed that the damned thieves were to blame. Obsessed with this idea, they now proceeded to bring upon themselves an epidemic of stealing without parallel in the West. At least that was what they called it, though to a cool-headed observer from Nebraska it looked more like "the bitter conflict which has raged incessantly between large and small owners."

In fact it was even more. For Wyoming in the nineties shared the outlook of that decade everywhere else; a decade of economic and moral monopoly, when righteousness belonged exclusively to the upper class, along with the means of production; a decade when the best people simply could not be wrong. The best people in this case were the Wyoming Stock Growers Association and their several rich and prominent eastern friends, and the climate of opinion they breathed was startlingly revealed in the hanging of Jim Averill and Cattle Kate. When the cattlemen shed crocodile tears because thieves went unwhipped, they forgot that thieves were not the worst to go free. At least six persons were shot or hanged in the years before the final flare-up, but not one person was ever brought to trial for the crimes—not even in the case of Jim Averill and the woman whose real name was Ella, who were hanged on the Sweetwater in 1889.

Averill and Ella ran a log-cabin saloon and road ranch up a desolate little valley off the Sweetwater, and they were nuisances. The man was articulate and a Populist of sorts, and had attacked the big cattlemen in a letter to the local press; the woman was a cowboys' prostitute who took her pay in stolen cattle. From this, aristocratic Dr. Penrose could argue later that "she had to die for the good of the country."

Die she did, with her paramour, at the end of a rope thrown over a tree limb and swung out over a gulch. There were three eyewitnesses to the abduction and one to the actual hanging, and a coroner's jury named four prominent cattlemen among the perpetrators. But before the case reached the grand jury three of the witnesses had vanished and the fourth had conveniently died. Afterward two of the men whose hands were filthy from this affair continued to rub elbows with the fastidious Teschemacher on the executive committee of the Stock Growers Association, and nauseating jokes about the last moments of Kate were applauded at the Cheyenne Club. Even Owen Wister joined in the applause, noting in his diary for October 12, 1889: "Sat yesterday in smoking car with one of the gentlemen indicted [*sic*] for lynching the man and the woman. He seemed a good solid citizen and I hope he'll get off."

The association tightened its blacklist. In a cattle economy where cows were the only means of getting ahead, the cowboys had long been forbidden to own a brand or a head of stock on their own, lest they be tempted to brand a maverick. Now more and more of them were "blackballed" on suspicion from all lawful employment within the territory. Likewise the association made the rules of the range, ran the roundups to suit itself, and kept out the increasing number of people it didn't like; hence many small stockmen, suspect of misbehavior by their very smallness, were also relegated to a shady no man's land outside the law.

*Russell sketched the sad condition of western cattle during the winter of 1886.*

If you call a man a thief, and deprive him of all chance to earn a living honestly, he will soon become a thief.

By 1890 a thin colony of blackballed cowboys had settled on the rivers and creeks of Johnson County and were waging war with rope and running iron on the big outfits. Then early in 1892 a group calling themselves the Northern Wyoming Farmers' and Stockgrowers' Association announced in the press their intention of holding an independent roundup, in defiance of the state law and the Wyoming Stock Growers Association. This was provocative, insolent, outrageous if you like; it was hardly the furtive behavior of ordinary thieves.

Also announced in the press were the names of two foremen for what was now being called the "shotgun roundup." One was a Texan, known as a skilled cowhand, who was lightning with a gun. His name was Nathan D. Champion.

Meanwhile the storied walls of the Cheyenne Club beheld the amazing spectacle of nineteenth century gentlemen plotting wholesale murder. The declared object of their expedition was the "extermination"—not "arrest," but "extermination"—of various undesirable persons in the northern part of the state. The death list stood at seventy. In addition to a hard core of nineteen most-wanted rustlers, it almost certainly included a large number who were merely thought to be too close to the rustler faction, among them the sheriff of Johnson County and the three county commissioners.

This incredible project was fully known in advance to Acting Governor Amos W. Barber, to United States Senators Joseph M. Carey and Francis E. Warren, and to officials of the Union Pacific Railroad, whose consent to run a special train was obtained; and none of whom found anything questionable in the undertaking. Twenty-five hired gunfighters from Texas raised the manpower complement to fifty, since the local cowboys were thoroughly disaffected and would not have pulled a trigger for their employers. A smart Chicago newsman, Sam T. Clover, had heard about the impending necktie party and was in Cheyenne determined to get the story for the *Herald*. He and a local reporter were taken along just as though the expedition were legal; it apparently had not occurred to the planners that they were inviting witnesses to murder.

They got started the afternoon of April 5, on board a train loaded with men, arms, equipment, horses, and three supply

*According to an old saw, "Where ropes were locks there was small need for keys."*

wagons. An overnight run landed them in Casper, two hundred miles to the northwest, where they descended, saddled their horses, and were off before the townspeople were up—except for enough of the latter to start talk. Their objective was Buffalo, the county seat of Johnson County, but when they arrived at a friendly ranch on the second night, they received new intelligence which determined them to change their course: Nate Champion and possibly a good catch of other rustlers were at a cabin on the Middle Fork of Powder River, only twelve miles away. They decided to detour and finish this group off before proceeding to Buffalo.

Rumors have come down to us of the drinking and dissension that accompanied this decision: faced with the actuality of shooting trapped men in a cabin the next morning, stomachs began to turn over, and three members of the party pulled out, including the doctor and the local newsman. But that night the main body rode on to the attack, through one of the worst April blizzards in memory. They plodded along without speaking, while beards and mustaches became coated with ice, and the wind lashed knife-edged snow in their faces. Halting before daybreak to thaw out around sagebrush fires, they went on until they looked down over a low bluff at the still-sleeping KC ranch.

Two innocent visitors, trappers, had been spending the night in the cabin. As first one and then the other sauntered forth into the gray morning air, he was recognized as not among the wanted men, and as soon as a corner of the barn hid him from the house, each was made prisoner. After a long wait Champion's friend Nick Ray finally appeared and was shot down. The door opened, and Champion himself faced a storm of bullets to drag Ray inside.

The fusillade went on for hour after hour. In the log shack Nate Champion was writing, with a cramped hand in a pocket notebook, the record of his last hours.

Me and Nick was getting breakfast when the attack took place. Two men was with us—Bill Jones and another man. The old man went after water and did not come back. His friend went to see what was the matter and he did not come back. Nick started out and I told him to look out, that I thought there was someone at the stable and would not let them come back.

Nick is shot but not dead yet. He is awful sick. I must go and wait on him.

It is now about two hours since the first shot. Nick is still alive.

They are still shooting and are all around the house, Boys, there is bullets coming in here like hail.

Them fellows is in such shape I can't get at them. They are shooting from the stable and river and back of the house.

Nick is dead. He died about 9 o'clock.

Hour after hour the hills crackled with rifle fire, and such was the emptiness of the country that while the besiegers were on a main road, such as it was, connecting civilization with a little settlement at the back of beyond, they could bang away all day without fear of interruption. Or almost. As it happened there was a slight interruption in midafternoon.

Jack Flagg, a rustler intellectual of sorts, had left his ranch eighteen miles up the Red Fork of Powder River on this snowy morning of April 9, on his way to the Democratic state convention at Douglas, to which he was a delegate from Johnson County. It was one of the oddities of the situation that the thieves were all Democrats, and the murderers were all Republicans. A rancher, newspaper editor, and schoolteacher, Flagg was an accomplished demagogue who had twisted the tails of the big outfits by means fair and foul. He was very much on the wanted list.

He was riding about fifty yards or so behind a wagon driven by his seventeen-year-old stepson; and since the invaders had withdrawn into a strategy huddle and pulled in their pickets, there was no sound of firing to warn him as the wagon rattled downhill to the bridge by the KC. Flagg started over to the house to greet his friends, and was ordered to halt by someone who failed to recognize him.

"Don't shoot me, boys, I'm all right," he called gaily, taking it for a joke. Under the hail of bullets which disabused him, he fled back to the wagon and slashed the tugs holding one of the team, and he and the boy made their miraculous escape.

The wagon Flagg left behind was put to use by the invaders. Since hours of cannonading had failed to dislodge Champion, they loaded it with old hay and dry chips and pushed it up to the cabin, where they set it afire. Flames and smoke rolled skyward until they wondered if the man inside had cheated them by shooting himself. Champion, however, was still writing.

I heard them splitting wood. I guess they are going to fire the house to-night.

I think I will make a break when night comes if alive.

It's not night yet.

The house is all fired. Goodbye boys, if I never see you again.

Nathan D. Champion.

Finally, he broke through the roof at one end of the house and sprinted desperately for the cover of a little draw, which he never reached.

Pawing over the body, the invaders found and read the diary, after which it was presented to the Chicago newsman. Its contents survived, to become a classic of raw courage in the annals of the West.

Next day, Sunday, April 10, the invaders were approaching Buffalo when they were met by a rider on a lathered horse, who warned them that the town was in an uproar and they had better

*In the old West, which depended heavily on both animals, cattle rustling or*

turn back if they valued their lives. They had just made a rest halt at the friendly TA ranch. Their only hope was to return there and dig in.

Sam Clover, ace reporter, was too smart for that trap. Deciding to take his chance with the aroused local population, he left the now deflated avengers and rode on into Buffalo, where he did some fast talking and finally got himself under the wing of his old friend Major Edmond G. Fechet of the 6th Cavalry, with whom he had campaigned during the Ghost Dance troubles in North Dakota. With the rest of the 6th, Fechet was now stationed at Fort McKinney, near Buffalo. So Clover rode off to the fort to luxuriate in hot baths and clean sheets and to write dispatches, while the wretched invaders prepared to stand siege for their lives.

*horse stealing could lead to summary execution without benefit of a jury trial.*

They worked all night, and by morning of the eleventh were entrenched behind a very efficient set of fortifications at the TA ranch, where they were virtually impregnable except for a shortage of food supplies. By morning they were besieged by an impromptu army of hornet-mad cowboys and ranchmen, led by Sheriff "Red" Angus of Johnson County. The army numbered over three hundred on the day of surrender.

In Buffalo, churches and schools were turned into headquarters for the steadily arriving recruits; ladies baked cakes to send to Sheriff Angus' command post; the young Methodist preacher, who was possessed of no mean tongue, employed it to denounce this crime of the century. The leading merchant, a venerable Scotsman named Robert Foote, mounted his black horse and, with his long white beard flying in the breeze, dashed up and down the streets, calling the citizens to arms. More impressive still, he threw open his store, inviting them to help themselves to ammunition, slickers, blankets, flour—everything. He was said to be a heavy dealer in rustled beef, and on the invaders' list; but so was almost everyone of importance in Buffalo.

The telegraph wires had been cut repeatedly since the start of the invasion, but on April 12 they were working again momentarily, and a friend in Buffalo got a telegram through to the governor with the first definite word of the invaders' plight. From that time on, all the heavy artillery of influence, from Cheyenne to Washington and on up to the White House, was brought to bear to rescue the cattlemen from the consequences of their act.

Senators Carey and Warren called at the executive mansion late that night and got President Benjamin Harrison out of bed. He was urged to suppress an insurrection in Wyoming, though the question of just who was in insurrection against whom was not clarified. Telegrams flew back and forth. At 12:50 A.M. on April 13, Colonel J. J. Van Horn of the 6th Cavalry wired the commanding general of the Department of the Platte, acknowledging receipt of orders to proceed to the TA ranch.

Two hours later, three troops of the 6th filed out of Fort McKinney in the freezing dark, in a thoroughly disgusted frame of mind because (a) they had just come in that afternoon from chasing a band of marauding Crows back to the reservation and did not relish being ordered out again at three in the morning; and because (b) they were heartily on the side of Johnson County and would rather have left the invaders to their fate.

They reached the TA at daybreak. Inside the beleaguered ranch house Major Wolcott and his men, their food exhausted, were preparing to make a break as soon as it was sufficiently light. They had eaten what they thought would be their last breakfast, and were awaiting the lookout's whistle which would call them to make that last desperate run—like so many Nate Champions—into the ring of hopelessly outnumbering rifles.

But hark! Instead of the suicide signal, a cavalry bugle! Major Wolcott crossed to a window.

"Gentlemen, it is the troops!"

From start to finish the Johnson County story reads like a parody of every Hollywood western ever filmed, and never more so than at this moment. Down the hill swept a line of seven horsemen abreast; between the fluttering pennons rode Colonel Van Horn, Major Fechet, Sheriff Angus; a representative of the governor, who would not have stuck his neck into northern Wyoming at this point for anything; and, of course, Sam T. Clover of the Chicago *Herald*. One of the guidon bearers carried a white handkerchief. An answering flutter of white appeared on the breastworks. Major Wolcott advanced stiffly and saluted Colonel Van Horn.

"I will surrender to you, but to that man"—indicating Sheriff Angus—"never!"

Forty-four prisoners were marched off to the fort, not including the few defectors and two of the Texas mercenaries, who later died of wounds. Of the ringleaders, only one had received so much as a scratch.

"The cattlemen's war" was front-paged all over the nation for some three weeks, with the Boston *Transcript* putting tongue in cheek to remark on the ever-widening activities of Harvard men. Then the rest of the country forgot it. Four days after the surrender, still guarded by unsympathetic troops, the prisoners were removed to Fort Russell, near Cheyenne. Here they were safely away from Johnson County, which had, however, been behaving with remarkable restraint. The weather was worse than ever and the march overland one of the most miserable on record. Apart from that, the killers got off at no heavier cost to themselves than minor inconvenience and some ignominy. They were never brought to justice.

They did, however, pay an admitted $100,000 as the price of the invasion, counting legal expenses and not mentioning the

*A brand was proof of ownership, but with mavericks the rule was "finders keepers."*

illegal. Of the sordid features of the Johnson County invasion which all but defy comment, the worst was the affair of the trappers. These two simple and unheroic men, who had been with Champion and Nick Ray in the cabin and had the bad luck to witness the KC slaughter, were hustled out of the state under an escort of gunmen in terror of their lives, and thence across Nebraska to Omaha, where they were piled onto a train, still under escort of gunmen and lawyers, and delivered at an eastern destination. The Johnson County authorities and their friends had been trying frantically to get them back, but no subpoenas could be issued because the cattlemen, still protected by the army, were not yet formally charged with anything. Counting bribes to federal officers and judges, legal fees, forfeited bail, and other expenses, it was said to have cost $27,000 to get the witnesses across Nebraska alone. The trappers had been promised a payoff of $2,500 each, and given postdated checks. When presented for cashing, the checks proved to be on a bank that had never existed.

Meanwhile the armor of self-pity remained undented. In their own eyes and those of their friends, the cattlemen were the innocent victims of an outrage. While awaiting a hearing at Fort Russell, they were kept in the lightest of durance, coming and going freely to Cheyenne. Major Wolcott was permitted a trip outside the state. When Fred DeBillier showed signs of cracking under the strain of captivity, raving and uttering strange outcries in the middle of the night, he was tenderly removed, first to a hotel and later to his home in New York, for rest and medical treatment.

Eventually the prisoners were transferred to the state penitentiary at Laramie, where the district judge who ordered the removal assured Governor Amos W. Barber that these important persons would by no means be required to mingle with ordinary convicts. They were then escorted to their new quarters by a guard of honor, which included Wyoming's adjutant general and acting secretary of state.

Public opinion was overwhelmingly against the prisoners, but it was poorly led and ineffective, and public wrath was dissipated into thin air. On their side, however, in the words of a newspaper correspondent, the cattlemen were "backed not only by the Republican machine from President Harrison on down to the state organization, but by at least twenty-five million dollars in

378

invested capital. They have the President, the governor, the courts, their United States Senators, the state legislature and the army at their backs." It was enough.

One sequel to the episode was an attempt to muzzle the press. A small-town editor who criticized the cattlemen too violently was jailed on a charge of criminal libel and held for thirty days—long enough to silence his paper. A second editor was beaten. But the latter, whose name was A. S. Mercer, exacted an eye for an eye in his celebrated chronicle of the invasion, published two years later and resoundingly entitled: *The Banditti of the Plains, or The Cattlemen's Invasion of Wyoming. The Crowning Infamy of the Ages.*

Thereupon his print shop was burned to the ground, and another subservient judge ordered all copies of the book seized and burned. But while they were awaiting the bonfire, a wagonload of them was removed one night and drawn by galloping horses over the Colorado line. Thereafter copies on library shelves were stolen and mutilated as far away as the Library of Congress until only a few were left. But two new editions have since been published, and so—in the end—Mr. Mercer won.

The same judge who had shown himself so solicitous of the prisoners' comfort granted a change of venue from Johnson County, not to a neutral county but to the cattlemen's own stronghold in Cheyenne. The trial was set for January 2, 1893. Nineteen days later over a thousand veniremen had been examined and there were still only eleven men on the jury. The prolonged financial strain was too much for Johnson County; since there were no witnesses anyway, the prosecution tossed in the towel, and the case was dismissed.

The so-called rustlers came out with the cleaner hands. Good luck had saved them from spilling the blood of the invaders; and while there was one unsolved killing of a cattlemen's adherent afterward, this appears to have been an act of personal grudge, not of community vengeance. The chain reaction of retaliatory murders that could have started never did; and strife-torn Johnson County settled down to peace. The roundups became democratic, with big and little stockmen working side by side. Montagu sons married Capulet daughters; notorious rustlers turned into respectable ranchmen and hobnobbed with their former enemies. One was mentioned for governor, and another rose to high position in—of all things—the Wyoming Stock Growers Association.

Yet, if bitterness has mercifully subsided, a certain remnant of injustice remains. The ghosts of old wrongs unrighted still walk in Buffalo, and, with the law cheated of its due, the pleasant little

town with its creek and its cottonwood trees can only wait for that earthly equivalent of the Last Judgment, the verdict of history.

*Cattle rustlers are dropped in their tracks by a posse on the brow of the ridge.*

# Picture Credits

CONTINUED ON PAGE 384